# BUCKET

## LIST

# ADVENTURES

# BUCKET
## LIST
# ADVENTURES

---

## 10 INCREDIBLE JOURNEYS TO EXPERIENCE BEFORE YOU DIE

---

### ANNETTE WHITE

Skyhorse Publishing

Skyhorse Publishing books may be purchased in bulk at special discounts for sales promotion, corporate gifts, fund-raising, or educational purposes. Special editions can also be created to specifications. For details, contact the Special Sales Department, Skyhorse Publishing, 307 West 36th Street, 11th Floor, New York, NY 10018 or info@skyhorsepublishing.com.

Skyhorse® and Skyhorse Publishing® are registered trademarks of Skyhorse Publishing, Inc.®, a Delaware corporation.

Visit our website at www.skyhorsepublishing.com.

10 9 8 7 6 5 4 3 2 1

Library of Congress Cataloging-in-Publication Data is available on file.

Cover design by Rain Saukas
Cover photo credit: iStock photo and author's collection

Interior photos courtesy Annette White

Print ISBN: 978-1-5107-1004-7
Ebook ISBN: 978-1-5107-1006-1

Printed in China

To my best friend and husband, Peter, who believed in me
even in the moments that I did not. To my mother, who
instilled in me her undying Italian work ethic. To my little
Lupita, who happily worked harder so I could escape to live my
dream. Most of all, to the dreamers whose aspirations see no
boundaries—you inspire me.

Peter and me touring a pineapple farm in Maui

# TABLE OF CONTENTS

# INTRODUCTION

What is keeping you from experiencing something truly incredible—turning a wondrous travel dream into reality? For some it is the obstacle of time, while for others it's the dilemma of limited funds or simply the fear of stepping out of their comfort zone. But, there is a place beyond those hurdles, a place where each morning you wake with inspiration in your heart and a fire in your belly, ready to tackle a goal with passion. Only a small fraction of people will ever live like this, but I have learned that most people can. You can find that place where your wanderlust runs wild and your diligence puts you on a journey that quenches your desire—*Bucket List Adventures* can show you how.

I am fortunate to be one of the few, a person who is living *my* ideal life. For more than eight years as a travel writer, blogger, and new experience collector I have been following my passion of checking the world off my bucket list, one incredible adventure at a time. It is a life where one day may be spent eating fresh Ladurée macarons in Paris, while the next will have me playing a game of hide-and-seek with the Sri Lankan children on the streets of Colombo or floating in the salty Dead Sea in Jordan. This lifestyle was not borne out of privilege: my family is not rich, and in fact are Italian immigrants who came to the United States with very little money. Rather, it is what can happen when you are determined to design a life that you are thrilled to be living, thus saying no to fear, and turning your "I can'ts" into "I cans".

It hasn't always been this way for me. Before following my calling for exploration, I instead followed in the family footsteps. My husband and I borrowed every dime to open a little Italian restaurant in my hometown. We settled into a beyond-full-time work routine that ate up over seventy hours a week of our lives. It left little time for anything else. Though the restaurant was rewarding and the food business is in my blood, there was also something else tugging at my heart. It was an urge to explore and try something for the first time—a *lot of* somethings. But, I too had countless anxieties and obstacles that prevented me from taking strides toward living an intrepid life, one that would take me away from the daily grind to travel the globe. I was uninspired, controlled by fear, and just going through the motions hoping that something would change, but nothing ever did. Einstein put it best when he said that the definition of insanity is "doing the same thing over and over again and expecting a different result." Doing nothing changed nothing. If going truffle hunting in Italy or diving the Great Barrier Reef was my deepest wish, then there were steps that had to be taken in order to make that happen. Nobody was going to wave a magic wand to cure my anxieties, free up time in my over-scheduled day, or put thousands of dollars into a travel fund for me. I needed to do those things myself. In other words, instead of just dreaming about my bucket list, I needed to actually live it. And that's exactly what I did, one tiny step at a time.

The result of these steps, which are revealed inside the pages of this book, has been a myriad of incredible experiences that span the globe. With over forty countries under my belt, this is a collection of my ten most extraordinary journeys—from walking amongst the

wildebeest on an African safari; to the Galápagos Islands to see the Blue Footed Booby mating dance; to swimming in a lake surrounded by thousands of jellyfish in Palau and so much more.

This is more than just a book of inspirational stories to whet your appetite; it is also a practical guide brimming with resources for active dreamers who are craving to create memorable adventures in their own lives. Each travelogue includes an informational guide that covers the "how-to" of checking the experience off your own bucket list: the best hotels, restaurants, tour companies, time of year to visit, etc. Beyond this, there are tips on how to find the precious free time that always seems to be lacking, how to create a money management system to fund your travels, and proven techniques on working through the fear that afflicts us all on some level. Most importantly, my book will give you the tools to create a life-changing bucket list of your own, plus essential travel tips for planning an unbelievable journey, and ultimately crossing your items off your list.

Imagine living a life filled with adventure, to be inspired to dream bigger and to have the means to turn fantasies into reality. Whether your goal is to go wine tasting through Tuscany, climb Mount Kilimanjaro, or simply have a family weekend getaway in the mountains, this book will inspire your imagination to have no limits and give you the know-how to design the type of life that you are truly inspired to live.

# PART 1: UNCOVERING YOUR DREAMS

# 1: SETTING GOALS WITH A BUCKET LIST

BUCK· ET LIST *noun*, INFORMAL.
1. A LIST OF THINGS A PERSON WANTS TO ACHIEVE OR EXPERIENCE, AS BEFORE REACHING A CERTAIN AGE OR DYING: A BUCKET LIST FOR A TERMINALLY ILL PATIENT.

The very words "bucket list" can stir up some pretty heavy-duty fears. It can be a reminder of our own mortality, and death is typically something we would rather not think about. But, the reminder that our time is limited is actually one of the best gifts we can be given. It is one that can guide us to achieve what is most important to us before it is too late.

On average, we all will have 22,170 days in our adulthood to decide how to spend; maximizing each moment should be a priority because that time will go by all too quickly. Instead of wasting precious hours on meaningless and mundane activities (how many times have you checked Facebook today?), we should direct our energy toward goals that will inspire us to wake up motivated each morning and push us to each live our ideal life. In order to do that, we need to be acutely aware that we are not immortal, and then we need a plan. A bucket list can be the foundation for this plan.

Have you ever noticed that we will have detailed architectural plans when building a home and binders full of intentions when creating a destination wedding, but absolutely no strategy for the direction of our lives? You wouldn't expect to construct your fantasy house without having a system for how to lay the concrete foundation; the same is true for your life. A bucket list can be the framework for your life's design. It is not simply an idle collection of goals you want to achieve while you are alive; it can lay the groundwork for the future, while also allowing you to dream bigger and giving you immediate motivation.

You may be thinking, "I don't need a plan, things happen for a reason." Just as often as I hear the term bucket list, I catch people claiming that things happen for a reason. Hearing that is like the sound of nails on a chalkboard to me. This is because many people use this phrase when they want to believe that they didn't have a choice in the outcome of whatever has happened to them. It makes them feel better thinking they had no control over racking up thousands of dollars of credit card debt, or having no time for an overnight getaway—that takes the blame off them. Of course, life can be unpredictable, so you cannot possibly be in control 100 percent of the time; sometimes there's an unexpected crack in the foundation. But, your current lifestyle is a result of the decisions you have made in the past. Take a look at your life; what choices did you make to get where you are today? Do you have a shiny new car in the driveway, but claim to have no money for that trip to the South of France you have been dreaming of since childhood? Is your schedule filled with reading the tabloids and surfing the Internet, but you believe you have no time to take a day trip to the mountains to learn to snowboard? For the most part, your own choices create your current situation, and a bucket list will help you to look at your future in a way that can be the guide to help make

Relaxing at a café in the South of France

decisions based on what you truly want. Without a plan, aspirations are nothing more than hollow ideas floating around in your head.

I had always been a fairly motivated person, consistently working on a few conventional goals: like finishing college, owning a business and my own home. But, it wasn't until I started my bucket list over ten years ago that my life completely changed. It forced me to reveal my deepest dreams, leaving the limitations behind. It was a place to put the fear aside and focus on the endless possibilities the world had to offer. It is the main reason that I chose to defy a conventional way of living, leaving behind the typical nine-to-five job. It is also why I have dared to eat worm patties on the streets of Vietnam, zip line through the Andes, fly through the air on a trapeze, and swim with whale sharks in Mexico. It was also the reason that I became a travel writer and started my travel blog, and why that blog now sees over a hundred thousand pairs of eyes each month. It got me in the mindset of truly believing that anything is possible, instead of just fantasizing about what I wished I could be and do. Without it, I undoubtedly would be a different version of myself today, one that conformed to societal expectations instead of designing my own life based on my undying passion for having new experiences.

## BENEFITS OF A BUCKET LIST

We fuel our bodies with food, our minds with education, and our hearts with love, but new experiences and dreams can nourish our spirit in ways that nothing else can. Whatever you want, there are benefits to turning them into a bucket list, and a well-crafted one can push you to lead your version of an ideal life.

### Forces You to Look at What You Really Want

Many people will live their entire lives without having any idea as to what they really want. They will follow society's conventional expectations of getting married, working the same office job for the next twenty years, buying a home, and having children—all without giving it a second thought because that is just what they are "supposed to do." But, if that path is not their true passion, then life will end up leading them, instead of them leading their life.

The process of writing a bucket list forces you to take a close look at what it is you truly desire, to analyze where you are versus where you want to be. It very well may be the career, children, and home, etc., but it may also be something entirely different. We may believe that what we want is to have more money or to land that big promotion at work, but delving deeper reveals that what we really crave is more freedom and to be passionate about what we do. Will that new position at work really help you achieve your future goals or will it only stifle your creativity and keep you at work more hours of the day?

When sitting down to contemplate what your future will look like, your dreams and what type of experiences you want to have will be brought to the forefront. By asking yourself what you truly want, setting goals and consistently reexamining your goals, you gain a self-knowledge that will propel you in the right direction instead of focusing on random things.

Inspecting a colorful sea urchin while snorkeling in Maui

## Gets you Excited

Many people's sleepless nights are due to having a mind filled with countless tasks for the next day: Johnny has to be driven to soccer practice after school, the prescription needs to be picked up at the pharmacy, work documents must be priority mailed . . . and the list goes on. These duties can also be the reason you walk around the entire day in a fog, oblivious to how you got from one place to the next, instinctively going through the monotonous routines of life. But, what if what kept you up at night were thoughts of planning your dream vacation to watch the sunset at Uluwatu Temple in Bali or going back to school to study French viticulture, to do the things you are truly passionate about? Then sleepless nights would be because of excitement, a reason to get up early in the morning, and stay up late at night.

Snowshoeing at Glacier National Park in Montana

When you are stuck in the rut of day-to-day life, it can be difficult to get excited about the day that lies ahead. A bucket list gives you a reason to spend that extra hour a day working, adding meaning to the extra effort, because the additional money will be why your dream of ice climbing in Iceland will come true. It can create an excitement deep in your soul and expose the passion you thought you had lost many years ago.

## Creates Focus

A bucket list will give you a sense of direction that allows your mind to focus on the target, instead of getting sidetracked dawdling on social media or watching reruns of the Kardashians (I am admittedly guilty of that sometimes too!). It will help you determine your end goal and the steps that need to be taken to get there, keeping your eye on the prize. For example, without a clear career focus, you may just take every promotion opportunity given, switching departments and ending up as the executive production manager, when what you really wanted was to be a marketing director. Without clear goals it's easy to get diverted, heading in multiple directions, and years later ending up in a place you really never intended. Even with goals, if you cannot remain focused you will lose momentum, which will lead to a loss of motivation and ultimately failure to achieve the result you desire. But once you create your bucket list, you will be able to continuously refer to it in order to reenergize your focus.

## Motivates You

Without motivation, your dream will be nothing more than that; it is the necessary energy that pushes you to accomplish your goals. If you think about it, most drive you have had in your entire life has been based on some form of a goal. You worked a part-time job in high school in order to afford a shiny new car, you suffered through endless piano lessons to be able to play at the year-end recital, and you ate salad for dinner every night in order to fit into a bathing suit by summer. Motivation is why race car drivers win trophies and business owners become millionaires, and it is the main reason that this is a published book, a project that took me over a year and a thousand hours.

In order to truly get motivated, you need to know what you really want, and writing a bucket list will help to determine exactly what that is. These goals will then be the root of your motivation. Also, having any sort of list naturally inspires you to want to cross things off of it, whether it is simply your weekly grocery list, daily to-dos, or a bucket list. Plus, having it written down will be a constant reminder of what you need to do, and will serve as the fuel that will drive you forward. This does not mean it will be easy, but once you set your list to paper and have announced it to the world, you have something to encourage you to push forward.

## Pushes the Boundaries of Your Comfort Zone

It has been said that life begins at the end of your comfort zone, so then why are so many afraid of stepping outside of it? I will tell you why. Being inside your comfort zone minimizes stress and risk, keeping you at a low anxiety level. This makes it very easy to never push the boundaries, because it's pretty darn comfy inside the safety of your little bubble. Everyday activities like taking a shower, cooking dinner, and going to work don't create any apprehension because they are familiar. However, flying across the globe, eating strange foreign foods, and not speaking the language of an area will undoubtedly cause trepidation.

Reeling in my first ever sailfish while on a boat in Guatemala

Unfortunately, if you stay inside of these boundaries you'll be missing out on the incredible benefits of taking a risk. Risk-taking leads to personal growth; expanding your mindset, teaching you valuable lessons, increasing your confidence, and limiting regrets. Your bucket list will continuously test these barriers, helping you to transform and grow. Once you step out of the norm for the first time, it can lead to a snowball effect, where each consecutive time you do it, it gets a little bit easier and your comfort zone expands bigger and bigger. That's when the world is truly at your feet.

### Makes You Feel Accomplished

There is a new gallon of milk in the fridge, the children have taken their baths, and dinner is on the table. You sit back with a glass of Cabernet and relish in the success of the last eight hours. It feels really good to finish your daily errands; there is a sense of satisfaction knowing that you completed everything you set out to do for the day. Just imagine the triumphant feeling after you've walked the five-hundred-mile El Camino de Santiago or skydived over Palm Jumeirah in Dubai. The sense of accomplishment can truly be overwhelming.

Accomplishment gives you a feeling of pride, which in turn builds self-esteem and increases life satisfaction and fulfillment. When you are living the bucket list life, you will be continuously making check marks next to your goals, and getting the addictive feeling of success often. It doesn't even have to be a gigantic long-term goal to generate the feeling of achievement; it can be as simple as learning how to make an origami crane or learning to ice skate. Plus, one of the best parts is that you are not waiting for someone to pat you on the back to tell you did a good job—it is a feeling you created yourself.

### Makes You More Interesting

My high school political science teacher once told me that the only thing I would be able to talk to my husband about at the breakfast table was going to be bacon and eggs. The class definitely wasn't my favorite, but her words have resonated with me ever since. It was humiliating at the time, making me feel dumb and insignificant, but I now understand that it was her intention to make me realize that people would find me a bore if there was never anything interesting coming out of my mouth. I would love to talk to her now about the dozen different types of bacon found throughout the villages in Italy and the secret recipe of the traditional egg coffee drink in Vietnam.

My husband and I at the famous Moulin Rouge show in Paris, France

Think back to some of the most intriguing people you have met at a dinner party or event. They were probably ones who were following their passions, traveling the world, and/or overcoming an obstacle to achieve a goal. With a bucket list you will have personal stories from around the world and extraordinary things you have done to contribute to the conversation. Plus, for me it's much easier to join into a conversation because when a person begins to talk about going wine tasting in Tuscany I have either done the same or have a relatable experience.

## Keeps You Active

Sitting home night after night on the couch leads to a sedentary (and very boring) life. Things like riding a mechanical bull, swimming with dolphins, or learning how to indoor rock climb gets you off the sofa and keeps you moving. Besides a few random Pilates classes, my bucket list is my main form of exercise, because there is always something adventurous on it. Some days will involve training for a 5k race, while others will take me to the golf course attempting to make an elusive hole in one. When the goal is centered on traveling, traipsing through airport terminals, and exploring city centers by foot, you could easily rack up the ten thousand steps a day that many of us try to achieve (my record was twenty-nine thousand or 14.5 miles while hunting for the Khamthiang Market in Chiang Mai). The best part is that when you are excited about trying something new or achieving a goal, you'll barely realize that you are getting a workout at the same time.

## Creates a Legacy

What stories do you want to tell to your great-grandchildren? How would you like to be remembered? What example do you want to set for future generations—one of a life full of passion, following dreams, and having meaningful adventure or one of unhappiness? We all want our lives to matter, to serve as an example for what a truly incredible life can be. A bucket list can help you to be that example.

When you are following your passions and accomplishing goals you will leave an inspiring legacy of your personal values for future generations. Family, friends, and even strangers will remember the best parts of you and be inspired to follow in your footsteps. Make sure the path is taking them in the direction you would want your loved ones to go.

## Allows You to Dream Bigger

Typically, when people create goals for themselves they are influenced by their current financial situation and personal time restrictions. They are usually thinking about things short term, instead of thinking of their entire lifetime. But, a bucket list is an invitation to dream bigger. When the time limit is before you die, instead of this month or year, it opens up the possibilities. It encourages people to put on it all the things they have ever thought about doing while taking away the limitation of fear, time, and money.

So make a bucket list and fill it with dreams that have no boundaries; things that scare the daylights out of you, make

Feeling on top of the world on the Exuma Islands

you pee-your-pants laugh, and inspire you to be a better version of yourself. Keep it close, to refer to it often as a reminder to never forget your dreams.

# 2. CREATING & CONQUERING YOUR BUCKET LIST

Sleep in an overwater bungalow in Bora Bora, hike Peru's Inca Trail to Machu Picchu, or drink beer at Oktoberfest in Germany—what's on your bucket list? For too many people it takes a terrifying illness, hitting retirement age, or some other life altering event to honestly begin thinking about the things they want to experience in their lifetime. In many of these cases, it will then be too late to turn these dreams into a reality. Life is uncertain, and you will undoubtedly be thrown curveballs throughout. You cannot be sure that in ten or twenty years you will be physically, emotionally, or financially able to do all of the things that you desire, like climbing the twelve hundred steps of Sigiriya Rock in Sri Lanka or hiking between the cities of Italy's Cinque Terre. Don't wait for that "perfect time" to begin—create your bucket list not because you are dying but because you want to live!

Maneuvering my personal underwater SUB in the Bahamas

There is no right or wrong way of designing a bucket list, no one specific prescription. It is a personal journey between you and your aspirations. Each one should be different because it is meant to reflect what you most desire in your own life. For example, mine includes learning to surf, skydiving, and rappelling down a waterfall to appease my adventurous side. If you are not a thrill seeker, your list may be entirely different. The important part is to come up with items that are meaningful to you; ones that will inspire you to wake up each morning with a fire in your belly. Retiling the bathroom floor has no place on this list, nor does cleaning the cobwebs out of the garage. Save those for your weekly honey-dos. With that said, don't worry if you didn't make each aspiration earth shattering, or even travel related; sometimes the simplest goals are the most rewarding. Giving a blood donation took less than an hour commitment, yet is still one of my most gratifying experiences. Also, don't exclude anything just because you think it is too difficult or frightening; it is meant to stretch your comfort zone. Do the same for the things you think are too simple. As long as it has meaning to you it should be on your list, because even the smallest achievement can give us the feeling of a great accomplishment.

The length of your list is also ultimately up to you; there is no magic number of goals that should be on it. You cannot put limitations on something that is meant to unravel your dreams. I do recommend having at least twenty-five objectives to start, with varying levels of difficulty. They can be as small as hiking a new trail at a local park or as big as running a marathon—some will be checked off in a weekend, while others may be lifelong journeys. Including short-term goals that can easily be completed will give you a sense of accomplishment and help to keep you motivated for the ones that may take years. By continuously working toward (and checking off) your goals, you will turn the sense of achieving into a good habit.

Don't pass judgment on your own abilities. You will be surprised at what you can actually accomplish. People put limitations on themselves by thinking that they can't do incredible things or because the big picture of an aspiration seems so overwhelming. You need to dream big, go beyond the realistic goals, and put down everything that you have ever wanted to see, touch, and experience. Be realistic, but also understand that we are capable of doing so much more than we think we can. Don't think it is too silly, just write it down.

Speaking of writing it down, one of the most important steps in creating a bucket list is recording it somewhere. Sounds simple, right? But even so, most people miss this critical step. Recording your list represents a sincere commitment, turning them into tangible goals—doable aspirations to work toward instead of wishful thinking. Studies have shown that people are 33 percent more successful with achieving their goals when they write them down, share them with the

Walking Jerash Archaeolgical Site—Jordan

world, and are held accountable with weekly updates. It's also very easy to forget all of your aspirations if you don't have something concrete to refer back to.

My first bucket list was created in a small, green, flowered journal, and then upgraded to a simple Word document. Afterward it graduated to a multi-tabbed Excel file. Now my over eight-hundred-item list is located solely online on my blog, which has been the easiest for me. Not only is it conveniently accessible, but it also holds me accountable by being visible to the universe. There are also many phone apps and online bucket list websites where you can record your list and share it with others (refer to resource chapter for examples).

Starting is the hardest part, so let's begin right now. Yes. *Now*. Living your own bucket list is as easy as following the Four C's: Cultivate, Commit, Conquer, Celebrate.

## CULTIVATE

Once you have made the decision to create a bucket list, you need to start cultivating ideas. You're bound to have a few items that you have always wanted to do in the forefront of you mind, and immediately write those down. But, how do you come up with other incredible ideas? How do you know what's out there in the world to choose from? The following are different methods to stimulate ideas for your list.

### Write Your Eulogy

At a time when I was suffering from a serious case of the blahs, a close friend challenged me to write my own eulogy. I thought that was the craziest and most depressing proposal. Why would anyone want to think about his or her own death? The answer is that by doing so you can learn a valuable lesson about what you want your life to look like when you are alive. What legacy do you want to leave? What do you want to achieve? What would you want your friends to say about you and your life after you are gone? What does your ideal life look like?

I took his challenge, without realizing the impact it would have. My eulogy read something like this:

*Annette was a devoted daughter, wife, and friend. She was always the first to laugh at herself and the last to judge others. She was a true lover of life—her biggest passion was trying something for the first time and sharing her adventures in order to inspire others to step out of their comfort zones. Her curious nature and eagerness to learn led her around the world, collecting thousands of memorable experiences and making friends of all nationalities, creeds, ethnicities, and races. These first hand experiences and the people she met were her best teachers in life. She designed an unconventional lifestyle that she was excited to wake up to every morning. It was filled with travel, adventure, giving back, and lots of laughter. She touched the hearts of people from all walks of life, though she would say that it was her heart that was touched by them.*

This ended up being an emotional and enlightening exercise, realizing the life I truly wanted to lead versus the one I was living at the time. The two were miles apart. I took these words and translated them into goals for my life; travels that would immerse me with the locals, ways to inspire others to live a life beyond fear, and adventures that would leave lasting memories. This eulogy and my bucket list became my life's mission statement.

## Create Categories

Breaking up your life list into different categories can make the brainstorming process much easier. This is also a great way to organize it once it starts growing. Divide a page into your selected categories and list at least five entries for each one. You will find that some goals fit into two different sections; that is no problem, just record it in one—the most important part is that it's on there somewhere. Following are only examples of categories. If you find many of your entries fall into a category not shown here, simply create it. This is your list.

- Local Experiences
- Adventure
- Career & Finances
- Charity
- Creativity
- Education
- Entertainment & Events
- Family & Kids
- Food & Drink
- Just for Fun
- Personal Growth
- Nature & Wildlife
- Sports & Activities
- Travel (Local, Domestic, International)

## Ask Yourself 20 Questions

Sometimes the biggest "aha" moments come from asking yourself a question that has never been asked of you before. It can lead to overwhelming emotions and enlightening answers. Play a game of 20 Questions with yourself to find what adventures you would be most passionate about. Asking yourself these questions will provoke answers that can determine the life that you want to lead. If you get stumped, just skip to the next one and come back later. Don't let your answers be controlled by fear or self-doubt, this is the place to dream bigger than you ever thought possible. Even I go back and ask these questions of myself from time to time, and as I have evolved as a person, so have some of my answers.

1. Where in the world would you like to visit?
2. If you had one month to live, what would you do?
3. What types of new foods do you want to try?
4. What cultural traditions are you interested in?
5. Are there any activities or sports that you want to try?
6. What events do you want to attend?
7. What has always been your biggest dream in life?
8. What classes have you always thought about taking?
9. If money and fear were not an issue what would you do?
10. Who have you always wanted to meet in person?

11. What would you like to do with family and friends?
12. In what ways do you want to improve yourself physically, mentally, or spiritually?
13. What skills have you wanted to learn?
14. Is there a charity you have always wanted to support?
15. What was your childhood dream—is it still relevant today?
16. If you won a multi-million-dollar lottery today, what would you do?
17. If you were on your deathbed, what would be your regrets?
18. What travel stories would you want to share with your grandchildren?
19. If you had three wishes what would they be?
20. Is there someplace you have always wanted to take your spouse, best friend, and parent?

## Use the Buddy System

Sometimes you can be gung ho about goal setting on your own and the ideas will flow easily, while other times you need a little help from your friends. Not only will they bring new ideas to the table, but also together you will be providing accountability and encouragement to each other. Connecting with like-minded people, especially if they share the same goal, can be a great support system to keep you motivated.

There are plenty of options when it comes to writing and tackling your bucket list with others. You can set up a girls' night at a wine bar, a special date night with your significant other, or get the entire family together to throw ideas around. Think about trading in your book club for a bucket list club, a group that can meet once or twice a month to create your lists, get motivation, and even accomplish goals together. One of my favorite ideas is to throw a bucket list party. You can supply decorative paper, sparkly pens, and the margaritas, then your best friends can hang out and conjure up ideas.

## Get Outside Inspiration

Now that you have ventured deep inside yourself to find experiences for your list, it's time to get some outside inspiration. In this modern day of television, Internet search engines, and social media, inspiration is all around you; you just have to be in the bucket list mindset to see it. Once you start cultivating ideas your instinct will automatically be on high alert whenever anybody mentions something worthy of a spot on your list. It is similar to when you've finally determined your dream destination is Italy and everywhere you look you notice either people going there, mentioning it in conversation, or it being written about in magazines. This is because your subconscious mind is already thinking about it.

Until this mentality kicks in, you can get inspiration from browsing Pinterest boards, watching travel shows, subscribing to adventure magazines, reading blogs (like mine, BucketListJourney.net—shameless plug), searching specific hashtags on Twitter, etc. The inspiration possibilities are almost endless. If that's not enough to get your brain juices flowing, you can also watch the movie *The Bucket List* with Jack Nicholson and Morgan Freeman. Though it did not start the bucket list phenomenon, it did bring the term to the forefront.

## Revisit and Review Your List

Revisit your list in a week or a month to double-check what you have with a fresh pair of eyes. Do this while remembering that putting something on your list is making a contract with yourself. Ask yourself if they are truly your goals or have they been added to your list out of social expectations? Delete items that you added not because you wanted to actually achieve them, but because you thought they should be on there. Be brutally honest with yourself. What do you want to see, do, and experience in your lifetime? Just because everyone has bungee jumping in New Zealand on his or her list does not mean it has to be on yours, unless it is really something that you want to do. Don't fill it with aspirations of other people, unless it truly resonates with your dreams. With that said, make sure that it is not your fear speaking when you remove something from your list

Remove anything that is impossible, *truly impossible*, not something that is frightening or seemingly undoable due to lack of confidence. If you are a woman, living in a Byzantine monastery on Mount Athos in Greece is not going to happen since females were banned in 1046. Competing in the NFL for a man over sixty with no athletic skill: I don't think so. I am a firm believer that I can do almost anything that I put my mind to, but I also know my limitations. My window of opportunity for being an Olympic gymnast is over, not to mention the fact that I can't even touch my toes, and becoming a famous country singer may involve not breaking glass when I sing. With that said, also force yourself to think outside of the box. If your goal is to compete in a Sumo wrestling match in Japan and you are a ninety-five-pound female, think about ways to tailor this target to something doable. Can you compete in an exhibition sumo match wearing a protective suit? Or is there a lightweight women's segment?

Make it a ritual of reviewing your bucket list once a month—have your feelings about any goals changed? Is there something that you heard about that sparked an interest? Don't be afraid to add items when inspiration strikes, or to delete when natural evolution has made the goal now lack meaning or you have truly had a change of heart. As I said earlier, fear, procrastination, or lack of motivation should not be the reason for a deletion. But as we grow, we evolve, and so should our bucket lists. Over the years your travel style will change, as will your adventure level. When you begin it may be all about your love of hiking National Parks in the United States, whereas a few years down the road you may have realized your passion for seeing the largest waterfalls all over the world or helping villages build community gardens in South Africa. As you discover more about yourself, a meaningful bucket list will have to grow with you.

Stopping to smell the roses in Guatemala

## COMMIT

Come each January, it is estimated that 45 percent of people make New Year's resolutions, and every year only 8 percent of them will succeed at the goal they set for themselves. Typically, the first couple weeks it is all rainbows and butterflies, you are 100 percent devoted to the goal. Then as time goes on your level of commitment starts to dwindle; you begin to get sidetracked and discouraged. Before you know it, winter is rolling around again and you are a part of the failure statistic.

You have already begun to stop the cycle by writing your bucket list, now you must truly commit to living it.

Commit by making a personal promise to yourself that will assist you in living your dreams. When I first decided to make my bucket list a priority in my life, this was the pact I made with myself:

Taking a falconry lesson at Dromoland Castle in Ireland

*I promise to never let fear make my decisions for me, and to take one step toward my goals each and every day.*

This commitment caused me to analyze every declined opportunity to see if the reason was based on fear. If it was, I forced myself to turn my no into a yes. It also caused me to be continuously making progress toward a goal by committing to doing one thing every day. It didn't have to be huge, on some days it was simply researching hiking trails and other days it was downloading a travel app to my iPhone. Maybe for you, you can only squeeze in a step every week. Whatever it is, make a commitment to yourself and stick to it.

## CONQUER

Okay, so you have this incredible list, now it is time to do something about it. A bucket list is not helpful if all the goals just sit unfinished forever. It is time to start turning your dreams into a reality. Time and time again we hear people mention the wish lists for their lives, wide-eyed with an excitement in their voices, the crackling of the wheels turning in the brain and an overwhelming feeling of hope. It's a contagious feeling; one that you wish would last forever. Then what happens? Unfortunately, that thought needs to turn to action and that's where the need for "instant gratification" scores a touchdown while hard work is left to watch from the sidelines. Taking on the entire goal seems like an impossible feat, so day by day the excitement dwindles until the goal is a distant memory like the wrinkle-free skin I had when I was eighteen. Don't worry, it's happened to me too. But, there are some techniques to help ensure your success.

## Be Accountable

Want to have better odds at keeping the commitment you made to yourself? Hold yourself accountable. You can do this by publicly announcing the contents of your bucket list or at least your active pursuit of one of your goals—share it with your family, friends, and even a couple of acquaintances. Not only will your enthusiasm be contagious, but sharing will make you feel obligated to complete a goal; you don't want to be seen as the person who goes back on their word. After telling a few people, there is no doubt that someone like Uncle Mikey will ask you how you are coming along with "that bucket list thing" at your next family gathering. Either you will have an impressive adventurous story to share or it will give you the little push you need to get back on track.

Even better, if you have started your list with friends, your children, or a spouse, make a plan to meet once a month to discuss the progress you have all made and to determine steps you will take before the next time you meet. Having these monthly get-togethers causes you to be answerable to someone, and it could be a huge support when you encounter challenges with a goal you are working on.

I held myself accountable by starting a blog and letting the entire world know my intentions. Even in the beginning when the readers were few, *Bucket List Journey* held me accountable every day. People would email asking what I was doing next, or they would congratulate me on one of my ventures. Several have even invited me to assist in one of their goals. I have been invited to Thanksgiving dinner at the home of one of my readers, on a sexy Playboy-style cruise with a stranger (I actually went!), and even was sent a gift card to a restaurant in Portland when I announced my plans to go there. Each interaction pushed me forward and strengthened my commitment. I didn't want to disappoint the people who were counting on me or to disappoint myself.

## Pick Starter Goals

You are probably looking at your long list of aspirations, confused at where to begin. Focusing on too many goals can be distracting, so start by picking two to three to work on, at least one long-term and one short-term. If you can't decide which ones to start with, read your list again to identify what excites you at the moment, what gives you goose bumps or a thrill in the pit of your stomach.

My first tandem goals were going to the movies by myself and driving through the hills of Tuscany. Of course, the theater task was completed almost instantaneously, which made me feel like I was making progress, whereas traveling to Italy took over a year and a half. Once the short-term goal was completed I immediately replaced it with another easier item while still continuing to make progress on the larger goal.

## Deadline Your Objectives

Setting deadlines can help escape the "someday" syndrome, a common excuse for why you won't begin today because you will get to it someday. The goals you choose to currently work on should have a

Searching for sea glass at Glass Beach in Fort Bragg, California

deadline different than "in your lifetime," as it will create a sense of urgency to propel you forward. Push yourself, but also be realistic. If you have just accepted a demanding new job that will require six months of training, then your dream of going to a month-long silent retreat in Bali may have to have a longer deadline than a year. Spend some time calculating what is practical: if you are committed to a half year of training for your position, then allow yourself three months for full transition into the new position after the training period. Then assess how long it will take you to complete the goal from this point, and that's what your deadline should be, keeping in mind that you will be able to complete little steps along the way.

If you are putting a deadline to your entire bucket list, then it's not really a bucket list by definition, because your lifetime is the deadline. What I can recommend is creating mini-lists within your list, for example:

- **Seasonal Bucket List** – Some items will only be able to be done in certain seasons, like seeing the tulip fields in Holland or dogsledding in Greenland. Each year create lists for summer, winter, spring, or fall.
- **This Year's Bucket List** – Instead of making a New Year's resolution, on the first of the year break your list down to the items you want to complete in the next twelve months.
- **30 Before 30, 40 before 40, or 50 before 50** – Choose goals that you want to do before reaching a certain age.

## Break Down Goals into Actionable Steps

Don't make the mistake of thinking it's not worth even beginning if you are only able to make a small start. If your goal is completing a marathon, put on your running shoes and walk around the block. If it is learning how to speak Italian, memorize one word a day or even a week. Every accomplishment starts with one single step; it doesn't matter how big or small, as long as you are making the effort to move forward.

Creating these types of baby steps is especially helpful when you are trying to tackle a larger, long-term goal. It is less daunting to focus on each small task, plus you will get a confidence boost with each little milestone reached, as you will realize that you are one step closer to your goal. When you are looking at the big picture in its entirety, it can seem overwhelming and intimidating, which can promote procrastination. Breaking it down into bite-sized pieces and concentrating on each one individually makes it seem more doable. For example, if your goal is to go hunting for truffles in Italy, this could be broken down into the following steps:

- Get a passport
- Research the best location for truffle hunting
- Determine when truffle season is

- Request time off from work
- Book a truffle hunting tour
- Research flights to Italy
- Book a flight to Italy
- Book a hotel
- Order currency
- And so on . . .

Take these steps, put deadlines to each one, and create a schedule. I can easily create up to a hundred steps for a large goal. This may sound tedious, but if you have committed to doing one thing each day, one hundred steps takes only just over three months of time before you are standing at the top of that mountain or crossing that finish line.

## Start Today

The more you procrastinate, the less likely it is that you will be able to do all the things in life you wish. Change that procrastination into determination by starting today. Make the first step of your chosen starter goal something you know you can complete within the next twenty-four hours. If your dream is to walk the Great Wall of China, begin by researching the best path. If your wish is to learn to crochet a scarf, start by finding a nearby class or set of instructional videos. Don't wait for what seems like the "perfect" time, because that time is today.

Sometimes we try to bargain with ourselves: "I will take that dream cruise through the Alaskan glaciers as soon as _____." You can fill in the blank: when your child turns eighteen, after your business has a more efficient staff, or possibly when you are debt-free. This bargaining tool makes us feel that our goal is actually possible, but the steps to achieve it will be taken at a later time—someday. Someday is not a guarantee. It is never too early to begin, don't wait for that someday that may never come. Go at life with a curious spirit, adventurous soul, and fearless mindset.

## CELEBRATE

When you are working toward a goal there are bound to be challenges. Being so focused on the task at hand can turn these obstacles into setbacks, especially when you are not taking opportunities to celebrate small victories. When you reach a benchmark, stop to celebrate your progress. Let's say you check off booking your hotel in Switzerland today, then reward yourself with a delicious piece of Swiss chocolate. You wrote your packing list for a trip to Venice in the spring—that's good for a scoop of hazelnut gelato. Marking our achievements, celebrating even the small successes,

Photographing the doors of Santorini, Greece

keeps us energized and encourages us to keep going forward with our goals. Don't only give yourself kudos for making the big check mark next to a large goal on your bucket list; recognize how far you've come and celebrate the journey all along the way.

After putting a big bold check mark next to an item on your list, make sure that the incredible memories and powerful feelings related to them don't slip away. Keep a memory book filled with keepsakes, post photos on social media, or write in a journal. Do anything that will keep the memory alive and motivate you to achieve the next dream.

# 3. WHY TRAVEL?

There were adorable African children at my feet, each wielding colorful twistable balloons. Some were wearing them as hats; others were making attempts at producing animals and a few of the younger ones were simply using them as pacifiers. One smarty-pants even tried to turn a bright yellow one into a water balloon, somewhat unsuccessfully. The laughter that encompassed the dirt courtyard and the smiles on their faces were priceless.

The orphanage, on the outskirts of downtown Arusha in Tanzania, was hidden down a bumpy dirt road and painted in a friendly pale blue. There were forty-eight children that called it home, many who came outdoors when we arrived to greet us with a shy "Karibu," which means "welcome" in Swahili. We were there to volunteer for the day and I came armed with fun—balloons that could be turned into animals. It was a simple toy that in a matter of minutes transformed bashful youngsters into creative, spunky kids.

When the memorable day was almost over, a little African girl came running toward me with her arms wide open, by pure instinct I scooped her up into my embrace. This was a thank-you that needed no words, one that crossed language barriers. It was a single moment that encompassed the power of a bucket list and meaningful travel; a moment that filled my heart with happiness, and hers too.

◆ ◆ ◆

Travel appears on many bucket lists for a variety of reasons. For some it is simply a time to reenergize your batteries, while for others it's to experience things first hand or disconnect from the stresses at home. For me, and many others who choose to take it one step further and travel deeper, it is because it has the ability to enrich your life in some way, shape, or form—you return a different person than when you

Spending the afternoon at Kibowa Orphanage in Tanzania, teaching the children how to make animal balloons

arrived. Just like in the case of the orphanage visit, it was impossible for me to leave those children without having been transformed in some way. It opened my eyes to hardships around the world, and to the importance of altruism. Travel is the best teacher in life.

Though many people associate having meaningful travel experiences strictly with volunteerism, there are many more ways to travel deeper, exploring the world purposefully and making your ventures matter more. It could be seeing a mother gazelle giving birth in the bush, taking a relationship-changing road trip with your elderly grandfather, or learning to make pasta from a nonna in Italy. These ventures can enhance your life just as much as building a home for poverty-stricken families.

You are the only one that can determine what type of travel experience will make a difference in your life, but here are several ways to get the most out of traveling:

## IMMERSE YOURSELF IN THE CULTURE

When many arrive to a foreign destination they make the mistake of visiting without ever really leaving their own world. They choose the route of being a tourist looking from the outside in, essentially sitting on the sidelines taking in everything going on around them yet never really participating. They are typically the people watchers, sitting at a Starbucks in Paris sipping a skinny vanilla latte, instead of eating croissants at Du Pain et Des Idées or shopping with the locals at the Marché aux Puces flea market. They are spectators of the city's people.

On the flip side of the coin, others gain a better understanding and have a more profound experience by being immersed in the culture, which is really just a matter of leaving the comfort of your hotel and being engulfed into the world around you. The deepest travel happens when you integrate into a community by actively participating, opening yourself to interact with the locals, and understanding the way others live. This can be as easy as actively participating in their rituals, eating traditional dishes from the region, or learning the history that makes the city what it is today. For me, in Florence it meant breaking away from the typical spaghetti with meatballs and eating a *lampredotto* sandwich made with tender slices of tripe, a Florentine street food tradition. In Greece it was about mastering the art of Greek dancing, where the women pranced in the inner circle and the men on the outer while shouting "Opa!" And in Warsaw, immersion was walking through the Jewish Ghetto learning about the rich history that went on behind the tattered walls.

The locals can give you the best insight into their culture, unlike any book on the shelves. Plus, some of the best travel tips and advice comes from talking to them. I know that connecting with the locals doesn't sound so easy to do sometimes, but try sitting at the bar when dining, striking up a conversation while standing in line, or talking to the taxi drivers—they definitely know their way around a city. This is

Meeting the locals at Jerash
Archaeological Site in Jordan

how I found out where the best Greek salad was in Santorini and which booth to buy the finest ahi tuna at while visiting Tsukiji Fish Market in Tokyo.

Learn some basic phrases in the foreign tongue and look for opportunities to interact with the city's people. Wander off the beaten path, drink at their pubs, and frequent their hangouts. Stay away from the tourist traps, but if you are there ask the workers at the souvenir stands the right questions. Ask the real questions about how it is to live, work, and eat in their town. Where are their favorite places to go? Be patient if you are traveling to a foreign country, as English is probably their second language. Interact with a curious, loving spirit—a willingness to learn.

Spending time lounging at a resort pool sipping on cosmopolitans is an entirely different experience than drinking a pint of Guinness at a neighborhood pub in Dublin. Put down the camera, turn off the cell phone, and just be present in a moment. There is a great value in learning a country's history and being immersed into its culture.

## CONNECT WITH NATURE AND WILDLIFE

Many brushes with nature are brief escapes from an otherwise stressful day; you may pause for a moment to look out your office window at an afternoon rainbow or spot a deer in the fields across from your child's school. For an instant, the accidental encounter energizes and calms you at the same time, but you may not be sure why. Connecting with nature means more than simply getting a little fresh air, rather it has the potential to make us aware of an existence bigger than the latest Apple product, and possibly even ourselves.

Hiking Pacaya Volcano in Guatemala

The world is an incredible collage of natural plants, animals, and landscapes—filled with unforgettable places organically created. Something spiritual happens when you are connecting with nature and experiencing wildlife. There's nothing quite like witnessing the peacefulness of a mother baboon cuddling her child in a Ngorongoro crater, the soothing sound of the rushing water of the Iguazu Falls in South America, or being amongst the stillness of the giant redwoods along the California coast. These experiences can spur creativity, bring happiness, relieve stress, and cause you to look at the world with a sense of awe.

Traveling gives you many opportunities to be among animals and consciously connect with them in their natural environment, not at a zoo or animal park. Look for places that allow you to interact with dolphins in the wild, participate in turtle protection programs, and spot birds in natural habitats; visit national parks, sanctuaries, and UNESCO World Heritage (www.whc.unesco.org) sites. Feel the grass beneath your feet, catch snowflakes in your mouth, or climb to the top of a deserted mountain.

## GIVE BACK

Just like the old adage says "it feels better to give than to receive." Simply put, giving feels good. Though giving should be a selfless experience, it is both beneficial for yourself as well as the recipient. Research has shown that there are incredible benefits to humanitarianism: it builds relationships, profits people less fortunate, strengthens communities, and helps you gain a different perspective.

Whether you center an entire trip on helping others or add a few volunteer aspects to your itinerary, there are plenty of opportunities to be charitable around the world. Giving blood can save lives, volunteering at a Cambodian orphanage puts smiles on dozens of faces, teaching English as a second language will change a child's future, and spending time helping at an animal sanctuary can mean being a part of saving a species from extinction. There are several organizations that create itineraries where you can join a development project trip, like Global Vision International (GVI; www.gviusa.com), Projects Abroad (www.projects-abroad.org), or Global Volunteers (www.globalvolunteers.org). There are also some simpler, less time consuming projects as well, like Pack for a Purpose (www.packforapurpose.org), where you leave a little room in your suitcase to pack items needed for community projects or lend money to a future entrepreneur through the Kiva (www.kiva.org).

## PUSH YOUR COMFORT ZONE

Just as I mentioned that one of the benefits of settings goals with a bucket list is its ability to push you to step outside your comfort zone, expanding your boundaries is also another way to get the most out of your travel experience. Each time you try something for the first time you will grow—a little piece of the fear of the unknown is removed and replaced with a sense of empowerment.

If you travel and want to stay within the comfort of your security bubble, then book a week at a resort hotel and never leave it. But, traveling deeper means pushing your boundaries. You need to walk away from a trip saying, "I can't believe I had the courage to do that."

On an international trip, many things will break you out of your comfort zone: dealing with the language barrier, navigating the streets, and ordering foreign food. But, you should also make it a point to do something that scares you just a little. Schedule something new and a little uncomfortable every day of your travel itinerary. Eat something bizarre, try an adventurous activity, and explore the nooks and crannies of a unique city.

## TRAVEL SOLO

Let's face it, sometimes you are the best travel companion for yourself—you can do what you want, when you want, and it makes planning so much easier when there aren't other opinions of what to do. Also, you are more open to meeting new people when you are alone; we tend to stick with our travel companions otherwise. Many people, especially women, will put their travel dreams on hold because they do not have the perfect companion who has the same available time, money, or desire to go on an adventure. But by doing so, you will not only miss out on what the world has to offer, but more importantly the feeling of empowerment you get from relying solely on yourself while on the road.

If I passed on opportunities due to lack of a travel buddy I would have never eaten gooey fondue in Switzerland or fed bananas to the monkeys at a temple in Thailand. Not only would incredible adventures have been missed, but also I may have never realized how perfectly capable I am of navigating the world on my own and on my own terms. Facing uncertainties every day and being able to overcome them on my own opened up more possibilities to achieving my bucket list goals.

## SHARE AN EXPERIENCE WITH SOMEONE SPECIAL

Have you ever been somewhere, seen something truly incredible and wished there was someone there with you to share that experience with? Just like traveling solo can be an enlightening experience, traveling with someone special can create cherished memories as well. A sunset that spreads over the water in Bora Bora, throwing tomatoes at the La Tomatina festival in Spain, or enjoying a wine pairing dinner in Argentina set atop a hill overlooking the city can be more magical when shared with someone else.

Traveling together can strengthen your relationships by building trust and creating the opportunity to learn more about your companion. A tandem bungee jump in New Zealand can bond a relationship. A girl's trip to Las Vegas can be one for the memory books. A weekend getaway with a parent can be their most special memory. One of my most

Working a pottery wheel in a Tuscan village

meaningful trips was to Yosemite National Park on Christmas day with my husband. We were spending the holidays alone and decided to take a spur of the moment road trip a few hours from our Northern California home. For three short days we sat by the wood fire making s'mores, drinking *Syrah* and talking about our dreams for the future. We woke up to a blanket of white, hiked waterfalls, and made a snowman. This would have been an entirely different experience if I had been traveling solo or with another companion. It was an opportunity to create special memories and getting to know each other even better.

## LEARN SOMETHING NEW

As I have said before, travel is one of the best educations you can have, it teaches you things that no textbook ever could. It is not difficult to learn something new, as many travel situations will force you to have to figure things out in a foreign destination. You'd be surprised how long it took me to learn how a Japanese toilet worked! But, where the real magic happens is when you are learning something new about a culture, a city's history, and about people of the land you are visiting, or even something new about yourself.

No too long ago, while sitting next to a young Japanese girl on the subway in Tokyo, she pulled out a couple colorful square pieces of paper and handed me one. She then began to fold the sheet, waiting for me to follow suit. We continued folding in complete silence and ten minutes later I realized that she was teaching me how to make an origami crane. It was unexpected, and memorable.

Look for deeper learning opportunities on your travels; take a cooking class in making a local dish, go on an historical tour of the city or learn to do the local dance.

## SUPPORT THE LOCALS

Many small businesses, especially in developing countries, rely on tourism for their economic survival. Spending your dollars at an international hotel chain and its restaurant is only partially supporting the natives of a destination. These companies do create local jobs, but a substantial portion of the profits may go to the large corporation owners and not the region's people. Further supporting the locals in the cities and countries you travel to would mean booking tours with local guides, eating at mom and pop restaurants, staying at independently owned hotels, shopping at the street market, or buying souvenirs directly from the craftsman who makes them. This will not only help the local economy, but also create a more authentic experience.

In Dublin, we chose to sleep at a small B&B whose owner sent us to the neighborhood bar where we shared fish and chips with the people who lived in the area. In Tokyo, we hired a native Japanese tour guide who in the end took us into her private home to teach us how to make sushi and then dressed us in kimonos. In Italy, I bought hand-stamped aprons straight from the craftsman who made them, and he allowed me to do some stamping personally. Have the travel globally;

Walking the rocky beaches of Nice in the South of France

think locally, mentality and it will pay you back two-fold in experience.

## NOURISH YOUR BODY, MIND, AND SPIRIT

For some, a true vacation means pampering themselves with deep-fried foods and glasses of sugary cocktails, plus pulling all-nighters while dancing on the bar at the hottest new club. The only real physical activity is walking from their room to the pool to the bar and back. Vacationers typically return home from these types of trips needing another vacation, their body feeling tired and their belly sporting some extra rolls. They may have had a good time, but they'll be paying for it for the weeks to come.

The opposite feeling occurs when you have just spent the week nourishing your body, mind, and spirit. This could be as simple as practicing meditation in Bali, going to a silent retreat in India, or attending a detox retreat in the Philippines. For me it was spending a peaceful week at a yoga retreat in Costa Rica. These types of trips feed not only your body, but also your soul. You return home feeling refreshed and revived, a better version of yourself.

◆ ◆ ◆

People travel for a variety of reasons and there are several different ways to get more out of your travel. With that said, the most important thing is that your experience makes you happy. One of my favorite things is watching people giggling as they are cheekily posing holding up the Leaning Tower of Pisa in Italy or taking a selfie with Elvis underneath the Las Vegas sign. Even though these touristy attractions are overrun with people, you can see the happiness on their faces, and calmness in the shoulders. If it is bringing you into a positive frame of mind that you otherwise would not be in with a boss hovering over your shoulder or children needing dozens of time-outs, then that may be enough meaning for you.

# 4. IF FEAR WASN'T A FACTOR

I was wide-awake at three in the morning . . . again, lying in my bed trembling from the inside out. It felt as if my innards were vibrating like a washing machine was running on spin cycle inside my body. Surely this symptom had to mean that I had some mysterious and deadly illness. It must be an ailment that was so rare that they probably didn't even have a cure, or worse, one that meant I would have to be quarantined in a plastic bubble for the rest of my shortened days. This wasn't my only symptom; there were also episodes of tunnel vision, tingling fingers, panic attacks, and lightheadedness. I had been to the emergency room so many times that I had started going to different hospitals for fear of being recognized as "a regular" by the nurses.

Each visit resulted in the same diagnosis. "You have anxiety," said doctor after doctor.

That just couldn't be, these symptoms were real and not some made-up condition. They were as legitimate as my pee being a fluorescent yellow the last time I showed up on Urgent Care's doorstep. It was just a fluke that it ended up being the new vitamins added to my morning routine and not something of a more serious nature.

I demanded a neurologist appointment, believing that my tingling and other odd symptoms must be an early sign of multiple sclerosis, lyme disease, or whatever else Google had suggested that I had on that particular day. I had MRIs, EPTs, EMGs and NCVs. The diagnosis always remained the same; the conclusion never wavered like my daily symptoms.

"You do not have a neurological disorder, you have anxiety," firmly stated the neurologist.

His words repeated in my head for days, if not weeks. Part of me was completely relieved while another huge chunk was utterly confused as to where to go from here. I had created a mess inside my body and mind, now I needed to figure out how to untangle the years of destruction.

It wasn't too long after the neurologist's diagnosis that I found myself curled up in the corner of my bedroom with an unsettling pit in my stomach and tears welling in my eyes. My body started to shake and the uncontrollable crying followed. Looking in the mirror that morning, it became dismally evident that the person who stared back was a shadow of who she could be. I desired a life filled with passion, new experiences, and travel, but how was I supposed to live that dream when anxiety had caused me to be stricken with a fear for just about everything in the world. Just the thought of being restricted to a hair stylist chair for even an hour caused heart palpitations, how would I ever be okay with flying in a plane for over twenty hours to Africa or traveling solo through Europe or swimming among the sharks in the Galápagos Islands?

I was tired of the restrictions fear was placing on my life and, in that very moment, I was finally ready to do something about it. Without really knowing exactly which direction to go and being fearful of taking medications, I started to read everything I could get my hands on about anxiety, fear, and living a passionate life. I devoured each word and took bits of advice from it all, creating a personal strategy. Little did I know, these eight fear-defeating habits would completely change my life. Maybe they can help you.

## EIGHT FEAR-DEFEATING HABITS

Fear is an emotional response to potential danger, which is a vital reaction when we need to protect ourselves from legitimate threats. But, we often end up fearing situations that are not a life-or-death crisis—we fear something that *might* happen. Having a physical response to an intruder in the home is significantly different than having the same response to the thought that your plane will crash before you have even booked the flight.

People can fear everything from cockroaches to clowns to the number thirteen. Even though the list of insecurities is countless, most fit under the umbrella of four main fears: the fear of failure, fear of dying, fear of change, and the fear of not being good enough. These internal fears can prevent us from having incredible new experiences—stop us from living an adventurous, passionate, and empowering life. Anxieties can cause us to turn down the promotion at work for fear of failing at the position, we don't ask our crush on a date for fear of not being good enough, or we never travel for fear of dying in a plane crash.

The toughest challenge may be overcoming the damage our own fears have created. But, a majority of the time your fears do not become a reality and then you wasted all the precious time worrying.

Covered in the mineral-rich black mud of The Dead Sea

What would you do if fear were not a factor? Would you volunteer at a children's hospital in Nepal or backpack through Europe? Would you dance the Flamenco with the locals in Spain or eat street food in Vietnam? The possibilities are endless.

Facing your fears can be an intimidating experience, because it can seem as if they are so powerful that there will not be a way out. Just like with tackling a goal, taking baby steps is the key and not getting discouraged when you don't see progress right away. It takes persistence and time.

### 1. Acknowledge the Fear

Many of us have fears that sit in the back of our minds, neglected, ignored, and unacknowledged. Even when the anxiety makes a physical appearance in our bodies we choose to just feel it, yet never truly name or understand it.

Start paying attention to how the physical reaction to fear feels in your body and acknowledge that sensation as a symptom instead of something greater. Not understanding or acknowledging the symptoms easily perpetuated my fear and anxiety. A slight tingle on a pinky toe could effortlessly turn into a self-diagnosis of gangrene, followed by thoughts of living with an amputated digit, and future visions of the manicurist's horrified faces while giving me a pedicure.

Accept that what you are feeling is anxiety or fear and not something else, and then take responsibility for it. When you are finally able to name the problem you can start moving forward on conquering fear. Face the fear and say, "I understand that this is just my fear of speaking in front of a large group and not something greater. I understand what you are doing to my body and it will pass." You can also write down all the physical feelings fear causes you, referring back can help you feel safe the next time it takes place.

I had spent so many years creating non-factual scenarios for everything that I was feeling, instead of simply calling them what they were.

Being able to finally sit back and say "my heart is beating fast, but I know that this is just because of the fear about boarding an airplane," or "my calves are tight, that must be from walking through all the street markets yesterday."

## 2. Challenge Your Fearful/Negative Thoughts

Norman Vincent Peale was quoted as saying, "Change your thoughts and you change your world." This couldn't ring more true, as our thoughts create the way we look at life and the interpretation of them creates the moods that we are having each and every day. Happy, positive, and optimistic thoughts create an entirely different interpretation of life than when our self-talk is plagued with fear and negativity. Changing our thought patterns is an integral part to working through the fear and creating a life of passion and adventure.

I had never analyzed or challenged my thoughts, never took a step back from them to assess what role they played. They just seemed to be something that had a life of their own: one bad one led to another which led to a downward spiral of negativity. The belief was that they were something that could not be controlled, much like aging or a natural disaster. But, what if these adverse thoughts were not unmanageable? What if they were a habit like overspending, avoiding eye contact, or saying "umm" when you speak? I put this possibility to the test.

For twenty-one days, the estimated time it takes to change a habit, every time I had a negative thought I would write it down in a journal. Then each sentence written was analyzed, asking myself questions like, "Is this thought a fact? What will most likely happen in this situation? Will this be important in five years? What is the best-case scenario? What would be a more positive way to interpret this situation?" After this analysis, underneath that unfavorable thought, I would write the positive and more factual version of it. For example:

**Fearful Thought:** "I will never be able to afford to travel the world."

*Unrealistic Positive Thought:* "I will be a millionaire soon enough and travel to every country in the world."

*Realistic Positive Thought:* "It may take some time, but I can curb my spending in certain areas, slowly saving enough money for my dream trip to see the kangaroos in Australia."

The first couple weeks of practicing this strategy produced a serious case of writer's cramp. My pessimistic mind was in overdrive. But, after the twenty-one day period, I noticed that not only were my negative thoughts easier to immediately recognize, but also many of my initial thoughts were switched to positive ones instead. Now, I can almost immediately notice when my self-talk is heading down a negative path and can consciously stop it before it spirals into an anxious episode.

### 3. Keep a Gratitude Journal

Over the years there have been many studies on the positive effects of having an attitude of gratitude. Robert Emmons is a leading scientific expert on gratitude and its affect on people physically, psychologically, and socially. His studies suggest that people who practiced gratitude had higher levels of positive emotions, a stronger immune system, felt less lonely, and had more happiness.

Just like with challenging your fearful thoughts, when you notice yourself thinking of something negative, switch it around to what you are grateful for about the situation. When you are stuck in morning traffic, be grateful for being able to listen to your music for an extra twenty minutes. If your travel partner gets a cold in Paris, which botches your dream date night, be thankful for room service. Instead of focusing on how cold it is while walking through the streets of Zurich, be grateful for the warm chestnut stands. If you get lost on the streets of Venice, missing the opening of the Opera, be grateful for being able to walk the streets of one of the most beautiful cities in the world.

You should also start each morning by listing five things you are grateful for. In the beginning it will probably be a struggle to come up with a mere five, being wrapped up in a world full of fear can disguise the good in your life. Think hard. Did you just drink a deliciously warm cup of coffee? Or did you connect with a friend by text? Or enjoy a heartwarming movie on television? There is always something to be grateful for—always.

## 4. Turn off Negative Television

Terrifying plane crashes seem to be a common occurrence. Cases of Ebola and yellow fever are clearly diagnosed at a rapid rate. Countless solo travelers are viciously robbed at gunpoint while walking the day-lit streets of foreign countries. According to television news, the world is falling apart at the seams, making many not want to explore it.

There is no doubt that television is an incredible innovation, but many of the shows breed negativity, which can affect your psychological health. The news is filled with disaster and reality programs are loaded with drama; this is what viewers feed off of. Watching these types of shows alters your mood in some way, this is why horror films can cause nightmares and puppy commercials make you feel warm and fuzzy inside. Studies have showed that being exposed to negative news is linked to making people more anxious.

Certain television programs can also create unrealistic expectations of life and feelings of inadequacy. Life is typically not like your favorite romantic comedy or fairytale. This expectation can make people disillusioned about what their relationships should be or how they should look. Our lives can feel mundane when compared to the seemingly perfect television character. If you ask any working nurse how their life compares to that of the staff on *Grey's Anatomy* I am certain they will give you a totally different perspective.

Change the channel; stop watching news, movies, or television programs that feed your fears.

### 5. Manage Stress with Exercise

Stress not only affects the brain, but also has an impact on the rest of the body as well. Feeling anxious or stressed? Swim some laps in the pool, perfect your downward dog in yoga, or hit the gym to pump some iron. Taking a little time out of your busy day to exercise not only improves your body, but it also has the power of improving sleep, self-confidence, and concentration, which all can assist in lowering stress levels. Getting sweaty also boosts production of endorphins, chemicals in the brain that act as natural painkillers—your brain's feel-good neurotransmitters.

I will be the first to admit to not being a huge fan of exercising. But, that changed when it became a part of my bucket list. I always made one of the goals I was working on a physical activity; learning to ice skate, hiking every trail at a local park, and running a 5k. Not only did the exercise help to release the anxious energy inside my body, but

Swimming with Sea Turtles in Maui

also the research and planning kept my mind focused on something other than the anxiety I was feeling.

## 6. Make a Fearless Promise to Yourself

We often make promises to ourselves about stopping a bad habit or changing our lives for the better. This is especially true as we conjure up ideas for our New Year's resolutions. During this time these promises result in gyms being flooded with newbies on January first, cigarette sales declining, and the local dog shelter getting overwhelmed with potential volunteers. Many of these resolutions that are made will only be forgotten in the upcoming months, if not weeks. We often make promises to ourselves that we don't live up to: I promise to eat better, to start exercising, and to spend more time with family. This time, you owe it to yourself to make one fearless promise and be able to rely on yourself to keep it. That vow is to *never let fear make your decisions for you*. This promise will dramatically change your behavior and improve your life.

After I had some control over my anxiety, I made the same powerful promise to myself. When opportunities presented themselves and I wanted to say no, I vowed to ask myself if those negative answers were fear speaking. If it was, I promised myself to say yes instead. This personal pact not only led to some of the most amazing adventures, but also pushed me into facing many fears head on, getting me out of my comfort zone.

## 7. Live the Bucket List Lifestyle

Creating a bucket list is only one small piece of the passionate life puzzle—actually living the bucket list lifestyle is the whole shebang. This lifestyle means waking up each day with the purpose of achieving goals, having new experiences, giving back, helping others complete their bucket list dreams and pushing the limit of your comfort zone. It keeps you focused on something else besides your fear. You will learn how to feel the fear and move past it in order to have a tick next to that goal. Plus, you will gain confidence each time you accomplish a feat and stepping out of the box will become the norm. You will learn that it's not about just succeeding, but also about failing and learning from those failures.

Having a bucket list, along with my fearless promise, has pushed me out of my comfort zone being the support system I needed to try so many new things. It has also made me realize that most things aren't as scary as you have imagined, that failing can be fun, that it is perfectly normal for not everyone to like you (or you them) and that perfection is a myth.

## 8. Expose Yourself to What You Fear

Mark Twain once said, "do the thing you fear the most and the death of fear is certain." As scary as it is, sometimes to beat the fear you just have to do it—probably more than once. Take that twelve-hour plane ride to Zurich, eat dinner alone in Vienna, and strike up a

conversation with a stranger in Dublin. Define your worst-case scenario of the unknown outcome, and realize that the worst rarely ever happens. You'll begin to notice that each consecutive time you do the scary thing it gets a little easier. Understand that your fear of flying will not go away just because you have taken one plane ride. Each time will get a little easier, but you have to be repetitive. Stanford neuroscientist Philippe Goldin told *Lifehacker*, "Exposure is hands down the most successful way to deal with phobias, anxiety disorders, and everyday fears of any sort."

My biggest fear in regard to traveling has always been flying. I admittedly was the one belly up to the airport bar prior to boarding. As time went on, I was able to skip the cocktail, because it wasn't necessary. Continuously doing what I feared the most made each time a little bit easier until I was finally able to board a plane without believing it would result in certain death.

So, I dare you to ask yourself, "What would you do if fear wasn't a factor?" For me if has led me around the world participating in cultural rituals, eating things I never even knew existed (blood sausage!!) and creating a lifetime of memories that mean more than any materialistic possession I could possibly own. Step by step it is possible to disown fear as a constant companion, and make it become a distant acquaintance.

# 5. OVERCOMING OBSTACLES: TIME, MONEY & BEYOND

Let's face it, it's much easier to set goals than to actually achieve them, especially when we hope that it can be done quickly without any difficulty at all. It's important to understand that the way to your dreams will have bumps on the path plus extreme challenges that may make you want to just quit the journey. Overcoming these hurdles is what will make the success so much sweeter. There are several types of obstacles you will face, like finding free time, saving more money, dealing with language barriers, and working through travel-related fears. The good news is that each one can be conquered, and tips on doing so are outlined below.

## TIPS TO FINDING TIME FOR YOUR BUCKET LIST

It seems that these days we are all just too busy, right? You don't have time to go to the gym or meet the girls for cocktails, for God's sake there's barely enough hours in the day to take a pee without multitasking while doing it. Your minutes are consumed with working your way up the corporate ladder or tending to the every need of the children, both of which never seem to leave even a leftover minute to focus on your dreams. But, the fact is that we all have the same twenty-four hours in a day—no more no less. It is what we choose to do with that time that is important. A big problem is people tend to associate being busy with self-worth—wearing busyness like a badge of honor. They get a sense of importance because they have so much to do, so many obligations, and people who need them. Your life can be richer and much more impressive if you're busy sitting on the beaches of Anguilla under a blue-striped umbrella with a fruity cocktail. The key to getting there is to take control of your time. There are always going to be obligations, but you need to make finding the time for your bucket list a priority and then utilize those hours properly.

### Create a Time Diary

If you do not have time to travel, what are you spending your time on? How much time do you spend watching television, talking on the phone, or on random unnecessary tasks? How many hours a week do you waste waiting in line because you shop or do your banking during peak hours? Put all your waking hours under a microscope by taking seven days to create a time diary that will keep track of what are you doing every fifteen minutes throughout the day. Include everything you do from the moment you wake up in the morning until the time you go to sleep; from eating a snack to feeding the dog to answering emails to commuting. After the week is over analyze your diary to pinpoint what's consuming your time and help to turn wasteful hours into something more productive by following these rules:

- **Eliminate Time Wasters** — Evaluate all the things you do each day and look for opportunities to eliminate the time wasters, all the unnecessary items that fill up your precious minutes.
  - Do you open your email a dozen times a day? Instead select predetermined times to check and answer your messages, limiting it to no more than twice in twenty-four hours.
  - Automatic notifications that pop up on your computer or phone while you are working can be a big distraction. Turn them off.
  - Eliminate junk email from reentering your inbox by using the unsubscribe button at the bottom of unsolicited emails.
  - Always keep your personal space and workspace organized so you're not spending too much time trying to find something.

- Avoid standing at the refrigerator door contemplating dinner by planning your meals for the week in advance. Also, cook in bulk so you always have leftovers available for a quick meal.
- Limit your choices — The more choices you have, the longer it will take to decide and the less productive you will be. Instead of having twenty winter sweaters in every different color and style in your closet, have just a few in the same color palette for easy matching. Instead of a refrigerator packed with different dinner options, have enough food to create just a few different dishes.
- Eliminate being pulled in a hundred different directions first thing in the morning by making a time-based daily plan the night before.
- If you find that you are on the phone with your girlfriends or family chatting about nothingness for an hour every evening put a fifteen-minute timer on the calls.

- **Look for Multitasking Opportunities** — There is never a time when I am watching television, getting a pedicure, or blow-drying my hair that I am not doing something else at the same time. It is the perfect opportunity to answer emails or research travel destinations. Look for opportunities in your day where you can safely multitask: listen to informational books on tape while driving, create your itinerary while watching television, or order travel products online during the few minutes you are waiting outside your child's school.

- **Consider Delegating** — Many of us have the mentality that no one can do a task as good as we can, so the thought of delegating at home or at work can be pretty frightening. This is especially true if you are a perfectionist, wanting everything done according to your high standards. But, in the grand scheme of things does it really matter if your bed doesn't have perfectly taut hospital corners or if the bushes have a couple of scraggly branches poking out? It's done, and one less thing on your daily schedule. If you want to free up time in order to focus on the things that are truly important, you need to delegate. Add a task to the children's chore list, hire a college kid to run errands, assign part of a work project to someone capable. There will be a learning curve when assigning duties, which means that you will have to teach people what your standards are and manage their work. But, delegation is a major reason that I am able to own a successful restaurant while also escaping around the world as a travel writer. It involves passing off everything from doing paperwork to editing photographs to shopping for supplies.

- **Learn to Say No** — For many saying no is exceedingly challenging. They end up responding yes to things that they really don't want to do for fear of hurting someone's feelings or simply out

Withstanding the snowfall in Big Fork, Montana

of guilt. But, learning to say no to others is a very big step to finding time for you. Putting too much on your plate can cause a stress that leaves you stagnant—don't take on more than you can handle and don't push aside something that is a priority to you. You must distance yourself from the thinking that declining an offer from someone is telling him or her that they are not important in your life. Saying no simply means that you have too many other obligations at the moment, plus it helps to set future boundaries between you and the person. Make sure to not give a specific reason for saying no, this will only give them an opportunity to find a work around. A simple "I'm so sorry but I can't this time" will do.

## Prioritize Dreams

Think about all the things you did today, how you chose to spend each minute of your day. Whatever you have accomplished was because you decided it was a priority in your life and something else was not as important. Going for a manicure after work may have been more important than researching a weekend getaway to San Francisco. Even though you may believe you have no choices, your life is filled with series of decisions, albeit most of those selections are based on the consequences you would face if the alternative happened. You may choose to go to a job you despise every day because the alternative would be the fear of not finding something better and not being able to provide for your family. This is a completely valid thought, but still know that it is a decision you made.

The key is to make your goals a priority, by eliminating the words "I don't have time" when referring to them. We all have time for what we choose to have time for and you need to make yourself a priority. That doesn't mean that the children won't get fed or the lawn will never be mowed, it just means that your dreams will be moving up on the priority ladder. Organize your tasks each day by what's most important to the least, making sure that a step toward your goals is near the top of that list every single day.

## Broaden Your Definition of Travel

The definition of travel doesn't have to equal a two-week trip exploring the Greek isles. It can also mean a weekend getaway to hike the red rocks of Sedona or a couple-day road trip driving along the California coastline. Stop defining travel by the distance the destination is from your departure or the length of time you will be away from home. Instead characterize it as a journey of exploration, relaxation, adventure, and learning. This sort of trip can be done a few blocks from your house or halfway around the world. You don't need to wait for a couple weeks off from work in order to recharge. Plan a micro-vacation, a brief getaway that can be from four hours to four days long and give you a momentary hiatus from the cares of everyday life. Use these tips:

- **Become a Local Tourist** – We can take for granted the beauty in our own backyards, so visit your hometown (or a neighboring one) as if you were a tourist. Treat it like it is a vacation; create an itinerary, make reservations for attractions, take a tour, and bring your camera. One of the most fun things my husband and I ever did was to become a tourist in San Francisco, just forty-five minutes south of my home base in Northern California. On one of our random days off together, we planned an entire itinerary filled with touristy experiences like riding a cable car, eating chowder at Fisherman's Wharf, drinking Irish coffee at the Buena Vista, etc. It was only an eight-hour getaway, but felt like a short vacation.
- **Use Holidays and Long Weekends Wisely** – Take advantage of long weekends and holidays by turning your two-day weekend into a three-to-four day getaway. This is easily enough time to

hop on a plane to explore another state. You can leave for the airport directly from work on Friday and roll straight into the office with a big smile on your face on a Tuesday morning.

Walking the 16th Avenue Steps in San Francisco

- **Add Onto Work Trips** – If you have a work position that requires you to travel, tag on a couple of days. The flights will typically cost the same for your employer, so take the opportunity to explore a city, outside of the conference walls.

- **Don't Underestimate How Much Time is Needed** – Many people would never dare to travel all the way to Europe if they only had a week available or to Africa if there was just ten days to spare. What a shame. I was gone a total of eight days on my trip to Tanzania, this included almost seventy hours of travel time. It left about five unforgettable days to go on a safari, indulge in traditional Ugali for dinner, sleep in the middle of Serengeti, and spend a very special afternoon with the sweet children at the African orphanage. These unbelievable memories far surpassed the feeling of jetlag.

## THE MONEY DILEMMA

Not too long ago instead of living my bucket list I was sitting on the couch watching the bills on the kitchen table pile up. There was a serious fear in even opening the envelopes, because there was no money to pay them. At that time, we had five mortgages (painful residue from taking advantage of the rental housing market boom and not foreseeing the crash), plus restaurant bills that wouldn't end even though our sales had plummeted. It would have been easy to drown in the poor-me syndrome, but I knew that no one else was going to get me out of debt, so I had to find a way. That's when I remembered something an old boss told me, "It's much easier to save money than make it." The light bulb turned on and I took the next month to focus on finding ways to save on my bills. I switched to a cheaper car insurance company, negotiated product pricing for my restaurant, changed employees' schedules, and canceled magazine subscriptions, plus went through every line of my cable bill eliminating unnecessary items. All this added up to the tune of almost five hundred dollars a month. I then switched all my credit cards with a balance to limited time o percent cards with minimal balance transfer fees. Part of the five hundred dollar savings went toward paying off these cards. Once they were at a zero balance, I changed all of them to rewards cards and paid any bill possible using these new cards, of course bringing them back to zero at the end of each month.

Afterward I took a look at the harder part, how to make more money. First, a significant amount of time was spent monetizing my blog, pitching partnerships with companies, and working with affiliate programs. At the time, this only amounted to an extra fifty to one hundred dollars per month, but an extra hundred bucks a month could buy me a plane ticket almost anywhere in the world after just a year. At the restaurant, when other businesses were raising their prices to recoup their losses, we lowered ours. If people were only going to be able to afford to eat out once a month, we wanted to make sure they chose us knowing that they would get value for their dollar. We also gave away free ten-dollar gift cards with no restrictions, knowing that this would get people in the door and most likely spending at least double that amount. This all was a fairly long and dedicated process, but in less than a year I was able to take my first very economically conscious trip.

There is a false perception that you need to be rich to travel, which simply is not true. I know dozens of travelers who live off of less than ten thousand dollars a year and travel every day of their lives. Being driven by their passion, they found unique ways to make it happen. They may use couch surfing sites for their lodging, earn extra money teaching English classes abroad, or survive off of economical street food for their meals. I am not saying that everyone has to be that extreme, it's just an example of the lengths people will go to follow their dream.

Of course travel will take some money and you may have to make some sacrifices (say good-bye to expensive frilly cocktails at trendy lounges), but it may not be as much as you think depending on where and when you go and the way you travel. A plane ticket can be bought strictly on rewards points and hotels can be secured cheaply with loyalty programs, plus every destination has free attractions to see. The trick is to use the savings techniques that professional travelers use and create a financial plan.

## Create a Financial Travel Plan

There are hundreds, if not thousands of financial books on the market giving advice on ways to save money. But, some of the techniques can seem like you are making too much of a sacrifice from your normal day-to-day living, which makes it difficult to adhere to. Saving doesn't have to be a complete downer; it can also be empowering and actually fun. Yes, fun. Start by picking a specific bucket list experience that you want your money to be spent on, because it is more motivating to be putting dollars in a jar labeled "Trekking the Inca Trail" than one that just says "future dream." Next, follow these steps to start putting your wanderlust into action.

- **Make an Expense Spreadsheet**
  Calculate your monthly expenses by creating a spreadsheet with two columns: Needs and Wants. Track every penny you spend in one month—it must all be on this sheet. The needs category should include things like rent, insurance, utilities, and other necessities. In the wants category, put all the things that are discretionary spending, the stuff you spend your extra money on. This would include dining out, clothes shopping, hobbies, manicures, and the things that you don't necessarily need. Tally both columns up putting the total at the bottom.

  Take a close look at your Wants category to see where you can cut back, even if it's not deleting the item altogether. Do you really need your triple-shot, non-fat, soymilk latte every morning? Can you commit to making coffee at home at least a couple times a week? If you skipped just three days in the week, you could be saving roughly fifty dollars per month. In just thirty days, you would have enough for a few mugs of beer at Oktoberfest in Germany or a week's worth of cappuccinos and pastries in Italy. Go through each expense in this column and commit to making one small change for each line item.

  Not only should you look at the Wants list, but also take a close look at the Needs. This is where I was able to also save a lot of money. Call every company in this section to try to renegotiate monthly charges or switch providers altogether. Switching my car insurance ended up saving me forty-five dollars a month and bargaining with the cable company to get any special deals that they had saved me thirty-five dollars a month. You can also go through every bill line by line and see if there are any extra charges that you don't understand. Call the companies asking for explanations and eliminate what is unnecessary. After you have gone through both columns, determine the amount of money you need from your paychecks in order to survive, add a small amount on top of that for incidentals and a few of your wants, then commit to saving the rest.

- **Open a Bucket List Savings Account**

  It may not be safe to store all your money in a jar, so go to your bank and open a savings account specifically for your dream bucket list adventure. If your bank doesn't offer accounts free of fees, there are plenty of companies online that do. Ally (www.ally.com) and Barclay (www.banking.barclaysus.com) have savings accounts with no minimums and no maintenance fees. The moment you get a paycheck, deposit your determined savings per month into the adventure account and don't touch it. The only withdrawals you should make are to pay for something to do with your goal.

- **Get Travel Rewards Credit Cards**

  Apply for credit cards that earn airline miles and/or hotel stays, and start using them for everything, even if it's just a pack of gum. But, make a commitment to pay them off at the end of every month. To earn even faster, you can also check your household bills to see if companies accept payments by credit card with no extra fees. Research the best program for your needs and hunt for the best signup deals; this is when they may offer thousands of miles/points for just getting accepted and charging a small amount in the first three months. My two most-used cards at the moment are the United MileagePlus Explorer (www.theexplorercard.com) and Hilton HHonors (www.hhonors3.hilton.com), but there are many others. The Points Guy (www.thepointsguy.com) has an entire credit card section, breaking down the advantages and disadvantages of many of the top rewards cards.

- **Sign Up for Travel Loyalty Programs**
  In addition to getting a rewards credit card, also sign up for airline, parking, and hotel loyalty programs so you can earn free flights and stays. Typically these programs are free to join, so enroll in them all. With that said, you will get more bang for your buck if you stay loyal to one company, as you will be able to build points quicker by doing so. Though I try to stick with the United and Hilton programs whenever possible since they are used in combination with my credit cards, I still belong to several others like American Airlines (www.aa.com), JetBlue (www.jetblue.com) and IHG (www.ihg.com).

- **Make Saving Fun**
  There are plenty of ways to save money, but the trick is finding the ones that can also be motivating, healthy, and just plain fun so it seems like you do not have to sacrifice too much. An easy way to do this is by turning your bucket list goals into saving techniques. For example, learning to cook doesn't only save money on dining out, but could also lead to a romantic dinner at home with your spouse. Here are some common bucket list goals that can actually help to put a little extra money in your bank account while still having fun.

  - **Run a Charity 5k or Marathon** — Cancel the expensive gym membership and get your friends together to do some outdoor training for a charity run. You will be getting into shape for free, while enjoying the fresh air and bonding with pals.
  - **Create Your Own Cocktail** — Forgo the pricy cocktails at the trendy bars and start creating your own adult beverages at home. This would be even more fun by throwing a BYOB

cocktail creation party and getting to sample all your friends' libations.

- **Throw a Theme Party** — Instead of going out to dinner with your best pals, plan a travel-themed potluck party at your home. Make the motif your dream destination and have the guests bring one traditional dish or drink from that country.
- **Learn to Cook**—With online cooking websites and YouTube videos, learning to cook is easier than ever. Plus, if you spend just ten dollars a day on dining out, it would equal roughly $300 per month. Cooking at home can cut this expense in half, affording you a plane ticket anywhere in the world in under a year.
- **Eat at a Food Truck** — If you have a hankering to go out to eat, trendy wheeled eateries and food truck events are popping up all over the world. They provide an inexpensive and social alternative to sit-down restaurants.
- **Be a Hair Model** — Many student stylists are in need of mane models to practice their skills on. If you are adventurous with your hair contact a local cosmetology school for a cheap cut.
- **Walk 10,000 Steps a Day** — It has been said that walking 10,000 steps is recommended for optimal health, but it also can save bunches of money on filling your gas tank or bus tickets.
- **Plan a Clothing Swap** — Instead of expensive apparel shopping at a boutique, plan a clothing swap with your friends. You can each bring ten lightly used items from your closet and take home a new wardrobe.
- **Read a Classic**—When was the last time you read a classic that was on your high school required reading list? You can download many of them for free on Amazon (www.amazon.com) in

their Kindle Store, or go to your local thrift store to check the dollar bin.

- **Create Your Own Beauty Products** — Homemade facials, deodorants, and shampoos can be made using products found in your kitchen cabinet for a fraction of the cost of purchasing them at the store.

## FACING THE FEAR OF TRAVEL

There are many myths, irrational beliefs, and misunderstandings when it comes to travel: traveling solo is unsafe, eating foreign food will cause food poisoning, and planes are just falling out of the sky. Just in the past few years I have been to over forty countries, taken hundreds of planes, dozens of trains, and walked countless streets alone. The worst things that have happened to me are my phone

Kayaking through a cave in northern Thailand

being discretely swiped (or misplaced, it's still up for debate) in Amsterdam and a case of mild food poisoning in Guatemala. Both of these incidents were unexpected nuisances, but not unrecoverable tragedies that would prevent me from ever exploring the world again. Of course tragic things can happen whether you are in a foreign country or at home, but they are not as common as you may think. You just need to know the facts and be prepared by taking normal precautions.

## Fear of Flying

To an experienced pilot, turbulence during take off, the sound of the landing gear retracting, and the noticeable reduction of engine power are all a normal part of their everyday job. To the fearful flyer, these same occurrences can be cause for sweating profusely while screaming profanities at the flight attendants. The fear of flying is quite possibly the number one issue that keeps people from traveling. Bumpiness, lack of control, claustrophobia, and unfamiliar noises can all contribute to this angst, especially when you are up 39,000 feet off the ground. But, in reality, the most dangerous part of your trip will probably be the drive to the airport.

According to the International Air Transport Association, an average of eight million people fly each and every day—365 days a year. That is equivalent to the entire population of Switzerland. The odds of being killed in a plane crash are 1 in 11 million. The chances are greater of you being struck by lightning, dying from a bee sting, or becoming the president of the United States. Most people are not afraid of driving in a car even though the odds of dying in an automobile accident are 1 in 5,000. But, there is sense of security that goes along with being in control.

Several years ago, I was the traveler with the armpit perspiration stains and cursing everyone under my breath, especially myself for being dumb enough to get on the damn plane in the first place. Prior to boarding, there was always a pit stop to the closest airport bar for a large glass of red wine, maybe two. During flights my husband would endure the death grip on his hand as my foot tapped uncontrollably. The beginning of descent was cause for counting and recounting the rows of seats between the nearest exit and me, just in case there was an emergency landing that required a rapid evacuation. I thanked the "Airplane Gods" after every successful landing—and vowed to never fly again.

Short-term fixes using alcohol, especially when an average flight to Europe is twelve hours, was not a permanent solution. As they say, "knowledge is power" and understanding the facts about the rare occurrences of airplane crashes or terrorist activity was a good first step to me coping with this fear. You also have to realize that television news programs sensationalize an isolated event. You will not be hearing about every car crash around the world, but an airplane crash will be replayed on every news program for weeks.

## Tips for the Fearful Flyer

- *Understand the Noises.* Not knowing the noises the plane makes during takeoff, landing, and in flight can lead to believing all these unfamiliar sounds are tragedies about to happen. Learn the sounds of the wheels retracting during takeoff, the chimes that happen inside the cabin, and the noise of acceleration, so that your nerves will be eased.
- *Distract Yourself.* Keep yourself busy with games, books, movies, or music. Sometimes one distraction is not enough for me, so I will use two—I'll flip through a magazine while listening to music or watch a movie while playing games on my laptop.
- *Use the Glass of Water Trick.* Ask for a glass of water, set it on your tray and watch how slightly the liquid moves, never spilling. This proves how little you are actually moving, even during most turbulence. The odds of that glass not spilling on a road trip are slim!

- *Research the plane's structure.* Take time to find out how airplanes are built and the safety measures taken each and every flight. How Things Fly (www.howthingsfly.si.edu) is a great resource for learning about a plane's structure, material, and aerodynamics.
- *Ask for assistance.* Make the flight attendants aware of your fear and they will keep you posted on noises, flight patterns, and such.
- *Visit the airport prior to your travels.* Spend time watching the planes taking off, landing, and listening to the noises. Take special note of how many people are arriving safely to their destination.
- *Consider getting more help.* Prior to departure, take an online course at Soar (www.fearofflying.com) or read the comprehensive guide at Fear of Flying (www.fearofflyingschool.com), plus visit Ask the Pilot (www.askthepilot.com) who covers an array of topics for the fearful flyer.
- *Realize you are not alone.* The rich, the famous, and businessmen fly safely all over the world all the time and thousands of people are flying right at this very moment.

## Fear of the Language Barriers

Many people have fears centered around trying to communicate with people from a different country. In my travel infancy, this was a big cause of intimidation for me, too. Of course speaking the native language of your destination makes things a million times easier, but in many larger cities it's not imperative anymore because English has become the universal language of travel. You can usually find someone who will speak it, plus many major attractions, restaurant menus, and road signs will include an English translation. Even without knowing a lick of the language, it is not a reason to stay home. Smartphones and translation apps have made it easier to find your way around, purchase a souvenir, or order a fancy cappuccino. Applications like Google Translate (www.translate.google.com) can be a lifesaver, as it translates paragraphs of text, images with words, and speech. Even before this technology, I have traveled through a city solely by using gestures; pointing, nodding, and employing the universal thumbs up sign. It's not the best way to get around, but it's better than sitting home on the couch!

Out of respect to the locals it is recommended that you learn a few words and phrases in the native language. Even if you get a laugh, most will appreciate your effort. Try to master how to say at least the basics: "Please", "Thank you", "Hello" and "Good-bye", plus my most-used phrases, "Where's the bathroom?" and "Can I have a glass of wine?"

## Fear of Solo Travel

Every year thousands of people travel on their own without incident. Preconceptions about the dangers of a country can fuel your fear, but the world in general is a hospitable place. Letting fear rule my decision to travel solo would have meant missing out on feeding bananas to the macaque at the Monkey Temple in Thailand and never soaking in the warm thermal baths in Switzerland. Don't let the grass grow under your feet just because you are afraid of doing something alone, but also don't travel solo being naïve, unprotected, and without having taken necessary precautions. A good rule of thumb is to follow the same safety guidelines in a different country as you would at home. Wandering desolate streets after midnight, getting sloppy drunk alone at a bar, or accepting rides from complete strangers is not safe at home or on the road. Most importantly, listen to your intuition. We all have different comfort levels, obey yours.

Sometimes the fear isn't about safety, but rather related to the embarrassment of just going somewhere alone, believing that people will feel sorry for you because you don't have a companion. In reality, some will question it, but deep inside most don't feel bad for you, they just wish they had the courage to do the same.

## Tips for Solo Travelers

- Be a planner—make your itinerary and plan your transportation from the airport to your hotel in advance. Leave a copy of your itinerary with a friend or family member.
- Understand the transportation system in each city, so you are not caught in the bad section of town without a way to get out. You can ask the hotel concierge about buses and subways. Plus, have them recommend reputable taxi companies, ones that won't overcharge because you are a tourist.
- Make your hotel reservations in advance, so you don't get stuck at the last minute without a place to sleep. Plus for extra safety, stay in a centrally located hotel with a twenty-four-hour reception.
- When you feel lonely, book group tours. You will not only meet other travelers, but feel safe with a local guide.
- Know the cultural norms of the country you are visiting and act respectfully. In some countries, eye contact can mean an invitation, while in others it means confidence.
- Be financially prepared by making sure to always have a little cash in the evenings so you don't have to hit the ATM after dark.
- Plans change, things go wrong, so always have a backup plan.
- Use your intuition—If your gut is telling you you're in a risky situation, change your path.
- If you venture to a bar, keep your eye on your drinks to make sure no one slips anything inside and don't get so drunk that you will make bad decisions.

## Fear of Getting Sick Abroad

Malaria! Yellow fever! Food poisoning! The fear of getting sick abroad crosses many people's minds at some point. It stinks being ill while on vacation, just like it stinks being sick at home. But, unfortunately there are nasty bugs everywhere. By taking the recommended precautions you can prevent many ailments, like getting vaccinations and not drinking the tap water. When it comes to eating the local food, realize that the residents' body systems are accustomed to the food and beverages, ours are not. Locals have a built-up immunity to some of the nasties. Trying different foods is part of experiencing the culture of the country you are in and most are safe as well as delicious, so just take extra care when choosing the foods you eat. If your plan is to snack on street food, choose a stall with the longest line of locals. This is almost always a guarantee that it will be tasty as well as fresh since their product is being turned over quickly. Also select whatever is deep-fried and cooked right in front of you instead of opting for anything precooked that may have been hanging out and unrefrigerated for hours.

No matter how many safety measures you take, you may still get sick. Most of these ailments will be easily cured with common medications, but some will need a trip to the doctor. You may be afraid that you will be unable to get the same type of health-care you can at home and in some cases this may be true. But, believe it or not, most countries have a very good medical system that is not inferior to the United States. In fact, many countries are known for their medical tourism and accredited facilities. Plus, some medications are less regulated overseas and can be purchased at a pharmacy without a doctor's prescription.

### Other Staying Healthy Tips

- Equip yourself with common medications prior to leaving, so you can avoid a doctor's visit or having to try to find a pharmacy. I always carry an over-the-counter pain medicine (such as aspirin), anti-diarrheal medication, nose spray, antibiotic ointment, cold medicine, and allergy tablets.
- Check with your health care provider to see what sort of medical coverage you receive while traveling. If necessary, get travel health insurance to be protected in case a visit to the doctor is in order.

- Wash your hands frequently, but also be aware that many public restrooms around the world will be out of soap, so always carry handy wipes and sanitizer.
- If it is recommended to not drink the water, be careful when it comes to salads, as they are probably rinsed in water, and the ice cubes in your cocktails. Stop by a market to load up on bottled water or bring water sanitizer tablets.

## Fear of Getting Robbed

There is something about going abroad that leads travelers to believe that there are con artists on every corner scoping out your valuables, which is just not true. Of course in rare cases it can happen, so you should be aware that most crooks on the streets are looking for an easy target. Don't be one of them. Targets of robberies are typically those who are distracted, carrying expensive equipment, or who leave their belongings unattended, which is why tourists are at a higher risk. Crime can happen anywhere, but pickpockets are statistically known to be more likely to take place in the crowded touristy sections of town; these are the areas you need to be the most cautious. You can go out and purchase expensive anti-theft pants and money belts, but by using common sense and taking simple safeguards, your odds of being a target will severely lessen.

## Safety Tips

- Stay alert, most petty crimes happen when people are distracted.
- Keep extra cash and a credit card in a separate location. This way if your purse or wallet gets stolen you will have backup.
- Don't carry a lot of money with you, just take what you need for the day.
- Keep your valuables in zippered, hard-to-reach pockets.
- Don't keep your phone or wallet in your back pocket.

- Use the hotel safe for your valuables instead of leaving them lying around in the hotel room. It is there for your protection!
- Don't put your purse on the back of your chair or leave your cell phone lying visible on a table while dining at a restaurant. This is especially true if you are eating on the patio of a street-side café where someone passing by could easily swipe your valuables.
- Wear your purse in front of you.
- Walk confidently and stay focused. When you need to look at a map, find a safe location away from the crowd.
- Make copies of your passport. Leave one at home and take one with you, storing it in a different location than the original. You can also take a photo of it to keep on your phone. If you lose your passport, you will want to make sure to be able to prove your citizenship.
- Make a list and take photos of the valuables (include make, model, and serial numbers) that you are bringing in case they need to be given to the police or your insurance company.

Only in Paris would you get souvenir matches at the Moulin Rouge.

# PART 2: TEN INCREDIBLE ADVENTURES

# 6. BEFORE ADVENTURING—PLANNING, PACKING, AND OTHER TRAVEL ESSENTIALS

You've been dreaming of a getaway for years, and it is finally time to make it happen—but you just aren't sure where to begin. Where should you go? How are you going to get there? What should you pack? Ugh! All the details can be frustrating, causing you to rethink even leaving in the first place. But really all you need is a little guidance to ease the travel planning pain and in this chapter, I take my years of experience to give you the tips and tricks I use when preparing for any trip.

Stalking sheep at Jerash Archaeological Site in Jordan

## PLANNING

### Choose a Bucket List Experience

You've created your bucket list, and it's filled with a multitude of incredible adventures. How will you choose which one to start with? Many times the answer to this will be by simply selecting the one that is closest to your heart. If you have always dreamed of hiking the towns of Cinque Terre, Italy since reading an article in the *New York Times* many years ago, then that is your answer. Otherwise, answering a few questions can help make the decision easier:

- *How much time do you have to travel?* — If you only have a few days to spare, then you probably won't want to spend all of it traveling to your destination, so think about sticking to just one city, state, or country. With a longer amount of time you will not only travel further, but possibly to multiple destinations as well.
- *What is your budget?* — There is a region to fit every budget, and every budget can fit into almost every region. Of course, if you have limited funds you will need to make more sacrifices when traveling to an expensive area, and the longer you are on the road the more money you will need.
- *What will the weather be like?* — Check the weather at your ideal destination during the months that you want to go. Is it going to be excruciatingly hot and humid? Is it tornado season? Also, consider the type of experiences you want to have in the area and the impact the weather may have on each one.
- *Is it peak tourist season?* If you are fortunate to have a flexible travel schedule, then avoiding the peak season will not only save you loads of money, but you can also avoid the long lines and hordes of tourists.

- *Are there deals?* Go to the airline websites to see if they are offering special deals to certain locations and also check out Kayak Explore (www.kayak.com/explore), where you can enter departure city and month, and it will return flight deals around the world.

## Book Your Flight

Your flight will probably be your biggest expense while planning your bucket list adventure, and there will always be a nagging feeling after you press the purchase button. Did you really get the best deal? There are some tricks to finding the lowest prices, without having multiple plane changes or a seventeen-hour layover at LAX.

- **Picking Your Dates**

  It's understandable if you have to take your vacation time when the children are out of school or on the exact ten days that your company has allowed you time off. But, if your dates are at all flexible there may be a better opportunity for saving money. You'd be surprised how much difference just a week or two, or even flying on different days of the week, can make in pricing. The ITA Matrix (www.matrix.itasoftware.com) is a good place to search pricing based on an entire month rather than just specific days. Though you cannot book directly through this site, it can be used to determine the cheapest dates for your travel. By looking at the monthly calendar you will be able to determine what day of the week or what time of year is the most economical. You'll most likely notice a trend that booking too late (within fifteen days), too early (five or more months in advance), or during peak travel season will be more expensive. A flight to Europe during the summer can easily cost a few hundred dollars more than booking your travel in March. Another thing to consider is the day of the week, generally Tuesday, Wednesday, and Saturday are the cheapest days to fly.

- **Booking Websites**

  If you are partial to a particular airline, possibly because you have a rewards card with them, check their website first but know that going directly through the carrier's site may not always give you the best deal with that airline. You should always check multiple booking sites to compare costs. It has surprised me on more than one occasion how some of these third party sites give cheaper fares than booking the same flight directly through the airlines' system.

  Also, airlines can change their pricing multiple times per week, so research your travel dates often. I recommend checking three times a week, for three weeks, so you can get a feel for pricing fluctuations. Try clearing your Internet cookies after each session, so the booking sites will not draw from your previous searches. If they do it is possible that you may not be given the best pricing because they know exactly what flights you are in need of and that you will have to book them at some point.

  If you are strictly looking for the cheapest flight and the carrier is not a concern, checking several booking sites is wise because each includes different airlines, and some won't include the budget carriers. After checking the best dates to travel on ITA Matrix, use those dates to search for flights on at least four other booking sites. I start with Tripadvisor (www.tripadvisor.com) because it is an aggregator, comparing rates from several different places like Orbitz, Priceline, and Expedia. This saves me the trouble of having to go to each of these sites separately. Then I open new tabs on my browser to check rates at Kayak (www.kayak.com), Skyscanner (www.skyscanner.net), and Momondo (www.momondo.com). The process really doesn't take long, and just entering a few dates can pay off big.

- **Flight Booking Tips & Tools**
  Still think you are not finding your best flight deal? If you
  choose to delve a little deeper into how to save money here are
  additional tips:

  - *Search on Budget Airlines* — Most of the larger booking sites
    don't include the budget or foreign airlines, like Ryanair
    (www.ryanair.com). Yet many foreign countries use smaller
    carriers for domestic travel, like the low-cost Malaysian air-
    line AirAsia (www.airasia.com). Check your destination for
    these budget airlines—it's sometimes more economical to get
    a cheap flight to the main city of a country using a well-known
    carrier, and then hopping on a budget flight from there.
  - *Try Alternative Routes* — While sometimes it is cost effective to
    fly into a cheaper hub in a country and then hop on a budget
    flight to your final destination, it may also be cheaper to fly
    into a different country all together. When I am heading to
    Europe I often fly into Zurich, as it seems to always be the
    cheapest flight from my airport, San Francisco International,
    then I pop onto another carrier to reach my final destination,
    sometimes saving myself hundreds of dollars. You can use the
    ITA Matrix to determine which destination is cheapest from
    your departure city.
  - *Don't Forget About Baggage Fees* — Different airlines have
    different baggage fee policies, with many charging roughly
    twenty-five dollars for the first checked bag (some even
    charge for carry-ons!). Make sure to factor this cost in
    when making your purchase decision and only fly with a
    small carry-on whenever possible.
  - *Check Alternative Airports* — If there is more than one airport
    in your destination, check pricing for them all. It may be
    more cost effective to fly into an airport fifty miles away,
    then take the train or shuttle to your final destination.

- *Don't Fly Direct* — Direct flights are the most convenient, but also the most expensive. Accept a layover. Better yet, turn a layover into another adventure. An eight-hour layover in Vienna led me to a fancy downtown restaurant to eat traditional wiener schnitzel.

- *Join Mailing Lists* — Most airlines have email lists that keep you updated on their latest discount offers, so join them all. Also sign up for Travelzoo's (www.travelzoo.com) weekly email that compiles the best travel deals of the week and Zozi (www.zozi.com) which specializes in offering discounts for adventurous activities and travel getaways.

- *Create Alerts* — Once you know where you are going, create an alert with the booking site. This way they will warn you any time the flight to your destination drops below the price at the time you created the alert. This works well with simple round-trip flights, not for multidestination flights.

- *Frequent Flyer Programs* — Even if you are not an active traveler, join the frequent flyer programs of the airlines. Just a few trips a year can get you free drinks onboard, lounge passes, or discounted upgrades.

- *SeatGuru* — This is not really a budgeting tip, but if you don't want to end up sitting next to the toilets or in the most cramped seat on the plane, check out the database at Seat-Guru (www.seatguru.com). Key in your flight and it will return the best seat choices, plus it gives reviews from past flyers who sat there.

## Get Your Travel Documents in Order

You've got your airline tickets and you're starting to get excited. Now it's time to get your travel documents in order so you actually can board the plane and enter the country. The best time to do this is once you have determined where you are going, as some documents can take up to six weeks.

- **Passport**

  If you do not have a passport, you will want to allow up to six weeks to get one. It is possible to expedite this service for an additional fee and get it in two to three weeks. I recently renewed mine by expediting and got the new fifty-two-page book in just ten days. If you already have a passport, check the expiration date—most countries will require that your passport be valid for six months beyond the date of arrival. You can get more information about applying and renewing online at www.travel.state.gov.

- **Visas**

  A visa gives a person official permission to enter, leave, and stay in a country for a specific period of time. Some countries don't require a visa, but many do, so it is always a good idea to check prior to leaving. Many times you can simply buy them at the airport when you arrive, while with some countries it needs to be done in advance. A few South American countries charge a reciprocity fee rather than requiring a visa. This is a cost that is based on what your home country charges the residents of the country you are visiting. US citizens can get information about each country's requirements online on the US Passports and International Travel website (www.travel.state.gov).

- **International Driving Permit**

  If you plan on renting a car in your destination overseas, you may be required to have an International Driving Permit. You can only apply for your permit through the American Automobile Association (AAA; www.aaa.com) or the National Automobile Club (NAC; www.thenac.com). In most cases this can easily be done through the mail, though you will need a passport photo.

- **Travel Insurance**

  Before committing to buying travel insurance, do your homework. Check with your existing insurance (medical, homeowner's, renter's, automobile) and credit card companies to see exactly what is covered while traveling. Some travel credit cards and insurance plans will cover minor health issues, while many may not cover adventurous activities, like hot air ballooning in Cappadocia or bungee jumping in New Zealand. You will need special insurance for that. Depending on where you are going and what type of adventures you will be doing, you may also want to consider purchasing emergency medical or evacuation insurance. World Nomads (www.worldnomads.com) is perfect for the adventure traveler, covering everything from parasailing to scuba diving. Allianz (www.allianztravelinsurance.com) provides financial safeguards for things like trip cancellation and emergency medical coverage. Clements Worldwide (www. clements.com) will have insurance policies that can cover your expensive travel gear that many other policies won't.

  If you will be driving a car, check with your automobile insurance to see what coverage they offer for automobile rentals and opt for the rental companies insurance when necessary. Plus always remember to take photos of the exterior of the car prior to driving it off the lot, just in case you missed any scratches or dings during the inspection. This would have saved me hundreds of dollars in France!

## Book Accommodations

Booking accommodations can be just as pricey as booking a flight, depending on what you are looking for. In this case too, it is smart to check several different websites in order to secure the best deal. My research begins with Booking.com and Expedia (www.expedia.com). These sites offer hotel searches where features that are necessary for you can be selected, like an airport shuttle or free Internet. Plus you have the ability to search by guest rating, rather than just hotel stars. This will bring to the top the highest-rated hotels by the guests that stayed in them. You can then read these reviews to make your decision. After making your selection, double-check pricing directly with the hotel's website; sometimes they will be having special deals strictly on their site.

If I am looking for more of a home environment, rather than a hotel, I will head somewhere else for information. Whether it's an oceanfront room in Costa Rica for a night, a rustic cabaña in Panama for a week, or a Tuscan villa in Italy, Airbnb (www.airbnb.com) can help you find it. What's cool about this site is that you can find accommodations in every price range, and if you are really on a budget there are shared rooms in someone's home. This site is for home rentals, not hotels, so be sure to read the reviews in order to be knowledgeable before booking. Another benefit is if you need some extra travel cash, you can list your home or just a room to be rented out.

## Create an Itinerary

There is something to be said for aimlessly roaming the streets of an energetic city, not knowing what you will find, popping into quaint cafes and talking to the locals. Though with a limited amount of time, you also don't want to leave "finding something interesting" totally to chance. In order to make sure you don't miss anything amazing, you should create a loose itinerary that leaves room for unexpected opportunity, like playing an impromptu game of stick ball on the streets of Havana or lingering over a glass of wine in a quaint bar in Rome. Being tied to a strict itinerary will cause you anxiety, wondering if you are going to make it to the next destination and cutting experiences short because you are scheduled for a museum tour at exactly two p.m., but it also can waste precious time when you don't have a plan. I never want to be spending hours in my hotel room trying to figure out what to do for the day, when I can actually be out doing it. Here's how I organize an itinerary:

- **Pick a place to store your itinerary** — In the beginning of my travel career, I spent a couple months creating a London itinerary, not wanting to miss a thing. I purchased an expensive map and spent hours putting little numbered stickies on all the places to be visited. These numbers coordinated with an Excel spreadsheet that listed the attractions by name along with other essential information. It was foolproof, or so I thought. On day one, while walking to Abbey Road, the map fell out of my purse and was gone. Countless hours of planning were down the drain in a matter of minutes. Since then I have never bought a paper map, especially since almost every airport and hotel has a free one you can pick up when you arrive. Instead, I create and store all my itineraries with the Evernote app (www.evernote.com). The app can keep maps, photos, and links to important websites that can be accessed on any of my devices. You can also set up an offline notebook in order to see your notes without Internet access, but keep in mind that you will need Wi-Fi to access any links.

- **Research** — If you want to get the most out of your experience, you need to know what you want to do and what will make the ultimate travel venture for you. Are you fascinated by a town's history, culture, or food? Do you want your trip to just be about crazy adventures and a city's vibrant nightlife? Answering these questions means that you need to do some research for the area you are visiting. Prior to going anywhere I do an online search of "unique things to do in XYZ," "traditional foods of XYZ," and "best restaurant in XYZ." I then scroll through dozens of the result sites quickly, making a list in Evernote of all the things that even slightly interest me. It is important to get past the first few pages of results to find more personal stories and blogs, instead of large generic sites that can give you only a touristy perspective. If the city or country's tourism board website does not come up within the search results, I always check their site for recommendations. I may also see if Netflix (www.netflix.com) has any documentaries on the destination that can be rented, plus browse a few travel guides at the bookstore. After I've got a rough list, more elaborate research is done on each attraction and restaurant to determine what will be kept on the itinerary versus what will be deleted. Keep in mind that you can't see and do it all, so put an asterisk by the items that are absolute must-dos.

- **Divide a City into Sections** — Many large cities will be split up in districts, like Paris with its arrondissements or the London boroughs. Look at an online map and determine the sections of a city you are traveling to. Create a header in Evernote for each district; if a town doesn't have sections, it can be zoned into four quadrants (NE, NW, SE, SW). If your travels will be through several small villages, your headers can just be the name of the village. Start taking the items from your master list and placing them in the sections that they are located in. This will make planning your day easier when you know what area you will be headed to and all the things you can do there.

- **Create a Calendar** — Make a calendar for each day of your vacation. You can either do this in a simple list format or create a table. Take a look at your "things to do" list, there are bound to be certain attractions/events that have to be done on specific days due to limited open hours or reservation availability, so put those on the calendar first under the appropriate day and time. If there are free hours on that specific date, then add anything that is in that same district to it, starting with the important items that have an asterisk next to them. Don't put specific times on these other entries—just squeeze as many as you can in before or after your scheduled event. This way you will have plenty of options on what to in the district that you will be in without having to be strict about the time.

- **Leave Room for Opportunity and Be Realistic** — Even when I am in a location trying to tick something off the bucket list I create loose itineraries, ones that leave room for unexpected opportunities, because a bucket list is just as much about the journey as it is the check mark. There are always times while exploring a city that something incredible sidetracks you, and if you are scheduled with events back to back you may have to miss out. Of course you're going to want to see and do everything on your trip, but also be realistic. Don't expect to land in Europe after twelve hours of travel and hit the ground running, jam-packing your itinerary from sun up to down. Leave room for meals, sleep, jetlag, and rest. Plus expect a few hiccups along the way: flights can be delayed, restaurants can lose reservations, and an attraction may pale in comparison in person to the photographs that got your attention on the Internet. In the Bahamas, our tour guide forgot to pick us up at the hotel, it rained for twenty-four hours straight, and the buggy we rented got a flat tire in the first half hour. Yes, it changed our itinerary a bit, but instead of the original plan, we met a lovely Bahamian couple who graciously drove us to the local fish fry where we ate cracked conch and drank bottles of Kalik beer. Sometimes the unexpected is the most memorable part of the journey.

- **Don't Forget the Extras** — Add your flight numbers, hotel addresses, maps, etc. to your itinerary file for easy access. All my itineraries include this information, plus the currency exchange rate. It is much easier to look at one file than have to

Exploring the old shipwreck in Point Reyes, California

scroll through dozens of emails or check different apps to find what I am looking for. This should not be a substitute for keeping all that information stored in emails or printed copies of confirmations.

## OTHER TRAVEL ESSENTIALS

### Currency and Credit Cards

It is best to take a mix of cash, credit cards, and debit cards on your trip; traveler's checks are no longer universally accepted. Choose at least two credit cards making sure that one is a debit card. I typically take three keeping one separate from the others just in case one of my bags gets lost. If one of these is a travel reward credit card it can be beneficial, not only because they give you points that can be applied toward future trips, but there are many other perks as well.

With my card, the United MileagePlus Explorer (www.theexplorercard.com), there are no foreign transaction fees to make a purchase, which are usually between 2 and 3 percent. Plus, I receive one free checked bag, priority boarding, two lounge passes per year, and luggage protection when flying with the airline. There are also many other rewards cards. Almost every airline and credit card company has one, so you need to see which one fits you best. The Chase Sapphire Preferred card (www.creditcards.chase.com) seems to be another leader in the bunch. Also, be aware that many countries use a chip-and-pin technology, so it's best if you have a card with a shiny square chip on it which many of the travel rewards cards already include. Some credit card machines may also ask for a pin number, if you do not know what it is call the company to get it.

Before you leave, notify the credit card companies and bank of your overseas travel plans, so your cards will not be blocked due to suspicious activity. This can be done either online or by calling them directly. Note that the sophisticated technology of American Express does not require you to place a travel alert to use their cards overseas.

When exchanging money, typically ATMs abroad give the best exchange rate, although most companies will charge a transaction fee. The second best exchange rate choice would be going to a bank in your destination (not the exchange booths in the airport or around town). Even though there are ATMs and banks in many locations throughout the world, it doesn't hurt to arrive with some of the local currency. I don't ever travel to a foreign country without exchanging a small amount of money in advance. I know most other experienced travelers would gasp at this, claiming that the exchange fees are way higher. But, there has been one too many times when I've had trouble getting my debit card to work in the ATM at the airport or the only exchange office is closed. Also, when there's an option, always get your cash in small bills. This can be used for street food, to catch a taxi, or shopping at the market when some vendors will not take credit cards or have change for larger bills.

Check the currency conversion before you go, so you know how much your dollars are worth in the local currency. You can easily check this online at XE Currency Converter (www.xe.com), or download their app in order to get exchange rates on the spot.

## Staying Connected

Though most people travel to escape being connected to their life back home, there are times when you may need to speak to the babysitter or access a map when you find yourself lost. The easiest and cheapest way to stay connected is with Wi-Fi using your own smartphone. There are plenty of options, like talking through Skype (www.skype.com), video chatting through Facebook (www.facebook.com), or texting through What'sApp (www.whatsapp.com) where you can keep in touch with other users of the app.

Skype is what I use most and is free, as long as the person on the other end also has an account. Or if you need to make a phone call to someone without Skype, you can load money onto your account and make the call for a fraction of the cost of roaming charges—just make sure to turn your phone to airplane mode so you are not using expensive data. In Ireland, I turned on my data roaming for ten minutes to get GPS directions and it cost me a whopping sixty-six dollars. In Ecuador, calling the airline to straighten out a canceled flight with no International phone plan cost me $180. If I had been wise enough to go through Skype the same call would have cost about three dollars. Lesson learned.

If you want to be more connected more often, opt for an international calling/data plan through your carrier. But be careful, each plan typically gives you only a certain amount of data, and watching YouTube videos or listening to Pandora can eat it up quickly. T-Mobile (www.t-mobile.com) is widely used amongst avid travelers, because they have reasonable monthly plan rates that include unlimited international data and texting.

If you can't bear to be without constant social media or chatting with your BFF, then purchasing a SIM card is also a good choice. These microchips give you a local number and cheap calling/data rates. They can usually be picked up at your destination airport or a local cellular phone store. In order to use them you must either have an unlocked phone or purchase a cheap phone from the country you are in. You can contact your provider to inquire about "unlocking" your phone, some will do it free of charge.

## Electricity

The different electricity in another country seems tricky to understand, but it's really not. A simple universal adaptor can work for you in most situations. I use the Insten Universal World Wide Travel

At the Blarney Castle in Ireland, getting ready to kiss The Blarney Stone

Charger that I bought on Amazon (www.amazon.com) for six dollars and it has taken me around the world with no issues. Either bring a couple of adaptors with you or just bring one and a surge protector that has multiple outlets. Where it seems to get problematic is when voltage comes into play. The US has 120 V electricity and many other countries have 220 V or 230 V. A converter is needed when the voltage is different if your electronics are not dual voltage. Check with each company to confirm, but typically electric toothbrushes, hair dryers, and flat irons are items that would have to be purchased special in order to have dual voltage. You can easily find each of these electronics or a converter on Amazon reasonably cheap.

## PACKING YOUR BAGS

Writer Susan Heller sums up the Golden Packing Rule in a quote: "When preparing to travel, lay out all your clothes and all your money, then take half of the clothes and twice the money." Let's face it, most travelers are prone to overpacking. I mean what are the chances you will need a purple sparkly off the shoulder blouse while trekking with gorillas in Uganda or all-terrain hiking boots while on a museum tour of Rome? Deciding what to pack can be stressful, especially if you want to plan for every potential circumstance under the sun. Limit your luggage size and frustration with a few techniques:

### Make a Packing List

If you are the person that always forgets something essential for a trip, create a checklist for every item you plan to take. This will ensure you don't end up in Argentina without deodorant and underwear. This list can be divided into two categories: "essentials," things needed for every travel outing, and "trip specific," items related to your next adventure. For example, if you were heading to Mexico to swim with whale sharks, an underwater camera would be trip specific where as toothpaste is essential. Generating a general list online with Packing List Online (www.packinglistonline.com) or using the app PackPoint (www.packpnt.com) is an easy way to get started. By inputting your destination, trip length, weather, and the basic nature of your visit, both of these will customize a packing list for you, and then you can make additions as needed. They will make sure you remember the commonly forgotten items like sunscreen, sunglasses, pajamas, and hats.

## Choose the Right Luggage

Choosing the right luggage will depend on how long you will be traveling, where you are going, and how you will be getting there, plus each airline's size and weight restrictions. Unless you plan on washing clothes, you will probably need a larger bag for longer trips, but when choosing your luggage you need to keep in mind the airplane carrier's regulations. Weight and size restrictions are specific to the airline and aircraft, so it is best to check the website for more information. In general, you are allowed to check suitcases less than fifty pounds and bring liquids up to 3.4 ounces each in your carry-on. If you are carrying on liquids, put them separately in a sealable, clear one-quart bag. Many airports require removing them from your bag so be sure to have them easily accessible. Most airlines allow one carry-on and one personal item (such as a purse or computer bag). My carry-on is always a dual-purposed bag. If I am heading to the shores of the Caribbean my carry-on might double as a beach bag, whereas a backpack as a carry-on would be more practical if I were going to be trekking to Everest Base Camp. Also consider your mode of transportation for your destination. If you will need to be moving locations often or are taking several trains, packing light is essential. Your luggage should be a size you can handle. It's a royal pain to lug your suitcases up and down European hotel stairs or metro stations without escalators. If you are taking a safari or jeep tour, they lend themselves to duffle bags that can be manipulated in trunks more easily.

## Plan Your Outfits

Determining what clothes to bring on a trip causes many travelers the most frustration. They always think they *might* need all five pairs of shoes or a different pair of sunglasses for each day. The trick to being efficient is planning your outfits and not trying to pack for every potential situation. You can't bring it all.

- **Check the Weather** — A few days before you depart, double-check the weather (www.weatherchannel.com) for your destination. This will allow you to be more precise with your packing. Keep in mind that the 70s with 60 percent humidity feels hotter than 70 degrees with no humidity.
- **Pack for Activities** — Examine your itinerary to see what type of activities you'll be participating in and what sort of clothing it will require. If you know you will be doing some light hiking in the sun, pack a hat and walking sneakers, or bring a fancy dress if your itinerary has a night at the symphony planned.
- **Color Matching** — Make sure that every piece of clothing you pack works with several other pieces, giving you a plethora of mix-and-match possibilities. I typically choose a three-color palette for every trip, selecting two neutrals and one pop color. Many times this will be black, light beige, and red or grey, white, and plum. If something cannot be used with at least two separate outfits, don't bring it.
- **Layering, Layering, Layering!** — Starting with the plane, I will always wear my heaviest clothes while flying. Not only does it help with my perpetual coldness and save room in my suitcase, but also it can be converted into many other outfits. I can mix and match four pieces of clothing to be appropriate for summer or winter. For example a pair of leggings covered with a skirt and sweater over a tank can easily turn into a warm weather outfit by eliminating the leggings and sweater. Also bring

versatile layering items, like a cardigan or light jacket. Both of these items can go well over a tee or button up shirt.

- **Versatile Footwear** — Most people gasped when I told them that I traveled through Europe for a month in March with only one pair of shoes; a pair of tall boots with enough traction for light hiking, style to pair with a casual dress, and durability to withstand the weather. Of course, this is not possible for every trip, but it is an example of how to make sure your shoes are as versatile as your clothing. Travel brands are getting smarter, they make water shoes that can be used for hiking or walking around the city centers, plus foldable ballet slippers for dressing up and saving space.

## Packing Medicine

Don't forget to pack the medications that you are currently prescribed, but also equip yourself with common medications to avoid having to find a pharmacy or visiting a medical office. Here's a list of the six things I always pack and have gotten me through every overseas ailment so far:

1. Over-the-counter pain medicine (such as aspirin)
2. Anti-diarrheal medication
3. Nasal spray for congestion relief (such as Afrin)
4. Topical antibiotic ointment (such as Neosporin)
5. Cold medicine
6. Allergy tablets

## Other Packing Efficiently Tips

The way you fold your clothes in your dresser or store your beauty products in a drawer at home isn't necessarily the most effective way to pack your suitcase.

- **Roll Your Clothes** — Instead of folding your clothes flat, roll them like you would a sleeping bag. You can roll each item individually or layer a few on top of each other. This method takes up less space than folding and helps prevent wrinkles.
- **Use Packing Cubes** — All my clothes go into different colored packing cubes; shirts go in one, pants in another, and so on. They are a great way to keep things organized, turning your luggage into a mini dresser. When I need a blouse, I just pull out the proper cube and they are all in there instead of having to rummage through the entire suitcase.
- **Maximize the Crevasses** — Use all the little nooks and crannies for packing smaller items, like putting socks and underwear inside your shoes or vacant corners.
- **Secure Breakables** — You can also wrap your breakables in socks and store them in your shoes.
- **Protect Valuables** — Keep your most valuable items with you in your carry-on luggage. It is not advised to check them in your suitcase, though if you absolutely have to use a TSA-approved luggage lock.
- **Be Plane Ready** — Put everything you need during the flight in your smallest bag that will be stored under the seat so you can reach it easily throughout the flight. This way you will avoid standing in the aisle trying to dig items out of your bag.
- **Bring a Plastic Bag** — If you don't want your dirty clothes mingling with your clean ones, bring an empty plastic bag to keep them in.
- **Get Doubles** — If you travel often, get doubles of all your cosmetics and grooming products. My cosmetic travel bag never gets unpacked—at the end of a trip I simply refill the empties and it's ready for the next trip.
- **Dress for the Temperature of Your Destination** — Not only should you wear layered clothing on the plane, but also be sure

those layers include an appropriate outfit for the temperature of the place you are going in case your luggage is lost. My husband ended up with just flimsy sport shorts and a T-shirt when we arrived in Dublin with forty-degree weather when his suitcase didn't make it to the airport on time. It was a very chilly night on the town for him!

- **Pack a Scarf.** — A scarf is not only fashionable but it is also a completely versatile thing to pack for travel anywhere in the world. It can be used to cover your head or shoulders when entering certain religious sites, for sun protection, as a bathing suit cover-up, or in some cases as a makeshift towel.

Don't let packing be the cause of frustration. Keep in mind that as long as you are not in a very rural area, you should be able to find everything you truly need at your destination.

# 7. EXPERIENCE NATURE ON THE GALÁPAGOS ISLANDS

Stepping foot onto Bartolomé felt like walking onto the set of a science fiction flick. I was half waiting for Darth Vader to appear and begin performing a space-landing scene from *Star Wars*. In front of me was a 360-degree lunar landscape view filled with a myriad of volcanic formations; parasitic spatter cones, lava bombs, cooled flows, and other compositions that only a licensed geologist could identify. There was a sporadic sprinkling of plant life; lava cactuses poking out of rocks, and a scattering of scraggly shrubs. The vegetation was scarce, and so was the wildlife—uncharacteristic for the Galápagos Islands. A couple of lazy sea lions greeted our *panga* at the dock with a careless glance, and a few sun-bathing lava lizards were dispersed about on the rocks. Our group of

Sporadic plants of the lunar landscape of Bartolomé Island

twelve expeditioners may have just doubled the population. The dust-colored, barren land was broken up by a long, wooden-planked walkway cutting through the middle of the island and leading uphill to a peak view of the strangely shaped Pinnacle Rock, one of the

A colorful marine iguana clings to a lava rock

most photographed natural structures in the group of thirteen main islands of the Galápagos. Our small pack took this vigorous path, but instead of photographing live creatures along the way, we picked up the deceivingly light lava rocks raising them high above our heads, flaunting our cartoon-like, super-power strength. I hoisted the

The planked walkway that led to the top of Bartolomé Island

largest one in an overhead press for a slew of "look at my muscles" self-ies. This may impress my Facebook friends more than another shot of a yellow warbler in the trees!

Bartolomé felt like an entirely different world—an unexpected natural display. The bizarre terrain was not what I had predicted from the Galápagos or what we had seen on the other islands; actually it was the complete opposite. The volcanic archipelago is generally known for being home to an abundance of wildlife with species that are found nowhere else on Earth; the giant tortoise being among the most famous fauna, an animal that inspired Charles Darwin's landmark theory of evolution. In fact, we had visited the Darwin Research Station in the village of Puerto Ayora on Santa Cruz Island a few days earlier. This breeding center was designed to preserve tortoise species. Sadly, a few years earlier they had lost a battle when Lonesome George had passed on, a one-hundred-plus-year-old male tortoise that was the last known of the Pinta Island subspecies. It was a breed that no one in the world will ever be able to see again.

My journey here had started in Guayaquil, the largest Ecuadorian city and a known gateway to the Galápagos Islands. It was an interesting place to spend a couple of days with a mix of stereo shops blaring music from their open doors, street carts selling freshly made empanadas, and the iguanas freely roaming throughout Parque Seminario. From here it had been an easy flight to Isla San Cristóbal, the oldest geological island of the Galápagos, a remote destination 620 km from the South American mainland. The next seven days were spent on a yacht with eighteen passengers and a crew of ten, including two naturalists who guided us through each island and the treasures they were known for.

I had come to this magical place not only to be immersed in a nature display unlike no other, but also to witness a unique courting event, a rare bird ritual: a blue-footed booby mating dance. Yes, I traveled all this way specifically to see the foreplay spectacle of a bird that had striking azure-colored feet. It was a feathered affair that up

Getting the staredown from a colorful Sally Lightfoot Crab

until that point had evaded me, and surely on the arid island of Bartolomé there would be no bird-wooing strut. Despite the wildlife shortage on Bartolomé, the rest of the islands had been the melting pot of animal life. There were plenty of land and marine iguanas along the trails of Española. Even when they weren't visibly present, the dusty imprints of their tails along the path proved that they had been there recently. We spotted the brilliant red bellies of the female lava lizards as they stood at attention to inspect who had entered their territory. Many multicolored Sally Lightfoot crabs were roaming the rocks near the sea's edge, and the Galápagos sea lions were lounging everywhere, tempting me to rub their soft tummies. If it weren't for the strict two-meter distance that must be kept, sea lion belly massages would have been doled out freely and often. I might have set up shop right along the white beaches of Española.

The separation rule was hard to keep at times, especially when

young pups wanted to play a game of chase, fearlessly waddling inches from my feet to sniff my camera lens. This lack of fear was one of the most intriguing aspects to the unique wildlife here. Unlike many humans, life on their land had not pre-disposed them to this emotion. The sunbathing

A female Española lava lizard showing off her brilliant red head seals barely glance your way as you get close enough to block their sunlight with a shadow. Groups of lava lizards bravely cross your path with a quiet confidence, and the giant tortoises do not retreat back into their shell when surrounded by travelers grabbing a quick snapshot on Isla Santa Cruz. It was truly bizarre. It seemed that everything and everyone, everywhere else in

Long tails of marine iguanas hang of the edge of the sheer rocks in the Galápagos

the world, was afflicted with a fear of some sort. But, not here—not in a place where the human footprint is kept to a minimum and natural predators are virtually nonexistent.

In between the fierce hunt for the blue-footed booby, daily snorkeling sessions were led by the naturalists, and proved to be fruitful

The brilliantly colored feet of the blue-footed booby

Keeping the required two-meter distance from a lazy sea lion

in marine life, which made it worth squeezing into a wetsuit that always seemed two sizes too small. On one morning's excursion a small motorized dinghy dropped us off at Devil's Crown, known for its swift current that will push you through the sea life with very limited effort—a lazy man's snorkeling trip. We started with floating through colorful schools of fish, as a few sea turtles glided by and royal blue starfish clung to the rocks below. It was peaceful until someone in our group yelled, *"There's a shark heading upstream."* The shark was about a hundred yards away heading against the current, and without thinking I began to frantically paddle not away from the creature, but toward it. Was I really chasing a shark? I stopped for a second to contemplate my decision and as I did, five whitetip sharks appeared directly below me. Amazingly, in that instant there was no feeling of uneasiness, just a sense of awe as they gracefully swam back and forth.

The same sort of surprise came on another snorkeling expedition just as disappointment started to set in when the naturalist beckoned

Lazy sea lions line the beach of Española Island

the snorkelers to come aboard the *panga*. This afternoon's water excursion at Sombrero Chino, also known as the Chinese Hat, would unfortunately be our last. There was a sense of serenity under these waters, an entirely different life that surely would be missed. We had come nose to nose with sea lions, spotted gigantic stingray stealthily moving about the sandy bottom, and even watched an octopus maneuver its tentacles through the rocks. As I was dismally making my way toward our dinghy, someone from our group started shouting *"Penguin, penguin."* Penguin? I was confused for a moment; there must be some sort of mistake. This was not the ice shelf in Antarctica or the beaches of South America's Tierra del Fuego. It turned out that these little critters were Galápagos penguins, the only wild penguins that live north of the equator. Though they have the smallest population size of all the penguins, these are ones that you actually don't have to brave the bitter cold to see. I instantly did a 180 and rapidly swam toward the reef of the sighting. The dinghy would have to wait—I had

The only wild penguins that live north of the equator

penguins to tend to. In the distance straight ahead, two Galápagos penguins perched on the lava rock could be seen. I propelled forward with one hand and took photos with the other, just in case they decided to plunge into the water before I arrived for a close-up. The pair chose to stick around for quite a while, posing for the small paparazzi of snorkelers. They gave us many different angles to work with, as if trying to find out what their "best side" for the camera was. For future reference Mr. Penguin, profile works best.

Back on the boat that same day, apparently the sea life was not ready for the show to stop. While napping on the sundeck, I was woken up by a voice on the loud speaker. "There are whales at the stern of the boat." A sundeck siesta turned into an unforeseen afternoon of whale watching. That is one of the beautiful things about nature: it can be delightfully unexpected. The boat turned around to see if we could get a better glimpse, the perk of touring the Galápagos on a small cruising yacht. Even the naturalists were at the back of the boat amazed by the spectacle as the whales jumped in the air and their spouts blew. Not a shabby afternoon in the Galápagos Islands.

The last morning we woke up early for one last chance at catching the yearned-for bird dance. Truth be told, I never understood the fascination with bird watching, until I came here—the islands are a bird lover's paradise. You could never tire of watching the great blue herons foraging while standing in a few inches of water, or marveling

The inflated scarlet red pouch of the male frigatebird, which can be the be as large as a football

at the ballooning red neck sacks of the male frigatebird, or even staring into the beady red-ringed eyes of the swallow-tailed gull. There are several species of birds on the Galápagos Islands, but not many as coveted as the boobies. There are three types that could be found: Blue-footed, Red-footed, and Nazca. Though we got a glimpse of them all, witnessing a blue-footed booby mating dance was more of a rarity.

On that final day in the Galápagos, it happened. Quietly crouching next to the dusty and dry ground, my

A brown pelican sits on a lava rock

The swallow-tailed gull is easy to identify, with its red rings around its eyes

eyes focused on one very popular female surrounded by the male version of a harem. It was our very last stop on a weeklong exploration of the island, Isla Seymour. I had been patiently waiting for seven days to witness what was about to happen. We stood a few feet away from the winged wildlife, not because the suitors would run scared if we ventured closer, but because we wanted to respect their privacy. Though we had seen them throughout the trip, it wasn't until now that they were strutting their stuff, all trying to impress one desirable lady. These birds really needed to be able to do some fancy footwork in order to woo their woman.

We sat silently. This event was the culmination of a spectacular nature show that came before it, the grand finale. The premating ritual included rocking side-to-side while exaggeratedly lifting their eye-catching baby blue feet—a blue-footed booby dance. I don't recall my husband ever doing a jig like this during our courtship!

Blue-footed boobies raising their azure feet during the mating dance

We watched as they did their seemingly choreographed dance, battling it out like a fierce episode of *Dancing with the Stars*. The male flaunted his lusted-after blue feet to impress his lady, at times raising his bill up toward the sky while spreading his wings. He then presented his female with an engagement ring of sorts, nest materials. She

The male blue-footed booby raising his wings in order to impress his lady during their mating ritual

accepted the offerings of her chosen soul mate and joined him on the dance floor.

Walking back to the yacht tears welled in my eyes, not only because this journey was coming to an end, but also because of the diverse terrain, plants, and wildlife we had been exposed to. We had walked in the footsteps of Darwin, came nose to nose with playful sea lions, climbed to the top of an extinct volcano, had seen species of animals that couldn't be found anywhere else in the world, and learned lessons that only nature can teach. It was a lesson in devotion, curiosity, and living a life without fear, teachings that we were lucky to bring home.

◆ ◆ ◆

# CHECK IT OFF YOUR BUCKET LIST

**Location/Facts:** Situated in the Pacific Ocean, the Galápagos Islands are a volcanic archipelago that lie 620 miles from the South American mainland. A province of Ecuador, it consists of thirteen main islands and six smaller isles. It is a remote destination that is a melting pot of unique wildlife, which inspired Charles Darwin's landmark theory of evolution following his visit in 1835. Having been called a "living museum and showcase of wildlife" it is home to wildlife species that are found nowhere else on Earth: the giant tortoise, Galápagos sea lions, flightless cormorant, the waved albatross and, of course the boobies.

**Getting There:** Galápagos is reached through the country of Ecuador by flying into either the capital city of Quito or the country's largest city of Guayaquil. If you don't plan on spending any time on the mainland, fly into Guayaquil, since it is closer to the islands and most flights from Quito to the Galápagos stop there. If you plan on doing some exploring in Ecuador prior to or after your trip, go to Quito. Its famous old town is an UNESCO World Heritage Site filled with colonial charm, bustling markets, and architectural buildings. Whichever city you choose, it will most likely require an overnight stay.

The Galápagos Islands has two airports, one on San Cristóbal and the other on Isla Baltra, just north of Santa Cruz. Which airport you choose will depend on how you have decided to explore the islands. The flight from Guayaquil to the islands is approximately an hour and forty-five minutes (about forty minutes from Quito to Guayaquil). Domestic flights can be booked through TAME (www.tame.com.ec), Avianca (www.avianca.com), or LAN (www.lan.com).

**Language(s):** Spanish is the official language in Ecuador and on the Galápagos Islands, though English is widely spoken on tours, plus in the restaurants and hotels.

**Currency:** The US dollar

**Electricity:** Plug type A/B, 110 V. The voltage and socket is the same as the US, so there is no need for an adapter or converter.

**When to Go:** Every month in the Galápagos has its highlights, and the weather makes any time of the year a good time to visit, so when

This sleepy sea lion barely lifted his head to see who was taking his picture

you go greatly depends on the type of experience you are looking to have. For example, in March on San Cristóbal and Genovesa you can catch a glimpse of the frigatebirds' inflated red throat pouches, in May your chances increase for witnessing the blue-footed booby mating dance on North Seymour, and in August you can catch a glimpse of the newly-born sea lion pups. There is always something incredible to see on the Galápagos. For a complete list of wildlife activity, check out the monthly calendar at Ecuador Travel Site (www.ecuadortravelsite.org).

The peak tourism months are June, July, and August, as well as mid-December through mid-January. You should book your trip well in advance during these times, as the number of visitors allowed on the islands is limited. Be aware that the prices are also often higher during this time. December through May is when the sea tends to be the calmest. In these months the weather is hotter and slightly rainy with temperatures typically in the eighties. On most days the sun will still make an appearance after the rainfall. June through November brings cooler temperatures (in the seventies) and colder water. Experienced divers prefer this time of year, as the currents bringing nutrients into the water draws more amazing marine life.

**How to Visit/Planning:** One of the biggest decisions to make when planning your travel to Galápagos is how you will choose to explore the islands. You can either take a cruise on a live-aboard boat or stay onshore using a hotel as your base. If you select the latter, it is possible to book day trips to some of the popular islands from Santa Cruz or San Cristóbal. Though this may be a more economical option, getting around independently can be challenging, as exploring most of the islands requires being accompanied by a licensed guide. Plus, you will have limitations to the islands you can reach due to the distance. The advantage to a multi-day live-aboard cruise is that they leverage the night hours by using them to travel between islands, so your days are not wasted. The small group yachts, under twenty passengers, are the best way to explore the islands and see more of the wildlife in a personalized environment. There are dozens, if not hundreds, of licensed vessels with a variety of stops and routes to choose from. Ecoventura (www.ecoventura.com) is the sustainable travel company who took me through the islands, and is ideal for those wanting a small group experience with educated naturalists. If you opt for day trips from the main islands, Sharksky (www.sharksky.com) offers good options. The best solution may be to take a four-day cruise, then spend a couple days on your own on a populated island, like Puerto Ayora in Santa Cruz or Puerto Baquerizo Moreno in Cristóbal.

**Getting Around:** Navigating between the islands will require a plane or boat. Though for getting around on the populated islands you can rent a bike for about fifteen dollars per day or catch a taxi for a couple of bucks to most destinations.

**Where to Stay:** If you are staying overnight in *Guayaquil*, try Hotel Oro Verde (www.oroverdeguayaquil.com; from $124), which offers shuttle service from the airport or for a more peaceful stay in a quiet residential area, Nazu House Bed & Breakfast (www.nazuhouse.com; from $86). In *Quito*, splurge at Hotel Patio Andaluz (www.hotelpatioandaluz.

com; from $210) centrally located in the historic district or hideaway at Las Terrazas de Dana (www.lasterrazasdedana.com; from $109), a modern ecolodge in the cloud forest of Mindo. In the *Galápagos*, stay in the lap of luxury at Finch Bay Eco Hotel (www.finchbayhotel.com; from $325) on Santa Cruz Island or the family run Galápagos Suites (www.galapagossuites.com; from $134). On **San Cristóbal**, try the simple Galápagos Eco Friendly (www.galapagosecofriendly.net; from $89) that has all you need.

**Where to Eat:** While in **Quito**, get your ceviche fix at Zazu (www.zazuquito.com) or indulge in traditional Ecuadorian dishes and pasta at Fried Bananas Café (www.newfriedbananas.com)—make sure to order the fried banana dessert made with vodka. In *Guayaquil*, try local foods with a trendy twist at La Pizarra (www.facebook.com/lapizarraec) or opt for Noe (www.noesushibar.com), known as the place to go for great sushi. On the island of *Santa Cruz* have a casual dinner at Calle de los Kioscos, an open-air market with plenty of cheap local food choices. For outdoor dining, head over to La Garrapata (+593 5-252-6264) for fresh tuna in a sesame and pepper sauce. For a local experience on San Cristóbal, get burgers at Cri's (www.facebook.com/CrisBurgerFactory) and eat on the tiny stools out front.

## NEARBY MUST-DOS

- Plan your trip around the month of May to get a better chance of witnessing the *blue-footed booby mating dance*, the courtship ritual of these popular birds.
- Take the steep climb to the top of the *volcanic cone of Bartolomé* and get a peak at the most photographed natural structure in the Galápagos, Pinnacle Rock.
- Do as the sailors did in the 19th century and *"mail" a post card at Post Office Bay* on Floreana Island. Sailors passing through used to leave letters to their loved ones inside an old barrel, in hopes that it would eventually get hand delivered by another

visitor passing through. This tradition still lives on, and you can leave a postcard addressed to anywhere in the world. With any luck another tourist from that location may hand deliver it upon their return home. Also, sift through the stack left behind and maybe you'll find one that you can personally bring to the addressee.

- Take a closer look at the giant tortoises at the **Darwin Research Station** (www.darwinfoundation.org) in Puerto Ayora, where scientists and volunteers are involved in conservation.
- Snorkel through the network of **lava tunnels known as Los Tuneles** on isle Isabela. The unique formations above and below the water include a series of arcs and tunnels that are a sanctuary of marine life.

## ESSENTIAL INFORMATION:

- It is a requirement to have a naturalist with you when exploring the protected islands; you cannot just venture off on your own.
- Though you may be able to hop onto a last-minute cruise when you reach the islands, it's best to book well in advance, at least three to four months ahead during non-peak times and six months to a year during high tourist months.
- When arriving to either of the two Galápagos airports, travelers must pay a $100 per person ($50 for children under twelve) Galápagos National Park (www.galapagospark.org) entrance fee at immigration.
- A visa is not required to enter Ecuador, though make sure your passport does not expire within six months of arrival.
- It is strictly prohibited to touch or otherwise disturb the nature or wildlife of the Galápagos. Do not feed the animals (not even a drop of water) or leave behind any sort of litter.

## PACKING TIPS:

- Exploring the Galápagos typically means being on a boat, so make sure that you load up on **motion sickness medication**. Some days can get pretty choppy, and seasickness can even affect those not typically prone to it.
- Be kind to the ecosystem by bringing **biodegradable** sunscreen, shampoo, conditioner, and lotions.
- A small pair of **binoculars** can go a long way when trying to spot wildlife from the boat.
- Limit plastic waste by bringing a **reusable water bottle**.
- Bring the right pair of shoes. Light **hiking shoes** are necessary for some of the islands and **water shoes** are needed for the wet landings when the panga can't bring you all the way to the shore or dock. A dual-purpose Keen-style active shoe would work well. Also, bring a comfortable pair of deck shoes to wear while just hanging out on the boat.
- Don't forget an **underwater camera** to capture the incredible marine life.
- Most tours will provide **snorkeling gear** (masks, tube, fins, and wet suit), but consider at least bringing your own mask. A properly fitted one can enhance your snorkel experience and lessen the chances of missing marine life because of having to fiddle with your gear.
- You can leave the **makeup and blow dryers** at home since you will most likely be in and out of the water several times per day.
- Bring a **small daypack** to take along on the hikes.
- Pack a **dry bag** to store all your electronics. It can get tricky moving from the small panga to shore while carrying your camera equipment and you want to make sure it is protected.
- If you are taking a cruise, there will be some down time and very limited Internet. **Bring a book** or **download movies** to your laptop prior to leaving home.

A troop of black marine iguanas warming themselves on a boat dock

- It gets hot in the Galápagos and a ***long-sleeved UPF shirt*** to protect you from the sun while hiking or snorkeling can save your shoulders from a brutal burn.

**Helpful Websites:** Galápagos Conservancy (www.galapagos.org); Parque Nacional Galápagos (www.galapagospark.org).

# 8. SPEND THE NIGHT IN JORDAN'S WADI RUM DESERT

Truth be told, I was nervous weeks before even getting on the plane. After all, it was a tumultuous time in much of the Middle East and that's exactly where I was headed. Every major news station highlighted this turmoil nightly; making the entire world, including myself, believe nowhere was safe to travel to in the area. Though all the signs pointed toward my final destination of Jordan being a relatively secure country, it was still surrounded by turmoil, sharing its borders with Israel, Syria, Saudi Arabia, and Iraq. It seemed like I was willingly going to be plopped in the middle of chaos.

I packed my bags carefully for the conservative Muslim country where masking your curves and covering your hair with a *hijab* is the

Wrapped in an Arabic head scarf overlooking the ruins of Petra

A Bedouin man, his camel, and his dog reflecting as they stand on a mosaic of cracked dirt

norm. Even though the weather would be relatively warm, there were no short shorts or little skirts in my luggage; they were replaced with lightweight long sleeved cardigans, lengthy loose T-shirts and colorful scarves. There is an amount of respect that needs to be paid to the culture of a country and I wanted to be certain to honor it.

Landing in the capital city of Amman was surreal. Just stepping foot in the Middle East was something that I never thought I would do, and looking around there was still a feeling of uncertainty. Some women were wearing a black *niqab*, a face-veil that left only their eyes uncovered, while others chose to only conceal their manes, and a few were in discreet Western wear. Many of the men wore red and white Bedouin scarves on their heads, with suits or a long *thobe*. It seemed like an entirely different world from my Northern California homeland, one that I was initially trepidatious yet eager to explore. But each

A small camel caravan roaming through the ruins of Petra

day that followed, actually each hour, the uneasiness lessened. I quickly began to realize what other travelers before me had already discovered: the Jordanian people's unity and generosity, plus their rich culture, is unlike no other. They are hospitable, kind, and eager to share. The only fears that would be experienced on this trip besides the plane's turbulence were the ones fictitiously created in my own head.

There are two main reasons that people visit Jordan and our itinerary was set to do both. The first is the ancient Nabataean city of Petra, the archaeological site whose pillared Treasury building is the most iconic photo of the entire country. It was easy to see why this place is so notorious: its impressive temples and tombs are carved directly into the reddish sandstone cliff faces. We not only explored the grounds during the day, but also attended Petra by Night where over fifteen hundred candles wondrously lit up the walk from the Siq to the Treasury. The

A camel sitting in front of the iconic Petra Treasury building

A caravan of camels moves through the arid valley of the desert

other reason many people come is to take a float in the Dead Sea, a salt lake that is over 1,300 feet below sea level making it the lowest elevation on earth. It's unusually high salt concentration creates a natural buoyancy making you float like a fishing bobber. Hordes of people flock here, some to benefit from its natural healing properties in the mineral-rich waters and others to take the quintessential photo of floating in the sea while reading the *Jordanian Times* newspaper. I was the latter of the two.

Both spots were incredible and beyond worthy of their popularity, but there was also an unexpected treasure, a place of tranquility and boundless empty spaces. Wadi Rum is 720 square kilometers of heart-stopping desert landscape, where a maze of sheer-sided sandstone and granite monoliths rise up from the valley floor. Its dramatic panoramic land is where you can follow the footsteps of Lawrence of Arabia, ride camels through the sun-kissed desert, and be amongst the semi-nomadic Bedouin people who still live in the area.

The burnt sienna rock hills rise from the valley floor

Driving down the seemingly endless dusty road into the largest wadi in Jordan it was easy to see why it was the filming location for *The Martian*, a movie set on Mars. Also known as The Valley of the Moon, it was dry and desolate, a place layered in countless shades of beige and desert red. The burnt sienna rock hills stood erect from the flat plains, and an occasional acacia tree or low shrub was scattered about.

Our shuttle arrived at the main barracks of Captain's Desert Camp on the edge of Wadi Rum, parking on a mosaic of arid cracked dirt. This was just a pit stop, as we would actually be spending the night at their private camp deeper in the desert. But, the twenty-person shuttle bus we were on wasn't able to maneuver us any further—we needed a better-equipped vehicle. Luckily, we showed up just in time for lunch, so before heading out we loaded our plates with traditional Jordanian food at their long buffet. A large, colorful pitched-tent lined with oriental carpets and cushioned bench seating was the dining room. As we snacked on dishes like *fattoush*, an older male

On the desert safari deep in the dusty valley of Wadi Rum

Having a cup of Bedouin tea with our guide, Mohammad

Bedouin musician was perched on a short stage playing the *oud*, an oriental instrument similar to the mandolin.

After lunch, three old Toyota 4x4 pickup trucks, fitted with benches in the open-air bed, were waiting for us. We were going on a five-hour desert safari, heading further into the landscape to explore before being dropped off at our barracks for the night. Though riding inside the cab was an option, I hopped into the back wanting to feel the wind in my hair and the sun on my face. We began driving through the desert, a cloud of dust trailing behind us.

The aroma of sage, cardamom, and cinnamon permeated the tent at our first stop for a cup of Bedouin tea. It was a teashop like no other, nestled between the rocks with a sand dune view from the seats inside. Tea is an important ritual for the Bedouins; there is never a wrong time for a cup, and this includes in the middle of the desert. The Bedouin are known for their hospitality and this friendliness almost

A camel taking a rest on the sandy desert floor

always includes a dose of hot tea. Saying no to this liquid generosity is just plain rude. The cup here was freshly brewed over the campfire and served in tiny glasses, with a generous amount of sugar. We sipped our brew, chatting about their tribal culture until it was time to move on.

Next, the trucks brought us to a place that appeared to be in the middle of nothingness, where a dozen camels laid resting on the warm sand making chewing motions and showing their large yellowed teeth. One had a newborn by its side that was just trying to learn how to use its wobbly legs. Considering this was our first camel sighting in Jordan, it was quite the spectacle. But that wasn't why we were here; it was for the inscriptions that were carved into the rocks that lay directly across from the herd of chomping animals. These petroglyphs depicted people, footprints and animals dating back to prehistoric times. The over 35,000 chiseled images and inscriptions dotted throughout the desert tell 12,000 years of stories about the people that have inhabited Wadi Rum, including the Nabataeans. They are believed to show information about hidden springs, pastures, and agriculture. This may have been just as impressive as the lazy camels that laid twenty feet away.

Dunes were common in the valley, but none as impressive as the expansive Al-Hasany red sand dunes that back up to Jebel Umm Ulaydiyya. Here the drivers put the trucks in park at the base of one of the tallest slopes claiming it had the best view from the peak. There was only one way to find out, and it involved a steep climb. We took off our shoes, sinking our feet into the soft sand and ascended to the summit. Once at the top, some of us sat cross-legged taking in the natural beauty of our surroundings, while others tried to capture the best jumping shots with a sea of sand as the background. On some days you can sandboard down these dunes, using them like you would a snowy ski mountain. But on this day, we instead jumped off the edge, running and rolling our way to the bottom. An impromptu dance party greeted us at the base, Arabic music was blaring from the trucks and our Bedouin drivers were shaking their hips with their hands high in the air. We all haphazardly joined in replicating their unscripted moves, our laughter bellowing throughout the desert.

After the spontaneous celebration, there were a few more stops before arriving at our camp for the night. First was Al-Qsair, what is left of the Lawrence house where legend has it that he stayed during the Arab Revolt. Its crumbled remains weren't much to be awestruck by, but the endless view of red sand dunes from the top of the nearby rock was breathtaking. Next was the Um Fourth Rock Bridge, a natural stone arch that stands almost a hundred feet in the air. If you dare to take the short but steep climb to the top, you can take the adventurous walk across the arch looking at the minuscule onlookers below. As evening fell, the last stop we made was in what seemed like the middle of Wadi Rum. This is where we abandoned our trucks since from here it was only a short walk to the camp. But before heading in that direction, we all sat quietly on the valley floor waiting for a performance of another kind. Nobody said a word as the sun began to set over the rocks, lighting up the desert in a flurry of color.

After five hours of exploration we ended up at a private camp deep in the desert. There were no other people or barracks in the visible vicinity; this was just for our Bedouin hosts and us. The area in and around Wadi Rum is primarily made up of the Bedouin people, a name meaning desert dweller in Arabic. They are a semi-nomadic group, most of whom are either goat herders or crop cultivators who migrate depending on the season and richness of the land. Today many also thrive on tourism, organizing tours and running overnight camps like this one. Their communities are easily recognizable around the barren parts of Jordan by the small cluster of goat hair tents; similar to the ones we would be sleeping in that evening.

Bedouin style tents at the camp in the Wadi Rum desert

Entering through a candlelit walkway, there were about twenty individual tents that surrounded a central courtyard. This patio had a campfire that was already blazing when we arrived. Comfortable and colorful cushions surrounded the fire pit, a place where we convened after dropping our belongings off in our individual tents. Our dinner had started to be prepared well before we arrived. With a cooking time of four hours, it had to be. The Bedouin staff were honoring us with a special feast, a *zarb*, an ancient and traditional cooking practice that is done underground. In the past, meat would be wrapped in palm leaves and placed in a hole in the ground that was layered in burning charcoal. It was then topped with sand to trap the heat. Today, a tiered iron pot is used and the meat is covered in foil. They called us over when dinner was about ready to be unearthed. Two men brushed away the mound of sand, then pulled the large layered cooking canister from the ground. The foil was punctured, allowing the steam and barbecue aromas to escape. Completely removing the wrapping revealed juicy lamb, chicken, and vegetables. This deliciousness was moved to the small makeshift dining room located directly behind the fire. Once again we were all silent, too busy feasting on a rare meal and licking our fingers clean of every last morsel.

After our casual dinner we sat back around the fire for some authentic entertainment that did not include a television or the Internet. Lively Bedouin tribe music began to be played as the natives taught us how to do the *zaghrouta*, a rapid ululation of a *la-la-la-la* sound that is used to express celebration. The trilling of the voices, instrumental sounds, and clapping hands echoed through the desert. After the music had tapered down, those who stayed up later spent the evening stargazing at the twinkling sky, drinking Jordanian Syrah, and smoking hookah. When the crackling of the fire started to dwindle and the bottle of wine was empty, I retreated to the cozy room in my goat-hair tent where there was no electricity or amenities other than a full-size bed, a wooden chair, and a box of candles. I lit one,

Exploring the peaceful sand dunes early in the morning

and fell into a peaceful sleep where the only sounds you could hear were from the faint voices of chatter from those still awake and the flicker of the flame.

I woke up the next morning well before any of the others in order to climb to the peak of an untouched sand dune and watch as the sun rose over the already picturesque landscape. At the top, with a view of the expansive desert valley below, I sat in pure silence. There was not even the chirp of a bird or the noise of a swaying tree being pushed by the wind. Miles from the nearest town, there was complete stillness. In our normal lives random noise is the norm, but not here. There may not have been a quieter place on earth than in the wee morning hours of Wadi Rum.

Back at the camp a slew of kneeling camels lined the walkway. Inside, our Jordanian guide Mohammad had set up a beauty shop of sorts on one of the benches in the dining area, where he was expertly

The camel caravan heads off deep into the dusty desert

wrapping traditional Bedouin scarves around campers' heads. These wraps would be helpful for our last adventure, a long camel ride through the dry desert back to the main camp. I approached the humped animals, picking my favorite of the bunch, selecting the one with the colorful red and yellow saddle. Holding on tight to the pommel, I boarded him as he was kneeling and he slowly stood to his feet jerking me forward. We then started on the journey back to where this experience began, following the paths that thousands had before. For centuries, camel caravans had moved goods through this very desert. The Nabataeans and Lawrence of Arabia had traveled the very same route. And then there was me, a simple travel writer looking for a story. Here in Wadi Rum there were about 12,000 years' worth to tell.

# CHECK IT OFF YOUR LIST

**Location/Facts:** Jordan is a mostly Muslim country located in the Middle East, sharing its borders with Israel, Syria, Saudi Arabia, and Iraq. Wadi Rum is a 720-square-kilometer dramatic desert in the southwestern corner of Jordan, near the Saudi Arabian border. Its diverse landscape consists of sheer-sided sandstone and granite mountains, natural arches, narrow gorges, and chiseled canyons.

**Getting There:** There are regular flights from the US on Jordan's national carrier, Royal Jordanian (www.rj.com), plus several other international carriers that will fly into Queen Alia International Airport located just south of Amman. From Amman, Wadi Rum is about a three-and-a-half-hour drive, though many visitors choose to stay in Petra instead, which is roughly an hour and a half away. From Amman you can take a bus to Petra, since there is no bus service that goes all the way through to Wadi Rum. A JETT (www.jett.com.jo) bus runs daily for around $14 USD and will drop you off in Petra where you could either hop on another bus or take a taxi. Your hotel can arrange a bus from Wadi Musa (or call 079 5235257 to book a seat), the main tourist gateway to Petra, to Wadi Rum that leaves around six a.m. and costs just under $10 USD (or call 079 5235257 to book a seat). Taxis run roughly $50 USD and many camps will be able to arrange taxi service. Viator (www.viator.com) offers a private transfer from the airport to Petra for $68.75 USD then you can take a bus or taxi to Wadi Rum from there or for roughly $200 USD. AAT (www.ammanairporttransfers.com) will give you a private transfer all the way to Wadi Rum. You can also get to Wadi Rum by renting a car, which can be the most flexible way to explore. The airport has numerous companies, many of which are also found in America (Dollar, Thrifty, Budget, etc.), so do a search on a site like Expedia (www.expedia.com) or Skyscanner (www.skyscanner.com) who will compare the rates from different car rental companies. The cost starts at around $40 USD per day. The roads are in good condition and the important signage will be in English as well as Arabic, but make sure you have a good map or GPS. Unless you rent a four-wheel drive you won't be able to truly explore Wadi Rum in your rental, but it will get you to the visitor's center where tour or camp guides can pick you up.

The cute face and crooked nose of a Wadi Rum camel

**Language(s):** Arabic is the official language. Many Jordanians in the urban cities speak English, though fewer will in the smaller villages, especially the Bedouin elders.

**Currency:** The local currency is the Jordanian dinar. Some places will accept American dollars, but it is not a guarantee so exchange some money beforehand. ATMs can easily be found in Amman (and there is one at the airport), but can be challenging in the smaller towns.

**Electricity:** Plug C / D / F / G / J, 230 V. Most outlets will be the same as the European with two round prongs. You will need an adapter and a converter if your devices are not dual voltage.

**When to Go:** The best time to visit Wadi Rum is from March to May or late September to November when the temperatures are moderate and rainfall is at a minimum. In the summertime the temperatures can soar up to 115 degrees, which will make exploring the desert next to impossible. In the winter the daytime temperatures may be comfortable in the mid-60s, but the evenings will get down to the low 40s, which will be chilly if you are sleeping in a tent with no heater.

**How to Visit/Planning:** For an overnight stay in a Bedouin tent it's best to book online directly with the camp (see the "Where to

Stay" section for recommendations) and have them arrange any tour experiences that you may be interested in. It is also very simple to make these arrangements once you get to the Wadi Rum visitor's center. For an easier option, Viator (www.viator.com) offers an overnight in Wadi Rum with transportation from Amman for $200 USD, though it only includes a two-hour jeep safari. If you feel more comfortable booking with a US tour operator who will plan your trip from start to finish then check the approved list on the Visit Jordan website (na.visitjordan.com).

**Getting Around:** You will need a 4x4 to navigate Wadi Rum on your own, though it is best to have a Bedouin guide who knows the area accompany you. You can hire a guide at the visitor's center who has his own truck or can hop into your rental. Otherwise most exploring of the desert is done on tours with trucks, camels, ATVs, or on foot. Taxis can be arranged by your chosen camp to get you to nearby places outside of Wadi Rum, like the city of Aqaba along the Red Sea.

Where to Stay:

WADI RUM CAMPS
There are several camps that offer a similar experience, glamping in a private Bedouin-style tent with shared bathrooms and dinner included. **Bedouin Lifestyle Camp** (www.bedouinlifestyle.com; from $35) is nestled beneath a rock face and run by two Bedouin brothers who want to share their culture. **Wadi Rum Night Luxury Camp** (www.wadirumnight.com; from $112) offers a more extravagant glamping night with a private terrace, bathrobe, and the finest linens. **Obeid's Bedouin Life Camp** (www.wadirumtrips.net; from $71) is a small family-run camp in the heart of the desert. In the private camp at **Captain's Camp** (www.captains-jo.com; $71) is where I spent the night surrounded by sandstone rocks and sand dunes.

PETRA

The Mövenpick Resort Petra (www.movenpick.com; from $117 USD) is conveniently located right across the street from the Petra Visitor's Center. A simpler, no-frills option is Al Rashid Hotel (Main Street, Wadi Musa; tel. 96232156800; from $38) in the city center which offers clean rooms and free breakfast. Petra Moon Hotel (www.petramoonhotel.com; $70) boasts a roof terrace that overlooks the beautiful Petra Mountains. The newly renovated **Sharah Mountains** (www.sharahmountains.com) is a family-run three-star hotel known for its cleanliness and hospitality.

**Where to Eat:** Restaurant options are limited in the area, plus you will most likely be eating all meals at your chosen camp where they are typically provided in the cost. However, if you want to venture, the **Resthouse** (tel. 962 2018867) located in Wadi Rum Village is a good choice since they serve alcoholic beverages. You can also get a decent buffet lunch or dinner here for around $15 USD. If you are staying in Petra before or after your visit, take a cooking class at **Petra Kitchen** (www.petrakitchen.com) and then eat your deliciously homemade Jordanian meal. Don't want to cook your own meal? Try the traditional lamb mansaf at the low-key **Reem Baladi** (Mid-Town on Tourist Street; Petra - Wadi Musa; tel. 0777312455). It's where the locals go! If you're not that hungry, head over to **TimeOut** (Tourist Street, Petra - Wadi Musa; tel. 96277780932) where you can get snacks and coffee while smoking shisha. With a couple extra days in Amman don't miss stopping by the most legendary falafel stand in town, Hashem (Al-Amir Mohammed Street, Downtown; tel. 96264636440). It will be challenging to snag a seat, but you won't be disappointed even if you are eating them in the overflow alleyway. Afterward walk a few blocks over to **Habibah** (www.habibahsweets.com; Al-Bank Al-Arabi downtown branch) who specializes in freshly baked *knafeh*, a cheese pastry soaked in a sweet syrup and topped with crushed pistachios.

## WADI RUM MUST-DOS:

- Get out of bed in the wee hours of the morning to get an unforgettable panoramic view of Wadi Rum in a **hot air balloon**. Royal Aero Sports Club (www.rascj.com ) offers a fifty-sixty minute birds-eye view for $182 USD.

- Do as Lawrence of Arabia did and ***ride a camel*** through the arid desert. Rum Stars (www.rumstars.com; from $98) offers multiday camel trekking, but a word of warning: going by camel is a bumpy ride, much more so than a horse. Camps will also arrange tours that can range from ten minutes to ten days.

- For the adventurous travelers who are not afraid of heights, stand on ***Burdah Bridge***, the natural stone arch that sits 262 feet above the rock below. It's a dizzying and challenging climb to the summit, but the photo op from the top is a once-in-a-lifetime. Many of the jeep safari tours make a stop here, but confirm this before booking.

- Strap your feet onto a board and take a wild ride down a sand dune. ***Sandboarding*** is similar to snowboarding, except if standing is too difficult it's perfectly acceptable to sit or lie down. Many full-day or more tours will include sandboarding, some of the jeep safari tours will offer a sandboarding option for an additional cost (around $14 USD). The Bedouin Lifestyle Camp (www.bedouinlifestyle.com) offers a free snowboarding option upon request with all their jeep tours.

- A ***Jeep Safari*** tour is the best way to see what Wadi Rum has to offer in the least amount of time. Common stops on a few-hours' tour can take you to Burdah Bridge, Lawrence's Spring, Al-Hasany Dunes, Nabatean Temple, and Khazali Canyon. Most, if not all, camps will offer a jeep safari, but you can also book one at the visitor's center for roughly $99 USD. It will be more cost effective to book this tour in combination with an overnight camp stay, as discounts will be offered.

## ESSENTIAL INFORMATION:

- Do not take any photos of the Bedouin people, especially the women, without asking permission.
- The stars in Wadi Rum are unlike any other place. If you want to get photos of them, be prepared with a tripod and know the proper settings for your camera.
- It's easy to get lost in the desert, so it's best to have a guide with you when exploring. If not, make sure to carry a compass and a map.
- US citizens will need a visa, which can be purchased at the airport in Amman. A single-entry visa that is valid for up to 60 days currently costs 40 JD (about $56 USD).
- Remember that some areas in Jordan, including some Wadi Rum camps, are dry (no booze will be easily available) so grab a bottle or two in Amman or Petra.
- Make sure to drink more water than you think you need. You are in the desert where it can be easy to get dehydrated. It doesn't hurt to stop by the pharmacy to pick up a dehydration powder that can easily be put into your water in case you feel dizzy.
- When there is a choice, hire the Bedouin people as much as possible to support their community. Many of them are available as drivers and guides at the visitor's center.
- If possible, leave your large luggage behind at your hotel. Traveling with just a backpack or duffel bag makes navigating the soft sand of Wadi Rum much easier.

## PACKING TIPS:

- Pack a *scarf* or a *hat* and *sunscreen* because there is not much shade in Wadi Rum.

- Wear comfortable walking shoes; *light hiking shoes* or *sturdy sandals* would work unless you plan on doing some serious climbing.
- Bring *tissues*, not so much for when you are at the camp, but you may have to make a pit stop behind a tree while on the safari, plus frequently there's no toilet paper in the restrooms throughout Jordan.
- A good pair of *sunglasses* is necessary to hold back the dust and sun.
- The sand will get everywhere so bring *durable clothes* that blend with the reddish-colored sand. Anything white will discolor quickly!
- It can get chilly at night, so bring **layers of clothes**. A pair of *warm pants* and a *sweatshirt* is a good idea.
- There can be some pesky mosquitoes out there; load up on the *bug repellent*.
- Many camps are lit by candles or turn off their lights at a certain hour, so bring a *flashlight* to find your way around at night.
- Jordan is primarily a Muslim country where many of the women choose to cover the curves of their body, hair, and/or face. Though this is strictly a choice made by the individual, not a requirement, you should still be respectful of their customs by bringing *modest clothing* (no skimpy shorts or tops). Loose, short sleeve T-shirts, ankle-length skirts, lightweight long pants, or capri-style pants are acceptable.

**Helpful Websites:** Wadi Rum Protected Area (www.wadirum.jo); My Jordan Journey (www.myjordanjourney.com); Jordan Tourism Board (www.visitjordan.com)

# 9. UNWIND AT A YOGA RETREAT IN COSTA RICA

In order to reach this place of pure serenity you need a large dose of courage and possibly an even larger one of Xanax. The flight from Costa Rica's main city of San Jose required boarding a tiny twelve-seater plane heading for the small town of Puerto Jimenez along the Osa Peninsula coastline. As far as I'm concerned, the words "tiny" and "plane" should never be in the same sentence. It is a frightening thought, especially on this day when the severe turbulence had me tightening the seatbelt until my stomach started to cramp and my knuckles turned a pale white. This was the beginning of a relaxing week-long journey to a remote yoga retreat, a place to nourish my body, mind, and spirit—only the relaxing part had yet to begin!

"Thank you God," I whispered to myself through clenched teeth after safely landing at the local airport. Looking around it was evident that the term airport was being used very loosely. There was only a short concrete landing strip blocked off by a chain link fence, which we had stopped only a few feet from. There were no flight attendants dressed in tailored uniforms, spinning baggage claim carousels, or long walks through barren hallways to reach the "arrivals" doors. At this airport, you step out of the plane, the pilot hands you your luggage, and you're on your merry way.

A dusty 4x4 picked us up just beyond the fence, and we traveled eight miles through the rain forest on a bumpy, dirt road. This small region of the country was primitive compared to the big city. The beaches were nearly empty, there was no commuter traffic, and the main town had only a few thousand residents, including the half dozen wandering dogs. We continued the drive, passing a light scattering of homes and barren pastures until we finally came upon an old wooden gate, surrounded by a fence that prevented even a glimpse of what was inside. As we approached, the hinge was unlocked and the doors flung open. I let out a long exhale and my shoulders dropped. I walked through those gates unaware of the education that would take place behind them, teachings that went beyond a perfectly aligned warrior pose. Through these doors was a place of tranquility filled with lessons of self-discovery. It has been said that yoga is the gateway to a meaningful life, and this would definitely be the perfect place to undoubtedly prove this theory.

◆ ◆ ◆

I arrived at my first class twenty minutes early in order to secure a spot

Getting to Zen before a hatha yoga class

in the absolute back of the room. It had been over a year since I had practiced any yoga; my mat was getting dusty in the back of the closet and my downward dog looked more like a lazy cat stretching. Plus the prospect of attempting to touch my toes was dreadful, almost as much as the thought of somebody watching as the endeavor failed miserably. "Looks like you had the same idea as me", I quietly said to the young girl who was placing her plain blue mat next to my damask-printed Gaiam mat that had been my "one personal item" in the cabin of an eight-hour flight from San Francisco—if nothing else, at least I would look the part.

"I'm a bit nervous, I do yoga at home, but have never been to a retreat," she replied whilst sitting in a perfect lotus position.

"Me neither. I can't even touch my toes," I regretfully blurted out. I'm not sure why this came out of my mouth. Perhaps to safeguard myself from the inevitable embarrassing stares in the future, or possibly just skittish jabber.

I quietly kneeled, sitting back on my heels, and resting my hands on my thighs in an acceptable *vajrasana*, one of my favorite postures next to *savasana*; kneeling and laying down are two things I didn't need much practice with, so at least I had that going for me.

The open-air yoga studio began to fill up with a mix of amateurs and yogis, the latter of the two taking up spots in the front next to the large, unscreened windows. Beyond these openings we could hear the

The second floor open-air yoga studio at Blue Osa

crashing of the waves in the distance, and see the white-faced monkeys playing in the trees. It was a serene setting, on the second level where the outside reflections of green foliage shined down on the wood floors. The high ceilings had timber beams running across the length, with three rotating fans hanging down in the middle. It was a peaceful place that seemed to blur the lines of outside and in, a perfect environment to free the mind and awaken the spirit.

Whether or not I was ready to be twisted into a variety of pretzel shapes, the bell chimed. This sound was not only used to indicate mealtimes at the retreat, but also a signal that class was ready to begin. Our instructor entered and commenced the session with a thirty-minute talk about the meaning of yoga practice and its connection with living a peaceful life. These talks became the tradition for every class that followed. Each day, important nourishing aspects of the yoga lifestyle were focused on. On the first day is was that practicing yoga is individualistic, and to listen to what your body was telling you; a sweet justification for hanging out in child's pose.

These monologues seamlessly led into a hatha practice, a sequence of *asanas* (postures) and *pranayama* (breathing exercises) designed to encourage a healthy mind-body connection. We went from downward dog to cobra to plank, none of which I performed perfectly, but to my surprise no one was staring at my lack of flexibility or coordination; they were all too deep in their own practice to worry about mine. This is something that can be said for everyday life too. Most of the time people really are too concerned with what's happening inside their own bubbles to look over and notice what's going on inside of yours. If nothing else, this realization was another push to live life without worrying about the judgment of others.

By the time we were halfway through with this introductory session I was so absorbed in each *asana* that everyone around me was practically nonexistent; my focused mind didn't have the capacity to think about self-doubt. This was about my body and me—no one else. I was beginning to understand the calmness that was happening in my mind. As we were entering *savasana*, the last posture of the day, the teacher had some parting words for us: "Leave this room with a peaceful mind."

Abiding by that mantra while here seemed to be easy, since every aspect of this retreat catered to these words, going beyond the walls of the traditional square yoga studio. It started directly to the left of the entrance where there was a tropical garden where herbs, fruits, and vegetables were being grown to use as ingredients in the kitchen. The kitchen focused on farm-to-table cooking, and each day things like parsley, mint, *Echinacea*, and red peppers were picked and brought to the chef who turned them into nourishing dishes with medicinal benefits. There was no need for a guilty conscience.

Most would think that healthy food equates to tasteless and dull, but that was far from the truth here. For breakfast I indulged in

Delicious deviled eggs topped with paprika

homemade chocolate-orange muffins, gluten-free banana bread, fresh cut fruit, and creative eggs (think ginger spiced scramble and Israeli *shakshouka*). The fruit that wasn't eaten during the morning meal was turned into a naturally sweetened juice available to quench your thirst throughout the day. Lunch and dinner were equally as delicious with fresh dishes like coconut crusted red snapper, green mango salad, cauliflower gratin, and flan topped with roasted pine-apple. On one evening they even treated us to crispy onion rings with a healthier twist, made by using extra-virgin olive oil and organic onions. Dining here wasn't about depriving yourself, it was about eating local fresh foods that were kind to your body and then reward-ing yourself with cheat dishes, like onion rings, that were made in the healthiest way possible.

Past the garden was the kitchen, where there was always a helping of whole apples, mixed nuts, or fresh juice on the counter. Snacks

An evening sunset along the Osa Peninsula

were always nutritious, there were no Oreo cookies or Doritos chips, and I didn't miss them one bit. Adjoining was the outdoor dining area, which the moderate weather allowed use of all year long. On the outskirts of the eating tables was a section of cushioned seating, which afforded a view of the green lawn and surrounding trees. Many hours were spent here sharing stories with the other guests, learning life lessons from the yogis, and sometimes simply petting the bellies of the resident canines. It was a place conducive to meaningful conversations rather than television watching and cell phone texting. A path veering to the left from these seats led to the secluded beach where long evening walks inspired creativity, and watching the beauty of a sunset was a main activity on your calendar.

My room backed up to the royal blue lap pool, which was surrounded by Ganesha statues and authentic bronze bells. The interior was decked out in a dozen shades of turquoise, a soothing color that encouraged tranquility. The hammock located at the entry was an

A laying goddess overlooks the brilliant blue lap pool

The relaxing hammock inside my yoga retreat room

inviting sight, a place to spend quite a few lazy hours reading, writing, reflecting, and even napping. The actual bed was covered by a mosquito net, something that made me feel like I was a little child hiding in my own tent. Nights in this room were not spent watching rerun episodes of *Friends*, but instead gazing at the ceiling, staring at blinking fireflies overhead, and falling asleep to the sound of raindrops on the roof.

Besides the three resident dogs, one cat, and countless amounts of friendly fireflies, the grounds were filled with an abundance of wildlife: howler monkeys in the trees, ginormous spiders that seemed to be permanently planted on their webs, jumping toads along the paths, and colorful macaws shrieking overhead. Each morning I was awakened not by the typical buzzing of the alarm on my iPhone, but instead by animal footsteps on the roof and birds chirping in the trees. Each evening I entered my room wondering what critter was going to be my roommate for the night. One evening it was a black centipede, another a pale green lizard, and on one particularly entertaining night, a giant cricket wanted to share the bed. It was an especially fun surprise when a larger, mystery animal, (most likely a monkey), sitting in the rafters pooped on my suitcase—the perils of living amongst nature.

My room had all the essentials, give or take a couple of extra creatures. However, what it didn't have was the energy to operate a hair dryer or flat iron, thanks to the sanctuary being solar powered. This, along with the encouragement to go makeup free, was an enlightening lesson in embracing my natural self. I abandoned the makeup, goopy hair products, and any hair-transforming electrical devices needing to be plugged in. In my day-to-day life, I actually don't wear much makeup; I own one tube of lipstick, a never-been-used blush, and there never seems to be a single eyeshadow in my makeup bag. But, and it is a rather large "but," for the past ten years I have been suffering from melasma, dark brown patches of skin on my face, which tend to get worse in the sun. The gobs of creams, painful lasers, and protective sunscreen can only do so much for me. Because of this, I feel a huge sense of security while wearing foundation, concealer, and powder to balance my skin out. Throw on a little mascara, and this is basically my makeup routine, one that admittedly makes me feel prettier.

The first morning I simply took a shower, put a comb through my hair, washed my face and was ready to go; a process that shaved thirty-five minutes off my normal routine. This ritual continued for seven days. I went to all meals, activities, and tours without wearing a stitch of makeup and my hair just combed and air-dried. It was liberating showing off the real me, without my painted security blanket or the comfort of electrical hair assistance. It forced me to emphasize my personality, which was frightening for someone whose confidence was built primarily on the way she looked. There were times that I wished my hair was a little bit straighter or my lashes a little bit darker, but in the end I realized that it didn't really matter. This meaningful

Showing off my surfing wound after learning how to hang ten

experience wasn't about who was the best looking or had perfectly lined burgundy lips; it was about self-discovery, and bonding over sharing a once-in-a-lifetime adventure.

Everything about being at this retreat supported nourishment in some form or another, including the planned excursions beyond the grounds. One afternoon there was the opportunity to learn to surf, something that had yet to be checked off of my bucket list. The first time I traveled to Costa Rica I rented a surfboard on the beach of Tamarindo, absolutely determined to catch a wave despite my lack of any prior experience. There was no knowledgeable instructor in sight, just my board and my desire. The reality of what happened that day was a little less than inspirational. The result was swallowing ridiculous amounts of water, lemon sized bruises on my hip bones, and pure exhaustion after an hour of attempting to stand for a mere half second; it was an epic fail. So, it was truly appropriate that the very next time I traveled to this country

After a rough day of learning to surf, I felt a need to relax

would be the time that I would learn to surf the right way—with a proper lesson, taught by none other than a hot surfer boy.

Just a half hour's ride from the retreat was our surfing spot, Playa Pan Dulce. When we arrived, there were only a few other surfers and the waves seemed manageable, even for a haphazard novice like myself. Our instructor with sun-bleached hair and a wicked tan greeted us. Our lesson immediately started on the sand as he taught us the three-step approach to riding a wave. Step 1: Lay on your board in a position similar to yoga's cobra, put your dominate hand forward and lift yourself up into a modified downward dog position. Step 2: Plant your back foot, and exchange your front foot with the hand that was there. Step 3: Stand up keeping your feet and arms perpendicular to the board. At this point you should look like you're doing a loose interpretation of warrior. Every step of this lesson seemed to remind me of yoga.

These moves were practiced a few dozen times on the beach before even taking to the water. Once the technique was embedded in my brain, it was time to execute the steps in the sea. Lying down on my stomach I paddled out into the ocean. Once far enough, I turned myself to face the shore and the teacher held onto my board. When the wave approached, just before it was underneath me, he gave me a forceful push. Though I quickly tried to execute what had been learned just ten minutes prior, my board and myself immediately tipped over. The second and third attempt looked much the same. While lying on my floating board for five minutes to catch my breath, I gave myself a little pep talk. Come on Annette. Get it together. You can do this. This little chat with myself seemed to work, because the next two tries resulted in standing up and riding the wave all the way to shore. It was like a *Rip Curl* commercial; perhaps not quite as smooth, but that didn't matter because I had just officially surfed. Everyone in our small group of ladies was able to stand up on their boards, a bond that we will now share forever.

The surfing outing not only exercised my body, but also gave a confidence to my spirit and I was looking forward to nothing more than rewarding myself by lounging around the pool with a fruity cocktail. However, that thought lasted a mere ten minutes before someone mentioned the option of releasing baby turtles into the ocean. Who needs cocktails and a pool when there are baby turtles to be helped? I immediately changed out of my bikini and put on my water shoes. Roughly a dozen of us were driven about half an hour on the gravel roads of Puerto Jiménez to the Osa Conservation Center. A conservationist greeted us and we were led on a 1.2-kilometer hike through the rainforest toward the hatchery that was located along the beach. This center moves turtle eggs from where they've been laid in the sand to a protected location in order to safeguard them from human and environmental predators. All species of sea turtles are considered endangered, but today we would be helping the Olive Ridley to beat the statistics.

In the hatchery the nests were placed on a grid pattern that indicated the age of the babies. This helped the center estimate when the turtles should hatch and be released into the ocean. We were each given plastic gloves in order to protect them from the oils on our fingers, and then we cautiously removed the turtles from their cozy nest and

A baby Olive Ridley turtle just before being released to the ocean

placed them into a blue plastic tub. There were twenty-six tiny Olive Ridleys in total, half of a nest. We carefully carried the bin back to the spot where the mom had laid the eggs, which was indicated by a stake in the sand. We carefully lifted each turtle out of the tub one by one, and placed them on the sand about ten feet from the water. For a brief moment they were in shock as they assessed this new environment they were placed in. Then they began to waddle toward the ocean's edge, some getting sidetracked along the way. When the tiny turtles neared the water, a wave swept them up and pulled them under. It seemed impossible that these tiny creatures could actually survive the depths of the ocean at such a young age, and in fact, an estimated one out of every thousand does. It was a sad but true reality, but their fate was no longer up to us.

Once all the turtles had found their way to their forever home we collected our things, headed back to the hatchery, and wished our babies the best. There's something special that happens to your soul when you help someone or something else; just another one of the many lessons I had now learned.

## THE LAST CLASS

On the last day of yoga class, I placed my mat in the middle of the room. It was remarkable how things had changed in the past seven days. I was no longer hiding in the back row, my flexibility had grown, the nutritious food had brightened my skin and the friends that I had made surrounded me.

"Yoga is a practice that takes you on a path to learn about and develop your mind and body. It can give you greater flexibility, improve your blood flow, improve your core strength, help you focus, and so much more," the yogi said on this final morning. "It will not only give you a calmness in your thoughts, but wellness and vitality of your entire being. I hope you have experienced some of this in the time you have spent here." With these words, a sense of gratitude washed over me. It is not often that we are able to spend a significant amount of time taking care of solely ourselves from the inside out. A time where children do not need to be dropped off at school, no conference calls need to be taken, and dinner doesn't have to be prepared. Everything here, from the nutritious and well-balanced meals, to the surrounding nature to the laid-back lifestyle; it all centered around creating peace in your mind, nourishment in your body, and fulfilling your spirit. It did its job well.

Yogis deep in their practice

◆ ◆ ◆

# CHECK IT OFF YOUR BUCKET LIST

**Location/Facts:** Costa Rica is a Central American country bordered by Panama and Nicaragua, plus the coasts of the Caribbean and Pacific. The Osa Peninsula is the rugged southwestern headland that has the Pacific Ocean to the west and Golfo Dulce to the east. It is a primitive haven of about five thousand where the rain forests are pristine, many of the streets are unnamed and white-faced capuchins swing in the trees.

**Getting There:** The Osa Peninsula can be reached by plane via Costa Rica's capital city of San José, The daily flights to Puerto Jiménez airport takes roughly forty-five minutes. My flight was with **Nature Air** (www.natureair.com), known as the world's first carbon neutral airline, reducing their carbon footprint to zero. Alternatively, you can fly with **Sansa Air** (www.flysansa.com). It is also possible to drive from San Jose, by renting a car with **Solid Car Rental** (www.solidcarrental.com), the trip would take about six to eight hours. Taking a bus can be tricky if you speak absolutely no Spanish and are not an experienced traveler, but it can be done. **Transportes Blanco Lobo** offers a daily bus service from San José to Puerto Jiménez, the main town in the Osa Peninsula. The cost is currently $13 and departs from the intersection of Calle 12 and Avenidas 7/9 Blanco Lobo Station at eight a.m. and 12:00 p.m. (tel. 2257-4121).

**Language(s):** Spanish is the official language, though English is widely understood.

**Currency:** Costa Rican colón, US dollars are widely accepted.

**Electricity:** Plug Type A/B, 120 V. Most outlets are the same as the two-prong American-style, though some will not include a spot for the third prong. So your 3-prong devices may need an adapter, though you shouldn't need a converter.

**When to Go:** The Osa Peninsula consistently sees average daytime temperatures between the high 70s to low 80s throughout the year, though there are two seasons; dry and wet. The ideal time to visit is during the dry season (mid-November to late April) when the rainfall is very limited. Though this time is also the peak tourist season, the Osa Peninsula doesn't draw the same crowds as the mainland, so you will still be able to enjoy lounging on the nearly empty beaches and hiking barren rain forests. Wet season is from May to mid-November, and during the peak months (September and October) the rainfall may prevent you from traveling to the more remote parts of the area, especially when the potholed dirt roads become challenging even for the most rugged sports utility vehicle. If you are looking for a bit of a bargain, traveling off-season in early May or November may be your best bet. The rains will have just started or ended during these months and retreats may offer discounted rates.

**How to Visit/Planning:** Yoga retreats in Costa Rica, including the Osa Peninsula, are generally weeklong, live-on-premise experiences. The hardest decision you will have to make is which retreat to go to, as each has different instructors and techniques. It's best to look at the upcoming retreat calendars on their websites to determine what falls in line with the type of experience you want. My relaxing week was spent at Blue Osa (www.blueosa.com), which is known for practicing morning silence, exercising sustainable tourism, having a secluded beachfront property, and healthy farm-to-table meals. Other good options in the peninsula are the Iguana Lodge (www.iguanalodge.com) or Ojo del Mar (www.ojodelmar.com).

**Getting Around:** The Osa Peninsula is a remote location and has very limited transportation choices while there. Most retreats will provide shuttle service from the Puerto Jiménez airstrip to the lodging and excursion operators will offer pick-up/drop-off services (fees may apply). Between spending time at the retreat and the extra tours your time should be pretty well filled up. But, if you have an interest in exploring on your own, it will require either renting a car, hiring a driver, or catching a ride in one of the few taxis.

**Where to Stay:** You will be resting your head at your chosen retreat on most nights, but if you need a night in San José before catching your early flight home, try **Adventure Inn** (www.adventure-inn. com; from $94) which includes an all-you-can-eat breakfast and a free shuttle to the SJO International airport. If you want to do a little exploring in the city, enjoy a night at the historic **Grano del Oro** (www.hotelgranodeoro.com; from $167) or Aranjuez Hotel (www. hotelaranjuez.com; from $46), just a short walk from the city center.

**Where to Eat:** Another perk to nourishing at a yoga retreat is that most offer delicious and healthy food. But, if you want to venture into the "big city" of the Osa Peninsula, head to the coastal town of Puerto Jiménez and indulge in the ceviche at the oceanfront **Marisqueria Corcovado** (www.marisqueriacorcovado.com). Or opt for a taste of Italy with a thin-crust, wood-fired pie at **PizzaMail.it** (piazza central; 506 2735 5483). For a special treat head north to Drake's Bay for a meal of fish tacos and tuna at **Gringo Curt's Seafood** (Agujitas de Drake; 506 6198 5899). If you spend extra days in San José try **Ram Luna** (www.restauranteramluna.com) for *Tierra Tica* (Typical Night) where every Wednesday and Thursday evening you can not only eat traditional casado, but also listen to marimba music and see authentic Costa Rican folk dancing.

## NEARBY MUST-DOS (BESIDES YOGA):

- Spend a few hours meeting the inhabitants at the **Osa Wildlife Sanctuary** (www.osawildlife.org), a center focused on rehabilitation. There will be opportunities for have contact with the animals, whether it be feeding a sloth, playing with a monkey, or petting a porcupine.
- Take a tour through a traditional cacao plantation at **Finca Kobo** (www.fincakobo.com; $32). See the different species and taste the fresh fruit from a chocolate tree.

- Hike amongst the monkeys and toucans at **Corcovado National** Park (www.corcovadoguide.com). With over one hundred thousand acres of tropical rain forest there are many picturesque trails to choose from.
- If you are an adrenaline junkie, go waterfall rappelling with **Everday Adventures** (www.psychotours.com). They will take you on a hike up a series of waterfalls. Once at the top, you will be instructed on how to tackle the rappel down two waterfalls (one 45 feet and the second 100 feet). A heart pumping bucket list experience! They also offer a fun tree climb where you will scale up the trunk of a 200-foot strangler fig. The combo package for both adventures is $130, totally worth the 5 to 6 hours of adrenaline.
- Take a guided kayaking tour through the mangroves with **Aventuras Tropicales** (www.aventurastropicales.com; $45). The paddle will take you through the Preciosa Platanares Wildlife Refuge to learn about the ecosystem through your experiences with nature.

## ESSENTIAL INFORMATION:

- Americans are not required to get a visa to enter Costa Rica, though they do need one upon exit. It can be purchased at the airport and the cost is $26 per traveler.
- If you only learn a few Spanish words before you go, make sure that two of them are *"pura vida,"* as it is worked into almost every paragraph, if not sentence. This literally translates to "pure life," but it goes beyond this definition. It is really a way of life in the Costa Rican culture, encompassing a mindset of not sweating the small stuff, letting go of what you cannot control, and understanding there are many people in worse positions than yourself.

- The Osa Peninsula is a rural area, so don't expect to be able to get your morning triple shot latte at Starbucks—this is part of the charm.
- If you rent a car, be cautious while driving because the dirt roads can be filled with potholes and there are virtually no street signs.

## PACKING TIPS:

- If you forget anything, make sure it is not **bug repellant**! The tropical, humid climate attracts many little pesky bugs that would love to eat you for dinner.
- Though most retreats will have **yoga mats** for rent and/or purchase, it's always nice to bring your own.
- A **small flashlight** is helpful at the solar-powered retreats where the walkways may be dimly lit. This will help you find your way around while making sure that you do not step on any critters in your path. You can easily use your smartphone as a flashlight too, but don't let bringing it out of hiding tempt you from the peacefulness of being disconnected with the real world.
- The Osa Peninsula's tropical climate and casualness lends itself to **simple, comfortable clothing**. A mix of Yoga, lounge, and beachwear works in most situations.
- Costa Rica is another country where the strength of the sun can be deceiving, so bring lots of **sunscreen**.

**Helpful Websites:** Costa Rica Experts (www.costaricaexperts.com); Go Visit Costa Rica (www.govisitcostarica.com); Book Yoga Retreats (www.bookyogaretreats.com).

# 10. TAKE A CULTURAL ODYSSEY THROUGH TOKYO

I ate beef that was creatively shaped like a brain, served to me inside of my private jail cell by women dressed in pink nurses outfits. I drank my coffee next to a dozen felines at a quirky cat café, confirming my preference for dogs. *And* I found out exactly what all the buttons on the Japanese toilets do (enjoying some outcomes much more than others). There are not many places that would provide such peculiar and unexpected forms of entertainment, but Tokyo is a city of many colorful facets; a mix of avant-garde and traditional. It is a town where the illuminated skyscrapers cohabitate with historic temples, unusual anime shops, and cherry blossom–lined streets. It is a destination where you can attend a lively tuna auction hours

After sumo practice the wrestlers wash their *mawashis* as they chitchat

before daybreak, eat skewers of *yakitori* in the seedy Piss Alley, or scramble across one of the biggest intersections in the world with hundreds of others. In other words, Tokyo is freakin' fabulous.

I arrived in Japan's humming capital city with a loose itinerary in hand, one that would have me up close to grunting sumo wrestlers, eating from modern vending machines, and drinking matcha at a traditional Japanese tea ceremony, while still leaving room for unexpected opportunities. It would be a four-day cultural odyssey—a journey to be immersed in the intriguing behaviors and beliefs of the people in this wildly unique metropolis.

It all started in the quiet Ryoguku neighborhood in the Sumida district of Tokyo where the first itinerary stop was quintessential of the Japanese culture. This is the section where many of the sumo stables reside, the training and living quarters of the powerful wrestlers who are considered the rock stars of Japan. Every wrestler belongs to one of these stables; once they have committed to one there is no turning back, they are part of a family.

The competitive full-contact sport originated in this country and on some days these stables allow a very limited number of visitors to take a peek into the life of the athletes by watching an intense morning practice. At the Hakkaku Stable the practice area was small, consisting of the dirt *dohyō* (ring), a viewing area big enough for under twenty guests, and a very small section filled with a modest number of free weights that couldn't begin to compete with the oversized gyms in America. Just over a dozen *rikishi* (wrestlers) were dressed in their *mawashis* (sumo belts) ready to begin. In the room the stereotypical robust body size of a sumo wrestler was apparent, although also varied greatly. There was everything from the round to the trim, but what they all had in common was that they were filled with pure muscle.

The practice was a mixture of faux matches, as well as the men performing ritual flexibility and strength exercises. I keenly watched as

Two wrestlers battle it out in a faux match at the sumo stable

each determined wrestler attempted to win a match by forcing the other outside of the ring or to touch the ground with anything besides his feet. You can't begin to imagine the intensity or discipline of this sport unless you are there live to witness the panting, grunting, and dripping perspiration. And I was close enough to the action to get sprayed with flying sweat.

A sumo stable practice is not your typical tourist attraction. The athletes are not putting on a show for you, they are in serious training and with a pending tournament closing in it was evident that they didn't have time to waste. There wasn't even so much as a glance at the spectators who were staring in awe with their mouths wide open. Toward the end of the morning session when the white belt wrestler, (an indication of higher rank) got into the ring, the junior wrestlers catered to him, handing him a towel to wipe his brow, giving him drinks of water when he beckoned, and even icing his pained shoulder. *How can I get myself one of these white belts and get that much attention?* He was the forerunner of this stable, with a legitimate shot

A big pot of *chankonabe*, the nutritious stew that sumo wrestlers eat daily as part of their bulking-up diet

of coming home from the tournament victorious. It was easy to see why; he could probably flip a car one handed.

The only appropriate thing to do after watching this process was to go to a *chanko* restaurant. *Chankonabe* is the nutritious stew that sumo wrestlers eat daily as part of their bulking-up diet. It is a hearty dish that is relatively healthy, low in fat, high in protein, and filled with tons of veggies. There are several chankonabe restaurants in Tokyo, conveniently located close to the sumo stables. But, Yoshiba is one of the most unique of its kind because it is housed in an old sumo stable with a *dohyō* right in the center of the dining room.

Though there were western-style tables with chairs, we opted for the more traditional experience by removing our shoes and sitting cross-legged on the floor. Shortly after, a burner was placed on the low table and a large silver pot on top of that, while inside was the uncooked chankonabe. The miso broth base was heated and used to

My husband and I cooking chankonabe at Yoshiba restaurant

cook the hodgepodge of ingredients. There was a little bit of every-thing in there: salmon, enoki mushrooms, fried tofu, prawns, scallops, small meatballs, vegetables, and even chunks of chicken. It was considered lucky to have this poultry in our meal because in sumo wrestling if your hands touch the ground you lose. Considering most animals have four legs they are at a serious wrestling disadvantage, but the chicken has an edge because he has no hands. Forget the "lucky duck," it was lucky chicken around here. We ladled enough of the stew to fill four large bowls and still barely made a dent in the pot. No wonder this was their meal of choice. The mild flavor of the broth allowed for each ingredient to shine and the lack of complex flavors gave the feeling of fresh, simple, and healthy eating. In the end, my belly was beyond full, protruding like a sumo wrestler's.

That evening the itinerary took us to an entirely different type of cultural show, one that was also full of drama and talented men, but minus the grappling in a dirt ring. The night was spent at a *kabuki* house. *Kabuki* is a unique form of Japanese theater that combines song, mime, dance, costume design, and elaborate makeup. A full kabuki performance, comprised of three or four acts, can last over four hours and is typically performed solely by men. Not sure about sitting for that length of time, we opted for buying a ticket for a single act at Kabuki-za, an introduction to this tradition. The audience, some dressed in their fanciest kimonos, quietly watched the performance, which was purely in Japanese. Even without translation it was easy for me to get the gist of the story, making me wish my ticket included the acts that followed. But, even though it seemed impossible after the lunch we enjoyed, by that time my stomach had started to growl again and it was time for dinner.

The food scene in Tokyo is on a different level and chankonabe was only a sampling of the feasting possibilities. There are unlimited choices of dining and drinks in this city that boasts the most Michelin-star restaurants in the world. Eating sumo stew was just the beginning for us. That evening we went to indulge in another unique

Even the server station at Alcatraz ER looks like a medical counter

tradition, a themed restaurant. The metropolis is exploding with restaurants that have quirky motifs; you can watch a sexy robot show while eating a bento box, or be served your dinner by trained ninjas, or dine in a replica European church. Though all of those options sounded equally as quirky, we headed to Alcatraz ER, a faux-medical prison where the menu was just as offbeat as the ambiance.

In order to open the doors to the restaurant we punched a big red button with our blood type;

The Alcatraz ER themed restaurant, where servers wear pink nurse uniforms

Drinking my Brain Shock cocktail out of the head of an old beauty school mannequin

choosing from A, B, AB, or O. We were then chauffeured by adorable girls dressed in pink nurses' outfits through a corridor to the jail cells, each one a private dining room. In our cell we were given a picture menu and instructed to bang on the metal bars with a steel cylinder pipe for service, which many of the patrons were already doing. We ordered the most bizarre items on the menu, a mix of drinks and food. The Brain Shock cocktail, which tasted like a very strong margarita, was served in an old beauty school mannequin head with haircut number 227. (For future reference, no one should ever ask for this style haircut, it was horrendous.) There was something a bit disturbing about the next mixed drink, the Peach Boobs, which was dispensed from a baby's bottle. After just a few sucks, I quickly realized that I prefer my cocktails in a martini glass. The Seared Beef Salad came to the table loosely in the shape of a brain. It didn't really take its true form until it was cut open and the stringy juices came flowing out. The

The Seared Beef Salad at Alcatraz ER, made to look like a brain

The fishmonger expertly slicing his ahi purchase that morning

last thing to arrive to the cell was the bright royal blue curry served in a hospital urine tin. That's just plain wrong!

The next morning, after our jail cell release, our guide Tomomi picked us up at the hotel bright and early in order to go to the market to purchase the freshest fish possible. It was sushi-making day and she, a Tokyo native, was going to show us how to master the art of the roll in her own home. Just as most of the world's leading sushi restaurants in the city do, we headed to the famous Tsukiji Fish Market to do the shopping. This is one of the largest wholesale fish markets in the world, where an average of 450 different species are sold on premise. The bustle of the mart starts well before daybreak, when wholesalers set up their goods for the notorious tuna auction. At five thirty in the morning, the auctioneer asks the question "How much do you bid?" and then a lively bidding war ensues. For the early-risers or jet-lagged tourists, a limited amount of visitors were allowed to watch this process. We arrived later in the day on a mission to find the freshest cut of tuna for our sushi class that afternoon, which wouldn't be hard since most of the stalls were expertly butchering their winning bids from that morning.

Just like the seriousness at the sumo stable, we quickly realized that though the market is a tourist destination, it does not cater to those who have no intention of making a purchase. Visitors were being shooed away while taking photos and beeped at when lollygagging in the middle of aisles. Plus navigating was like a serious game of frogger, as there were speedy electric carts, busy shop owners, and determined shoppers to evade or get flattened. Our local guide safely led us to a trusted stall where we would be supplied with the greatest catch, a shop where the owner Kusumoto was butchering the ahi he had purchased at the auction a few hours earlier when we arrived. He had made his hundred-and-forty-pound buy that morning based on a small slice in the fish's tail and a tiny piece of flesh that he was allowed to rub between his fingers. It was all about texture and color. We watched how he accurately cut the tuna using a special four-foot-long knife, picking out a large chunk for us. It was a pound of perfectly pink ahi for our sushi.

At Tomomi's home, in a quiet neighborhood on the outskirts of the bustle of the central city, we learned to make sushi in an environment that felt more like we were long-time friends just coming over for lunch than tourists. It was a hands-on experience where we took part in steaming rice, grating fresh wasabi, and even making tamago from scratch, rolling the thin layers of egg in a

The result of the sushi-making class given by Tomomi

rectangle pan. After artfully constructing our colorful sushi that was overstuffed with the ahi from the market, we sat down to enjoy a delicious Japanese meal made by two Americans. As we were finishing our handmade sushi lunch, Tomomi had an unexpected surprise. She wanted to dress my husband and me up in kimonos, a traditional Japanese garment that is typically worn by women on special occasions. For me, the process started with a layer of padding because women in kimonos should have a cylinder shape rather than the curvy figure known to be appealing in America. I needed a little extra padding just under my breasts because she said that I had big boobs. Yep, those are the words that came from her mouth and I will never forget it, because that has never been said to me before. Ever. With my small-by-American-standards B-cups, I was considered well-endowed in Japan. After the padding was in place the strategic kimono fitting began. The purple-flowered cloth was carefully layered left over right; if you do it backwards you are dressing a corpse. The *obi*,

Red lanterns dimly light narrow passageways

kimono belt, was then wrapped tightly around my upper waist, which made me stand a little taller. She expertly tied a decorative knot in the back. If only we had had these for the night we were at kabuki, I would have been the belle of the theater.

It had been a delightful afternoon, but that evening we wanted a grittier dining experience so we headed over to Piss Alley, a name bestowed upon this section of town in the 1940s due to its lack of toilets. Today this narrow alleyway is also known as Omoide Yokocho or Memory Lane, and is filled with over seventy tiny, cramped restaurants plus a handful of drinking holes, most with no more than a half dozen seats. Squeezing through the tight passages would definitely challenge the bulky sumo wrestlers we had seen the day before.

This area was more of a local hangout than a hotspot for tourists, a place where suited men with their neckties loosened occupied many of the stools. Nevertheless it is still known as the district to go for some of the best *yakitori* (meat skewers) in the city. We strolled

Just one of the dozens of small yakitori restaurants

through the thin walkways that were dimly lit by the red-tinted lanterns, following the crowds and the smell of barbecue. We jammed onto barstools and into hidden corners of several of these yakitori restaurants sampling things like *toriniku* (white meat skewer) and *tsukune* (chicken meatballs). As the lights began to fade and the evening came to an end, while licking our fingers we confirmed that rumors where true, the yakitori here was second to none.

Day three in Tokyo was all about drinking, which of course in a town like this meant to expect the unexpected. It started early in the morning where we traded in our skinny vanilla lattes at Starbucks for an odd cat-themed café. The Calico Cat Café in Shinjuku is a furry place that gives you the opportunity to play with unique feline breeds while drinking a hot cup of coffee. We entered into what some might consider a kitty-lover heaven, and the first noticeable thing was the strong aroma. It smelled like a litter box—a dirty litter box. There were lazy cats sprawled all over the place, most didn't even glance our way when we passed by. The only time they seemed to be interested in anyone was when you waved a little food in their direction, then you would have a flock of feline friends.

There were unique breeds that lived here, many that I had never seen back in the United States. Some were striped like a tiger, some had mushed faces, and others had stubby little legs like a Corgi dog. We spent a few minutes attempting to get the attention of some of the kitties by shaking toys in front of their faces. They didn't even flinch, as if to silently say, "Where's my food?" Between the foul smell and the shun of the felines (a dog would never do that), we left before even finishing our brew.

Still needing a caffeine fix, we went on the hunt for a vending machine that could ease our pain. It is hard to walk a block in Tokyo without passing half a dozen of these dispensers that sell everything from beverages to dog food, hair products, umbrellas, and hamburgers (yes, I said hamburgers). We quickly found a digital machine that dispensed chilled

A kimono-dressed woman making the matcha tea during a traditional Japanese tea ceremony

Learning the proper way to hold the tea cup during a the ceremony

coffee drinks and bought a couple of Wondas, a chilled beverage that tasted like a creamy Frappuccino and made the promise to kickstart our day. It did its job well.

From here we headed to the next drinking experience that was quite a bit more refined than kitty cafés and tin dispensers. I will be the first to admit that I am not dainty. When you hear a loud bang in a store it's probably because I dropped something. But we still made our way to Happo-en Japanese

Garden that sits in the Shirokanedai district of Tokyo to participate in a very graceful Japanese Tea Ceremony. Through the stone pathways, abundant koi pond, and peaceful waterfall of the garden lies the wooden Muan teahouse. A woman dressed in a brilliant kimono waited for us in the doorway of the quaint six-seat building. We sat watching as this eloquent lady silently prepared the traditional matcha tea, a fine-powdered green tea, following a ritual of technical steps. Once the matcha was prepared, the cup was placed in front of me with the picture on it facing toward me. I was instructed to hold the bottom of the cup with my left hand and to wrap my right hand around one side. Before drinking, the cup must be rotated exactly two quarters of a turn clockwise, so the picture is facing out. Take one sip to taste the tea, then finish the matcha with three to four more sips, leaving a drop at the bottom. The last splash must be slurped making a very unrefined noise. Afterwards, I turned the cup two quarter-turns clockwise so the picture was facing me once again and took two fingers from my right hand to wipe the rim. My technique was not perfect, but I still managed to finish the tea ceremony without breaking a thing.

That evening drinking had to be something a little less sophisticated; it took all my mental energy to make it through the tea ceremony. I had heard of the perfect place. On the flip side of Piss Alley was Golden Gai, a neighborhood in the Shinjuku ward of Tokyo that squeezes in over two hundred miniature bars into a network of six narrow alleys, made only for pedestrians. Most bars in this section of town seat less than ten drinkers and cater to the locals. But, some welcome traveling foreigners like myself and I was looking forward to planting my butt onto one of their limited stools to drink the night away.

We aimlessly wandered through the dimly lit alleyways looking for someplace two Americans would be welcomed, as some were solely for the locals. The FOREIGNERS WELCOME signs posted near the front doors, advertised "foreigner charge" scribbled on chalkboards, or more simply just by the menus written in English were all good indications of acceptable drinking holes. We decided on Nessun Dorma, which means None Shall Sleep, mostly because we saw through the window smiling foreigners sharing beers, plus there were a couple of vacant seats at the bar. This particular place had a 700-yen cover charge just to claim one of the limited stools. We squeezed our way to the seats, causing each of the already drinking guests to have to push in their chairs in order for us to get by. Even though they had a back bar filled with hard liquor and offered specialty cocktails with obscene names, we followed the lead of our new Canadian friends seated next to us and ordered a Japanese beer and settled in for the night.

On our last day in Tokyo we ventured to the outskirts of town to witness what is known as America's favorite pastime, but here it's done Japanese style. From the Gaiemmae metro stop, we followed the crowd to Jingu Stadium where we would be attending a good

Jingu Stadium where the Tokyo Swallows play ball

old-fashioned baseball game. The spotlessly clean stadium seemed to resemble those in the US, a perfectly manicured field surrounded by tiered blue seats and a jumbotron displaying the action. But, it became quickly evident that they do things a little bit differently in Japan when the cheerleaders came out for the preshow. Cheerleaders in baseball? Of course, the husband thought this was a brilliant idea. Though the technical part of the sport ran pretty much the same, there were a few noticeable differences in addition to the aforementioned girls with pom poms. There was chanting and singing for just about every reason: an out, a new batter up, or a steal. Then came the banging together of miniature plastic baseball bats in rhythm with the loud music of the band that sat in the stands. Also, when a player scored a run, the crowd opened tiny clear umbrellas and waved them high in the air. My absolute favorite addition to the Japanese version was the stadium vendors selling fresh edamame—the peanut substitute. In the end the Tokyo Swallows team lost, but attending a baseball game in Japan was a winner to us.

After the game, there was only one thing that I couldn't possibly leave this vibrant city without doing: walking across a street crammed up next to thousands of other people. Shibuya Crossing is notorious for being one of the busiest intersections in the world, where a crowd of up to 2,500 hustle across during one change of the light in the midst of rush hour. I patiently waited on the sidewalk surrounded by a mass of bodies. When the light turned green I walked into the center of the crosswalk like Scarlett Johansson in a memorable scene from the movie *Lost in Translation*. Standing in the middle of the blaring music, automobile congestion, flashing neon lights, and a sea full of people I raised my arms in the air and looked to the sky, taking it all in. This was a city with a hundred different personalities and this felt like the center of it all—the perfect place to end an unforgettable odyssey.

# CHECK IT OFF YOUR BUCKET LIST

**Location/Facts:** Tokyo is the capital city of Japan, an archipelago in East Asia. The country is located east of the Korean peninsula (its closest neighbors are Korea, Russia, and China) and Tokyo is centrally located within the country along the Pacific Ocean. The 845-square-mile metropolis has a population of over thirteen million and is divided into 23 central city wards; the main ones being Shinjuku, Shibuya, Chuo, Shiyoda, Minato, and Shinagawa. These wards are further split into districts and neighborhoods.

**Getting There:** There are two main airports that service Tokyo, *Narita International* and *Haneda International*. If you are flying into Tokyo from the United States your choice will mainly come down to price and distance to the city center. Narita International sees the most foreign visitors (and will most likely be cheaper), but is located further from the city center, about 37 miles (60 km) east of central Tokyo. Taking a taxi from here to Tokyo would be quite expensive (well over $100 USD); the better option would be taking the JR Narita Express (N'EX; www.jreast.co.jp/e/nex), which takes about an hour and costs roughly $27 USD. Haneda has fewer international flights, but is located in Tokyo and closer to the city center. It easily connects to central Tokyo by the monorail (www.tokyo-monorail.co.jp; around $5) that runs every three to five minutes. You can also take a limousine bus for roughly $9 (www.limousinebus.co.jp) or taxis are available at the arrivals terminal.

**Language(s):** Japanese is the official language and very few people speak English, with the exception of the younger generation.

**Currency:** Japanese yen (¥). Many restaurants and stores will not accept credit cards, so make sure to bring a substantial amount of cash, either Japanese yen or US dollars to be exchanged upon arrival.

**Electricity:** Plug Type A/B; 100 V, 50 Hz. Note that most Tokyo outlets are American style two-prong, though if you have a three-prong American appliance you will need an adapter.

**When to Go:** Tokyo is a city that experiences the four seasons and is becoming a year-round destination, though the locals will tell you that spring and autumn are the ideal times to visit. In the **spring** (March to May) is when daytime temperatures are comfortable (60s to 70s). The end of March through mid-April is the peak time to see the brilliant cherry blossoms that invade the green space, begging for a picnic under the blooms. **Autumn** (September to November) is another great time to visit (especially October) when the fiery fall colors create a picturesque scene of foliage. Though rare in Tokyo, beware that September is the primary month for typhoons which may bring strong weather patterns that affect flights. The **summer** (June to August) is the busiest foreign tourist season, so expect long lines at museums and even more densely packed streets. It is hot and humid with daily high temperatures in the 80s. With the muggy heat and higher room rates, I recommend avoiding this time of year. If you don't mind the chilly weather, **winter** (December to February) is another travel option since there is very little rain. The day temperatures range from the 40s to low 50s.

**How to Visit/Planning:** With twenty-three wards and countless neighborhoods, planning a trip to Tokyo can be quite intimidating. So the big question to ask yourself is whether to book a tour or try to navigate the city on your own. The answer very well may be both. Tokyo is so vast that it can seem intimidating to maneuver without a tour group, but it can be done. The best way to do so is to design your itinerary based on the city's wards, listing the attractions and metro stop for each. It is also possible to hire a personal tour guide for a half or full day. We hired Tomomi from Tokyo Tours (www.tokyotourswithtomomi.weebly.com) for a full day. She not only expertly showed us through the Tsukiji Fish Market, but also taught us how to make sushi in her home, escorted us to the sumo wrestling stable, and dressed us in kimonos. For the best experience, I would recommend doing Tokyo on your own with a couple of half- or full-day tours thrown in.

**Getting Around:** With the proficient public transport system, it's easy to get around Tokyo. There are trains, buses, and taxis, but the subway system is most commonly used and can take you just about anywhere in the city. The subway can seem daunting at first, but it is fairly easy to use and much cheaper than pricey taxis. Plus, there's plenty of English signage to show you your way. It's best to plan your journey in advance, take the subway to the station nearest your destination, and then either walk or catch a taxi to your final stop. Each station has several different exits, so make sure to not only know the name of the metro stop, but also the exit. At most ticket stations you can get a rechargeable Suica or Pasmo card for a 500-yen (a little over $4) refundable deposit, then you load them up with money. Each of these cards used to be for separate lines, but are now pretty much interchangeable, so it really doesn't matter which one you get. They don't give you a discount on your subway rides, but allow you to breeze through the turnstiles with just a tap of the card. Plus you will not have to bother with doing any math as the correct amount will automatically be deducted from the card. There is also an array of unlimited day passes available, which would only make sense on days when you'll be hopping on and off the subways all day. Tokyo Metro (www.tokyo-metro.jp) sells a 24-hour unlimited ride for around $6.

**Where to Stay:** With so many wards in Tokyo, choosing a hotel location can be mind-boggling. But, if you want to be where the action is, Shinjuku or Shibuya may be the best district to stay for your first visit; both are conveniently located with easy access to shopping, restaurants, nightlife, and public transport. Plus, they look like the Tokyo you typically see on television with bustling streets, towering skyscrapers, and flashy neon lights. In Shinjuku the *JR Kyushu Hotel Blossom* (www.jrhotelgroup.com; $213) is just a three-minute walk from the south exit of Shinjuku station. For a more budget-friendly gem try *Tokyu Stay* (www.tokyustay.co.jp/e/; from $115) that has locations throughout the city including Shinjuku and Shibuya. If you want to venture to other wards, the **Tokyo Station Hotel** (www. thetokyostationhotel.jp; from $260; Ginza ward) is conveniently located in the heart of the city and right above the Tokyo JR station. For a unique cultural experience stay at a *ryokan*, an old-school Japanese inn typically with tatami-matted

Barbecuing our own meat at a yakiniku restaurant in Tokyo

rooms, low tables, and communal baths. **Ryokan Sawanoya** (www. sawanoya.com; from $85; Taito ward) will give you this traditional feeling or opt for the updated **Andon Ryokan** (www.andon.co.jp; from $71; Taito ward). If you want to avoid the bustle of the city, head off the beaten path to the original boutique hotel, **Claska** (www. claska.com; from $135; Meguro ward).

**Where to Eat:** Being that Tokyo has over 200 restaurants with at least one Michelin star, you should make it a mission to eat at one. Splurge at the three-starred **Ishikawa** (www.kagurazaka-ishikawa.co.jp/) with their ¥19,000 (about $162 USD) set menu or get the signature *shoyu soba*, soy-broth ramen for under $11 at **Tsuta** (Toshima-ku, Sugamo 1-14-1), the first ramen shop to be awarded a coveted star. For your sushi fix, get up early (people start lining up at three a.m. for the five a.m. opening) to wait in line at the famed **Sushi Dai** (5-2-1 Tsukiji, Tsukiji Fish Market 6th Bldg.). For a very local experience head over to the Shinjuku's Piss Alley (www.shinjuku-omoide.com), and eat at one of the many yakitori stalls, **Kabuto** (Shinjuku 1-2-11, tel +03 3342 7671) is amongst one of the favorites. If you are an adventurous eater try **Izakaya Asadachi** (Shinjuku 1-2-14), famous for serving things like pigs testicles, grilled salamander, and frog sashimi.

Flexibility and stretching is an important part of the sumo wrestling sport

## TOKYO MUST-DOS:

- Head to the Ryoguku neighborhood and **attend an asageiko**, wrestlers' practice at a sumo stable. Many stables that allow visitors will require appointments by phone at least a day in advance and some request a Japanese speaker accompany you. Though you can attempt a visit on your own, it's much easier with a guide who speaks Japanese; **Tokyo Tours with Tomomi** (www.tokyotourswithtomomi.weebly.com) escorted me to practice at **Hakkaku-beya** (1-16-1 Kamezawa, Sumida-ku, Tokyo). When navigating on your own you can try the following stables:
  - **Oshiogawa-beya** | tel. +81 (03) 3643-8156 | 2-17-7 Kiba, Koto-ku, Tokyo | Subway: Tozai Line to Kiba Station
  - **Wakamatsu Stable** | tel. +81 (03) 5608-3223 | 3-5-4 Honjo, Sumida-ku, Tokyo | Subway: Toei Asakusa Line to Honjo-Azumabashi Station

- *Futagoyama Stable* | tel. +81 (03) 3673-7339| 8-16-1 Kita Koiwa, Edogawa-ku, Tokyo| Train: Keisi Main Line to Kei-sei Koiwa Station
- *Musashigawa Stable* | tel. +81 (03) 3805-6343| 4-27-1 Higashi Nippori, Arakawa-ku, Tokyo| Train: Train JR Yamanote Line to Uguisudani Station
- *Oshima Stable* | 3-5-3 Ryogoku, Sumida-ku, Tokyo | Sub-way: Sobu Line to Ryogoku Station
- If you want a quick (and free) peek go to *Arashio-beya* where you can see the action from the windows out front. 2-47-2, Hama-cho Nihonbashi Chuo-ku Tokyo | tel. 81-(03) 3666-7646)

- Drink at Shinjuku's *Golden Gai*, a neighborhood in the Shin-juku ward of Tokyo that squeezes in over two hundred minia-ture bars into a network of six narrow alleys, made only for pedestrians. There's plenty to choose from, but some aren't as welcoming to tourists as others. You can try *Bar Plastic Model* that is a bright white bar that has Rubik's Cubes and a vinyl record player; or *Albatross* that has seating on three floors and a rooftop terrace that boasts a view of the cities lights. If you are a movie buff than pop into *La Jetee*, a place that is dedicated to film.

- Eat at one of the many *themed restaurants*. The place that I noshed on beef in the shape of a brain was *Alcatraz ER* (2-13-5 Dogenzaka Harvest Bldg 2F, Shibuya; +81 3-3770-7100). If 90s video games is more your thing, head over to *8bit Café*, grab a Nintendo console, and spend the night mastering Donkey Kong (3-8-9 Shinjuku | 5F, Q building, Shinjuku; +81 3-3358-0407). Or opt for *The Robot Restaurant* (B2F Shinjuku Robot Bldg, 1-7-1 Kabukicho, Shinjuku-ku) in Shinjuku that takes dinner and a show to another level. There will be loud music, dancing, and robots fighting, plus a little sushi to dine on if you should choose. To get a taste of anime *@Home Café* (www.cafe-athome.com) offers the quintessential "maid café" experience. Be charmed by waitresses dressed as French maids as you are served food and drinks that are meant to look simply adorable.

- Baseball isn't just one of America's favorite pastimes, the Japanese are passionate about it too, so hit up a *baseball game* (www.japanball.com). They just do things a bit differently at the games. Though the Yomiui Giants at the Tokyo Dome draw larger crowds, you can also see the Tokyo Swallows play at the outdoor Jingu Stadium.

- Attend the *Japanese tea ceremony* at Happo-en Garden (www.happo-en.com/) that sits in Shirokanedai district of Tokyo. Not only is it a beautiful representation of a Japanese garden, but you can also schedule to participate in a traditional Japanese tea ceremony where you will be drinking matcha in their wooden Muan teahouse.

## ESSENTIAL INFORMATION:

- Tokyo is vast which makes planning an itinerary a bit of a challenge. It's easiest to not think of it as one big city, but instead consider each ward its own city.

- In Japan, you are required by law to carry your passport with you at all times. Though you probably won't have an issue, the police can stop you at any time and you must be able to show your document.

- You must mind your manners in Japan. Doing things like blowing your nose in public is considered rude.

- Some of the places will require removing your shoes to enter; you'll know which ones by the line of shoes sitting at the front door.

- Download an English—Japanese dictionary; this is a country where English is limited. Many signs will be in English, but many people do not speak it.

- Good service is the norm in Japan. Tipping at restaurants is not expected, and may not even be accepted, as they believe that you pay for good service in the initial cost.
- Many of the futuristic Japanese toilets will take some practice to master. They feature a dozen different buttons that will spray jets of water and blasts of air. Practice makes perfect!
- Be courteous and walk to the left. If someone is heading straight for you, step to the left, not the right.

## PACKING TIPS:

- If you are using the subway as your primary mode of transportation, then **comfortable walking shoes** are a must. The closest metro station may be several blocks from your final destination.
- As mentioned before, it is a Japanese custom to remove your shoes inside many locations, so bring a pair that **easily slips on and off**.
- Japan is a modest nation where the women **dress conservatively**. You may feel uncomfortable if the only things you pack are bootie shorts and skimpy tanks.
- Carry a **small hand towel** since paper towels or hand dryers in restrooms are rarely provided.
- When traveling by train, it's wise to **pack light**, as storage places are limited.
- If you are traveling in the summer it can get excruciatingly humid, pack **mosquito repellent** and a **water bottle** to keep you hydrated.
- Don't worry if you forget to pack something, Tokyo has a little bit of everything and more.

**Helpful Websites:** Japan Guide (www.japan-guide.com); Japan Rail Pass (www.japanrailpass.net); Go Tokyo (www.gotokyo.org).

# 11. GO ON AN AFRICAN SAFARI IN SERENGETI

The nurse came barging toward me wielding a syringe filled with a clear liquid. Shouldn't there have been a warning? At the very least a three-two-one countdown? I urgently closed my eyes, yet it was a bit too late. My body cringed as she stuck me in the arm with a pinch and the burning fluid spread intramuscularly. I wanted to instantly curse the inflictor, telling her the extent of her horrendousness in a flow of profanities that needed earmuffs to muffle them. But, the truth was it barely stung; I had paper cuts that hurt worse. What a colossal waste of the last eight hours spent worrying about another fear that never came true. The vaccination tally for the day was four. There were shots for yellow fever, hepatitis A, and a polio booster, plus a live oral dose of typhoid. Added to that were malaria pills and a few of anti-diarrheal meds for the road, definitely wouldn't want to be caught in *that* predicament amongst the hyenas in Serengeti. I was completely protected when I hopped on the flight to Tanzania's Kilimanjaro airport.

"Medical document." I wasn't sure if this was a question or statement. Either way, the burly woman at the arrival door repeated it a second time, before I could barely comprehend the first. I dug deep into my carry-on and produced a paper record of my vaccinations. She took a quick glance and shooed me on my way. Those who could not hand over this document were sent across the hall to the barren vaccination office. It was rumored that this is where they were giving out yellow fever shots for those who had not bothered to get one prior to arrival. But the truth in at least one case was that they took twenty-five dollars in return for a yellow fever stamp and no needle pokes were actually given. Either way, I was perfectly content about getting mine done back in the States.

In downtown Arusha, the meeting place for the safari tour

I grabbed my suitcase from the creaky carousel, walked out of the smudged glass doors and took a deep breath. Holy shit. I was in Africa.

◆ ◆ ◆

My glamping tent in the Rongai hills overlooking Seronera Valley

Unzipping my green canvas tent a maximum of two inches, I peeked through the small slit no bigger than the size of my thumb. A dozen pairs of shiny eyes in the distant trees stared back. The gazelle had retreated into the woods for the night, though not far enough for my taste since I could still get a glimpse of their fixed gaze. I

Wildebeest roaming the dusty dry plain

quickly closed the crack and secured the two connecting sliders of the zipper with my luggage lock. There would be no unwanted animal entry here.

By now I was sort of getting used to animals ogling me and vice versa. We had spent the entire day in Tanzania's oldest and most popular national park, Serengeti, a place that easily earns a spot on many people's bucket list. It was not only an UNESCO world heritage site, but also home to one of nature's grandest spectacles—the largest migration of mammals on the planet. The annual wildebeest migration is when more than a million land animals stomp the dry-grass plains in search of greener pastures. The wildebeest don't travel alone; hundreds of thousands of Thompson's gazelle and zebras join them in this trek, plunging through crocodile-infested waters in their effort to escape death from hunger, thirst, and predators.

Even when the pounding hooves of the migration ceases, travelers come for the notoriously brilliant game viewing; roaming herds of buffalo, hyenas that will beyond a doubt cross your path, plus thousands of baboons, impala, and eland. Today we had been those

One of the Big Five animals, the African elephant

people—three travel writers and our knowledgeable driver—on a quest to see the incredible wildlife that they are known for, plus a personal pursuit to spot the Big Five, the five animals that are said to be the hardest to hunt on foot. This highly coveted group include the African elephant, leopard, lion, Cape buffalo, and the ever-so-elusive rhino. We had made headway on the game drive in the afternoon, seeing a male lion nearly hidden in the tall, dry grass. He paced back and forth, and then let out a powerful roar proclaiming his territory. Another cat crossed in front of our rugged Land Rover, eyeing a young zebra in the

African elephant exploring a tree trunk

A safari jeep exploring the park leaves a trail of dust

distance. I was grateful not to have been wearing black and white; I wouldn't want to be mistaken for dinner. There also was a sighting of a solo Cape buffalo toting a tiny bird on his back. Plus, African elephants were a dime a dozen, like duomos in Italy or temples in Thailand. That only left the leopard and rhino to spot for the upcoming day. I was feeling pretty confident.

After the long, dusty day on safari, we were all just looking forward to a warm bed, decent food, and a hot shower. We were driven through Serengeti via a maze of desolate, nameless dirt roads. "Are you lost?" I questioned the driver. I wasn't sure how it was possible to not get disoriented when your only frame of reference was a boulder, a hill, or a tree. "No, no. It's just around the cluster of acacia trees up ahead." About a half hour later we saw signs of human life: glimmering lights on the slopes of the Rongai hills overlooking Seronera Valley. As we approached the glow, there was a small group of roughly ten green canvas tents. My first thought upon seeing them was, "Oh no, I am not

You must always be careful of animals crossing in front of your jeep

a happy camper." Typically, I just don't see the point in having to spend hours setting up a temporary home in order to sleep on the hard, uneven ground and pee in the bushes. Besides, I can easily make s'mores on the gas burner of my stove at home. Seeing the cluster of tents at Osupuko Camps was not a thrill, especially since the night before had been spent in a luxury, octagon-shaped room with floor-to-ceiling windows, elephants roaming in clear view, and Maasai escorts to assure our safety while walking the grounds. This was much different.

A closer look made me realize that these tents were not your typical flimsy popups; they were large, stand-up versions made of heavy canvas. My personal abode had two full-size beds, a shower, and flushing toilet. This was my kind of outdoor sleeping—glamorous camping that didn't require me to squat in the wilderness amongst the leopards and baboons. We were glamping in Serengeti.

Tucked under the covers that night, in my room alone, it was an adjustment getting used to the evening noise; the wind blowing against the walls of the tent, random animal calls and light footsteps outside the zippered and locked door. But, eventually I fell into a deep sleep, dreaming about the wilderness that had been already seen and what was yet to come.

The sunrise was our wake-up call, along with the smell of bacon and sound of birds in the trees. After a quick breakfast cooked by our hosts, it was back to our game drive. Venturing deep into the Serengeti in our

Two zebras in a protective embrace

now-dusty beige safari jeep, we drove through the open plains where the land is blessed with a high concentration of animals. The display at the break of day was nature's show of predator versus prey; unruly-maned lions prowled the plains, a high density of cheetahs laying on a termite mound masterminded a siege, and the insectivorous aardwolf had a dinner of thousands of insects using its long, sticky tongue. Zebras were passed by the hundreds, many with their head and necks wrapped around each other in what looked like a tender embrace, though was actually a way of protecting each other from predators.

In the early afternoon we parked next to the hippo pool where several dozen were sloshing about in the water in a large cluster. They were huddled so close together it was difficult to tell where one ended

There is never a shortage of grazing zebras in the Serengeti

The Serengeti hippo pool where dozens slosh around in a tight cluster

and another began, until they popped their heads up and opened their mouths wide showing their large pointy teeth. The male monkey nearby stood out with his bright-blue colored private parts, quite an interesting choice of testicle color made by Mother Nature. Lastly, there was number four of the Big Five, the leopard, who was lazily lying on a high branch in an acacia tree.

Male vervet monkey

The men of the Maasai village gathering to greet us

The women of the Maasai village preparing for the welcome dance

As the sun started to warm and the top layers of clothing had to be removed, it was time for the typical safari afternoon meal; a box lunch that was picked up from a local food stall before our departure in the morning. The feast on this day was peanuts, green beans, a muffin, an apple, and a beef sandwich. Many safari drivers and their guests will gather at a local "safe" spot to eat lunch, but ours wanted to enhance the experience even more by choosing remote locations; under a kigelia tree, beside a riverbed, or overlooking the savannah. Even though we had to eat inside the car for safety, it was much better than a tourist-infested picnic bench at the parks gates.

All of the noontime meals were too much food, so we had already gotten into the habit of saving our uneaten portion for the sweet children of the Maasai, a colorfully dressed ethnic group who graciously accepted our offerings. Most anywhere you go in the towns or countryside of Tanzania, plus along the route from Arusha to Serengeti, you will see the Maasai people grazing their livestock on the open plains.

Their royal blue and red frocks give them away every time. Not only are they scattered throughout the main roads, mostly herding their cattle but, their villages are also sporadically spread on the long stretches of land. These homes are easily identifiable: the small cluster of cow-dung huts with straw roofs sit alone on long stretches of otherwise barren land.

A couple days prior we had been welcomed into their tribal community, paying a visit to one of their villages. The chief's son took us into the inner circle of their living quarters, which consisted of eight small huts. There was one for each wife and their children, plus one for the husband who alternates which woman stays with him each evening. In this polygamist lifestyle, the more wives the chief has (and the more cows), the more respected he is. *And* the more brides, the less work each one is responsible for, so we were told that many of the women did not mind when another lady was brought into their community. The women do most of the work inside of each village,

Playing with the sweet children at the village

while the men are in charge of creating wealth, which is mostly from their herds of livestock, and being the warriors. Not only are the cattle and goats used for currency, they are also used for nutrition, providing meat, dairy, and occasionally blood which is mixed with curdled milk and drank either for celebration or healing.

The interior of the chief's shelter consisted of three tiny rooms, each no larger than a typical closet in the United States. One room was designated for the husband and wife; one for the children, and the main area was a kitchen. The bedrooms were mostly vacant besides the blue tarps that lined the hard dirt floors. The cooking room housed a couple of ceramic mugs, a teapot, and a towel.

The residents had welcomed me into their society with a lively *adumu*, or aigus dance, which consisted of chanting in combination with the men jumping high to show off their stamina and the women performing in a rhythmic bouncing motion. I was brought into the center of the group to participate in this tradition, hopping up and down with a half a dozen children at my feet. The children standing next to me took my breath away; many were toting bottles of dirty water and their sweet faces were covered with flies. This always made it an even easier decision to give most of my meals away.

After lunch, we were left with only one animal of the Big Five to spot, the rhino. Though this mammal had been evading us, there was plenty else to see on our hunt through the

A grey-crowned crane strutting its mohawk in the low grasslands

sunburnt savannah that afternoon. Spotted hyenas dined on other predators' leftovers, ostrich poked their long necks over the grassy plain, and warthogs kneeled on their front legs eating the low grass. Plus, there were birds, lots of birds. The birds in Serengeti are like nothing I had seen anywhere else in the world. With over a thousand species, each was unique. The shimmering blue back of the malachite kingfisher could be easily spotted in the trees, so could the black-and-white-spotted wings of the red-and-yellow barbet. The elegant grey-crowned crane strutted around with its Mohawk of golden-colored feathers. The Nubian woodpecker could be heard pecking in the distant trees. Then there was the largest flying bird in the world, the kori bustard, who looked like a small plane overhead, and their oversized nests resting in the trees were certainly roomy enough for a small human to rest.

We drove for hours seeing some of the usual suspects of animals and some that I had never known existed. Our African naturalist took us to all the spots that the rhinos usually hung out, but we were coming up empty. If anyone could spot this animal I had faith it would be him. He could identify any fauna here from a quarter mile away just by its shape and swagger. But, the truth is that Serengeti was home to only just over thirty rhinoceros, a miniscule number compared to the vast open space. Unfortunately, their horns are still in demand in parts of the Middle and Far East, which results in heavy poaching. Though conservation efforts have been proving successful, it was still a battle for survival.

As this last day on safari came to an end and the sunset was lighting up the acacia lined woodlands, it was evident that the Big Five would be minus a Big One.

◆ ◆ ◆

Back in the city, five of us sat at Arusha City Park for our last lunch in Africa before returning home; three writers, one driver, and one safari tour owner. We sat on blue plastic chairs at a wobbly table covered with a Pepsi-advertised tablecloth, the country music of Dolly Parton playing on the radio in the background. In front of me was a plate of traditional *ugali*, a stiff porridge similar to polenta, made from maize flour. Surrounding the grits were plates of *samaki* (fish), *ng'ombe Choma* (diced barbecued beef parts), and *ndizi machalari* (bananas and beef). As instructed, I took small sections of the cornmeal with my fingers, rolled it into a ball and sopped up all the other goodies with it. As we ate, Natasa, the owner of the Shadows of Africa tour company and a resident of this town asked, "what was the most memorable part of your experience?"

I looked down at the meal in front of me, gazed around at the locals sitting at the surrounding tables and answered, "You know, I am dusty and tired, yet I sit here still in disbelief of where I am right now and where I have been in the past few days. There couldn't possibly be just one memory, there are many. This has been a trip that has changed me and the way I think about the world. It is one that is not possible to return home the same as I came, and for that I thank you."

# CHECK IT OFF YOUR LIST

**Location/Facts:** Serengeti National Park is located in the Serengeti ecosystem that spans east-central Africa. The 12,950-square-kilometer park is in the Mara and Simiyu regions of Tanzania, which is famous for the annual migration of over a million animals.

**Getting There:** Most Serengeti safari tours begin in the town of Arusha, which is served by only one international airport. ***Kilimanjaro International Airport*** (JRO) is 29 miles from the city center and accepts regular international flights via Amsterdam on KLM airlines. Alternatively, you may be able to find a cheaper flight on other airlines into Nairobi, and then take a one-hour connecting flight into Kilimanjaro on Kenya Airways. Arusha can also be reached from Nairobi by bus using ***Riverside Shuttle*** (www.riverside-shuttle.com) or ***Marangu Luxury Shuttles*** (http://marangushuttles.com). The journey takes 6 to 8 hours and costs around $35 USD one-way, tickets can be purchased online or at the Nairobi airport.

Typically, your tour operator will pick you up at the Kilimanjaro airport once you arrive. But, if you have opted to arrive days earlier to explore Arusha, you can hire a taxi or shuttle from the airport to bring you into town. A taxi ride into the city center will cost about $50 USD and take about forty minutes. Also check with your airline, some will offer shuttle service to town for around $10.

Arusha is about an eight-hour drive from Serengeti, though

A protective mama baboon embraces her baby

A group of wildebeest walking through Serengeti

most safari tours will split up the driving time in two to three days, visiting other parks along the way. If you want to avoid the long drive, and not visit other parks, there are flights from Arusha to one of the airstrips inside the park for about $100 to $150 each way. Check times and prices with Coastal Aviation (www.coastal.co.tz), Auric Air (www.auricair.com), Regional Air (www.regionaltanzania.com), or Air Excel (airexcelonline.com).

**Language(s):** Kiswahili, commonly called Swahili, is the main language. English is widely spoken throughout the country.

**Currency:** Tanzanian shilling is the currency, but US dollars are widely accepted and favored in many places.

**Electricity:** Plug Type D/G, 230 V. The voltage in Tanzania is different than the United States. You will need to purchase an adapter plug and a converter for those devices not dual voltage.

**When to Go:** *April and May* are the "long" rainy months in Tanzania, when it tends to rain all day. This is also when some camps shut down, so the best times to visit Serengeti is anytime other than these two months. The temperatures stay relatively even throughout the year with highs in the low 80s and lows around 60 degrees. My trip was in late July when the weather was pleasantly cool in the mornings and moderately warm in the afternoons. Wildlife viewing is at its peak during the dry season from late *June to October*. Travel in late *January to March* for the best chance to

Zebra and wildebeest peacefully cohabitating in Serengeti

catch the wildebeest calving, when thousands of calves are born each day. Though the exact time varies every year dependent on the rainfall, *June through early October* is typically the best chance for witnessing the migration.

**How to Visit/Planning:** The easiest way to visit Serengeti National Park is by booking an all-inclusive safari tour, which will include meals, transportation, accommodations, and park fees. Most companies will offer packages that fall under the budget, moderate, or luxury categories. The differences between the three are in the lodging style and dining options. My visit was the moderate package with **Shadows of Africa** (www.shadowsofafrica.com), which had us sleeping in everything from a luxury tent to a five-star hotel. They are greatly recommended, though there are several other reputable companies to choose from too. You can also try these highly ranked alternatives: **Easy Travel** (www.easytravel.co.tz), **Roy Safaris Limited** (www.roysafaris.com) or **Duma Explorer** (www.dumaexplorer.

com), plus check the **Tanzania Association of Tour Operators** (www. tatotz.org) who aim to list the most trustworthy tour companies. If you are a confident and adventurous traveler, it is possible to explore Serengeti on your own by booking lodging and either hiring a driver or renting a car. This will just take a lot more effort in the planning and with the countless tour operators offering reasonable prices it may not be worth your time.

**Getting Around:** If you have booked a tour package it should include transfers from the airport as well as transportation during the game drive, plus to and from the lodging. If you plan on staying in Arusha for a few days before or after your safari you have a few options for getting around the city. *Dala-dalas* are the shared minibuses that run along the major roads and cost roughly 600 TZS, $0.27 USD. They are very cheap, yet tend to also be crammed with people. Motorbike taxis are also an economical choice, but may not be the safest option. It is the quickest way to get around, though be sure to ask for a helmet! Taxis are the easiest, quite affordable and plentiful. Rides within the city center run about 13,000 TZS ($6 USD), this price may be higher in the evenings. Taxis in Tanzania are not metered, so be sure to negotiate prices before getting in.

**Where to Stay:** When booking through a safari company your lodging will be taken care of. But, if you're spending time in Arusha enjoy the pure luxury of **The African Tulip Hotel** (www.theafricantulip.com; from $230) on Serengeti Road or **Kibo Palace Hotel** (www. kibopalacehotel.com; from $230). Either would be the perfect way to start or end a safari. For more budget-friendly accommodations book at **Planet Lodge** (www.planet-lodge.com; from $94), **Mvuli Hotels** (www. mvulihotels.co.tz; from $62) or **Korona House** (www.koronahouse. com; from $60) that are all just outside the hustle of the city center.

**Where to Eat in Arusha:** On safari with a tour company your meals will be included. But, while in Arusha for a rather unique experience pop by **Khans BBQ** (Mosque St, City Center), which is a car parts shop during the day and a bustling sidewalk BBQ stall at night. If a fine dining experience is in the cards try the delicious food from the Belgian chef at **Onsea House Arusha** (www.onseahouse.com) whose Mount Meru view only adds to the ambiance. Eat at **The Station** (www.thestation.co.tz) to feel right at home and see what Mama is serving up that day, besides her warm hospitality. **The River House** (Dodoma Road, Arusha) is the perfect place for lunch when paired with a stop at the **Shanga Shanga** (www.shanga.org) workshop that employs people with disabilities to create arts and crafts for sale.

## SAFARI MUST-DOS:

- Brave the strong smell of barnyard and ask your guide to make a safari stop at the **Hippo Pool** in Central Serengeti. This is where there are roughly two hundred playful hippopotamus sloshing around in the shallow waters.

- Get a unique perspective of the park hundreds of feet above the ground with **Serengeti Balloon Safaris** (www.balloonsafaris.com; $539 USD per person). It is a once-in-a-lifetime photographic and wildlife viewing experience from a hot air balloon.

- See if you can get luckier than me by **spotting the Big Five**, the animals said to be the hardest to hunt. Make it a challenge to see at least one of each in the group; the African elephant, leopard, lion, Cape buffalo, and rhino.

- Witness what has been called the "Greatest Show on Earth," the **annual wildebeest migration** where more than a million land animals migrate in search of greener pastures. Expert Africa (www.expertafrica.com) has detailed migration maps, including locations of the best camps in Serengeti.

- **Meet the Maasai** people and learn more about their culture. Many safari tours will make a stop at a village, but confirm that this is included as it is an experience not to be missed.

- Sleep in a luxury tent, while *Glamping in Serengeti*. Even though I was worried at first, there's nothing quite like the experience of sleeping amongst the wildlife when only a thin piece of canvas separates you. My stay was at the Serengeti Osupuko Camp (www.osupukolodges.com) and it was one of my favorite memories.

## ESSENTIAL INFORMATION:

- All visitors from the United States and other countries require a *visa* to enter Tanzania, which is available at the airport upon arrival. The cost depends on your nationality; $100 USD for Americans and $50 for residents of UK/European Union. For the most up-to-date regulations visit www.tanzaniaembassy-us.org.
- It is a requirement to show proof of a *yellow fever vaccination* upon arrival in Tanzania if you are coming from (even via a layover) yellow fever prevalent countries. Check with US Passports and International Travel (www.travel.state.gov) and the Centers for Disease Control and Prevention (www.cdc.gov) for the latest information regarding this. It is best to also contact your doctor early about your travel plans for other vaccine recommendations and how far in advance you need to get them.
- Though a disaster is unlikely, *Travel Insurance* that covers medical and emergency evacuation is highly recommended since the wilderness can be unpredictable. See the Planning Chapter for insurance recommendations.
- Don't forget to *set aside some cash* (either Tanzanian shillings or US dollars) for extra things like tipping your safari driver and the few handicraft stops along the way.

## PACKING TIPS:

- If you wear white it will get dirty from the dust and black or dark blue will attract tsetse flies. It is recommended to **wear earth tones** in order to blend with the dirt that will collect on your clothes.
- Though many animals will walk right next to your jeep, some of the wildlife, especially birds, can only be seen from a distance. So, **binoculars** and a **zoom lens** are highly recommended.
- The mornings and evenings can get chilly, but the afternoon sun will warm you right up, so **layering your clothing** is key.
- Bring a **hat** that can protect your face, ears, and neck. Even when it's not blazing hot outside, you can easily get sunburned while spending the day poking your head out of a safari jeep.
- A **pocket flashlight** comes in handy for navigating the pathways when you are staying at some of the lodges, or the camps in Serengeti. Plus some places will turn off the electricity at specific hours during the day.
- Pack a **swimsuit**, because some lodges will have a pool that is perfect for a relaxing dip.
- Instead of bringing an expensive pair of **sunglasses**, bring an old pair (preferably polarized). It gets dusty out there and scratching the lenses becomes easier. Also, the dust can cause problems with wearing contact lens, so make sure to have a pair (or two) of prescription glasses handy. A pair with a cord that wraps around your neck would be best.
- Pack a little **bottle of soap and/or hand sanitizer**. It will be used frequently, especially before and after eating boxed lunches. Plus, many bathrooms will have a sink, but no soap.

- The roads are very bumpy, so ladies you won't be disappointed if you are wearing a **sports bra**. Even if you are small-breasted, the girls will be bouncing.
- If possible, bring **soft-sided luggage** (for example, a duffle bag). This type of luggage is easier to manipulate in the limited storage areas of the vehicles.
- A small bottle of **eye drops** can be helpful with all the dust.
- Bring a roll of **toilet paper** or package of **tissues**, 50 percent of the time you will need it in the restrooms.

**Helpful Websites**: Serengeti National Park Official Site (www.serengeti.org); Expert Africa (www.expertafrica.com).

# 12. SWIM IN JELLYFISH LAKE IN PALAU

I had traveled from San Francisco to Tokyo to Guam to reach my final destination of Palau, a tiny speck of a country that didn't even register on Google Maps without having to powerfully zoom. It is certainly a place that very few know much about. Frankly, the first time I had ever heard of it was a month prior to my arrival. A Micronesian country in the western Pacific Ocean, Palau is probably best known for its uninhabited Rock Islands, a group of unique formations created by ancient coral reefs. The limestone islets are topped with jungle-green foliage, while the bases have succumbed to slow erosion creating a distinct mushroom shape, fitting for a scene in *Alice in Wonderland*. The surrounding turquoise waters have been

A mushroom shaped isle of the UNESCO Rock Islands

called the "underwater Serengeti", as well as the "seventh underwater wonder of the world"—home to diverse marine life and special hidden treasures. These islands, and their well-deserved inclusion as a UNESCO World Heritage site, are the main reason that many make the long trek here. But, not me—I didn't come here for islands that looked like fungi, I came to this dot of the world to swim in a lake surrounded by thousands upon thousands of jellyfish.

Within the first hour of landing in Palau, its Hawaii vibe was overtly evident. It possessed the same humid weather that turns my hair into a frizzy mess, and a Polynesian laid-back attitude that is contagious as soon as you exit the airplane. It was also a destination famed for its signature diving and snorkeling that took place throughout the more than two hundred islands of the archipelago. But there was something that Hawaii lacked and this country had: a large swimmable lake crowded with jellyfish.

Layers of blue on the waters of the Rock Islands

The tide goes out, offering a picturesque view of a stuck boat

Though pulsating plankton was the primary reason I had traveled this far, Palau had many other natural wonders to offer up, centered around its pristine, warm waters. Each of the days prior to being escorted to the main attraction we were guided through the gems of the notorious Rock Islands. The premiere one was the Milky Way, a blue lagoon named for its opaque turquoise waters, caused by the limestone clay found on the

Covered with the white limestone mud from the bottom of the Milky Way

floor of the inlet. This mud is known for its therapeutic properties. Though not scientifically proven, it is believed that coating your body in the white limestone mud has youth-enhancing properties, making your skin look five years younger. This is one age-old belief that I was willing to put to the test. Who wouldn't want a free rejuvenating facial and all-over body rub with a chance of dialing back the years? Anchoring our boat in the center of this natural pool, our guide jumped into the shallow waters. He skillfully dove to the floor of the inlet, scooping up the muddy clay and transferring it into a plastic bucket. We eagerly coated ourselves with this muck that was the consistency of smooth, wet cement. I made sure to not miss an inch of exposed skin, making certain that each spot would have the potential of being a half-decade younger. I put a double layer on my face and even loaded the crevasses in between my fingers and toes. After twenty minutes of drying in the sunlight the mask turned chalky gray and started to crack. It was time to see the results of the mask. I jumped into the baby blue water to rinse off. The clay mostly disintegrated with the water's touch, but the remainder easily disappeared with a few quick rubs. Afterward, the skin on my body felt silky smooth, but much to my dismay it did not instantly melt away the years.

Besides bathing in the Milky Way, the perfect eighty-two-degree water lent itself to easily jumping out of the boat and snorkeling just about everywhere it stopped; I may as well have permanently attached the snorkel and mask to my face. At the Blue Corner, we ogled a parade of gray- and white-tip reef sharks from the top of the water. Divers who dove deeper underwater were encircled by up to thirteen different species, but the safer distance at the surface was perfectly fine for me. The thousand-foot vertical underwater wall at the Big Drop Off looked like a pretty picture covered in endless colorful corals. The nooks and crannies along the reef's edge offered protection for camouflaged stonefish as well as other sea life. One of the most interesting undersea jewels was Clam City, a colorful mollusk garden in the sea. It

Exploring the nooks and crannies of the Rock Islands by kayak

is a place where clams that are more than four feet long could be seen in shallow enough waters that even us snorkelers got a clear glimpse. These guys were seriously big enough for a small child to hide inside. It didn't matter where we swam, every one of the snorkeling locations looked like the perfect scene from a million-dollar aquarium.

When our masks were finally detached from our faces and the indentation on my forehead had faded, we explored the archipelago in a different way. Kayaks led us along the edges of the islets squeezing us between rocks and deep into desolate caves, spaces that motorboats could not possibly fit into. We gawked at the motionless sea cucumbers on the sandy floor, yelled inside the caverns just to listen to the reverberating echo, and chased the surface turtles, quickly learning that they were much quicker than our paddles.

Kayaks are the best way to explore inside the caves of Palau

The journey to Palau had been magical up until that point and we hadn't even reached the pièces de résistance. Surely the colorful parrotfish and moray eels could just not possibly compete with Jellyfish Lake.

Truth be told, when I first announced my plans of venturing solo across the Earth to a location that most had never even heard of, people called me brave. After sharing the purpose of this journey, they called me crazy. Maybe in this case it was a little bit of both. All the natural wonders of this country were beyond impressive, but what I had travelled over twenty hours for wasn't to rub clay all over my face or spot large crusty clams, it was to swim in a lake surrounded by countless jellyfish as they gently pulsated around me in a hypnotizing dance. Most people would try to avoid this sort of encounter, rubbing themselves in protective creams at the beach and keeping a three-foot radius when seeing one washed up onto the sand. But, at Jellyfish

Lake you will be smack dab in the middle of an estimated thirteen million creatures. There is no amount of cream that could protect you from that.

Jellyfish Lake certainly is an anomaly. The fourteen-acre land-locked saltwater lake is home to literally millions of jellyfish that are deemed relatively harmless since they have lost their sting. Over many years, the golden *Mastigias* jellies have adapted to their conditions, evolving to not need their predatory stingers. So, the chances of having to ask strangers to pee on a plankton prick would *most likely* not happen. See, I am not that crazy.

When we arrived to the entrance of the lake on Eil Malk Island, the rules that must be abided by were laid out plain and simple:

1. Don't hold the jellyfish.
2. Don't kick the jellyfish.
3. Do not remove the jellyfish from the water.

Only one jellyfish could be seen from this dock at Jellyfish Lake

The guidelines seemed pretty reasonable, as I wasn't planning on playing a game of patty cake or kickball with any of them, and they definitely would not make as good of a souvenir as a magnet. Heck, I was nervous about being within inches from them, so any touching would definitely be an accident probably done while flailing my arms in fear when one came too close. Passing the entrance booth, we took the fifteen-minute hike up a steep rope-lined trail. It was a heavily forested path with mossy, limestone stairs that needed careful maneuvering. Over the peak and at the bottom of the other side was a small wooden dock that led to the deep turquoise green lake. Standing on this dock preparing my snorkeling equipment, one solo golden jellyfish could be seen in the briny water. Just one. I was worried. This didn't look anything like the photos on the Internet where countless animals enveloped the adventurous swimmers. It was like Glass Beach in Northern California where the photographs on Pinterest present a shoreline blanketed in saturated colored glass, but in reality it was muted tones, and mixed in with mostly pebbles. It had me briefly questioning whether Photoshop was made for good or evil, and also the technical process for easily multiplying one jellyfish into a thousand.

Just as the guide saw the concerned look on my face, the few visitors were urged to jump into the green lake and swim about a hundred feet out, toward the sunlit waters. Jellyfish didn't just enjoy basking in the sun; sunlight was critical to their survival, so much so that the agglomeration migrate from the west end of the lake to the east each and every day in search of it. It was a repetitive daily pattern, pumping water through their sepia-toned bells to follow the warm rays shining down from the sky.

Following the instructions, each foot I swam closer toward the light, the jellyfish population grew. It started with that one lonely one by the dock then doubled, tripled, and quadrupled until they completely surrounded me. Then I was worried for an entirely different reason. Contrary to popular belief, these jellyfish were not completely stingless, but instead the sting is so mild that unless you are unusually sensitive it is unnoticeable. Remembering this fact at that moment created a nervous pit in my stomach and the rapid-fire questions swirled through my brain. *Are they really harmless? Could it be possible that one hadn't lost its sting, defying evolution? It*

There's no escaping being completing surround by jellyfish when you are in the sunlight

*would surely find me. Are there medics close by?* Unfortunately, there was only one way to find out.

The first five minutes in the water were spent panicked any time a jellyfish would brush up against a limb, lightly bumping me like a rubber ducky in the bath. I frantically swam in circles, trying to keep my eye on every one of them, which was impossible since they crowded me in every direction. Though we were not supposed to touch them, the effort was futile, as their eight broccoli-like tentacles didn't seem to give them a good sense of direction. One would bonk me in the head, then another in the leg and one more on my back.

After this initial frenzy, a sense of security started to set in and their lackadaisical

The broccoli-like tentacles of the golden jellyfish

One jellyfish wants to get up close and personal

movements completely mesmerized me. Some were the tiny size of a lime, while others were larger than my head. It seemed like a bizarre underwater dream world where incalculable sepia-tinted parachutes oscillated around me in what seemed like slow motion. It was like a never-ending movie that I could have watched forever.

It wasn't until my fingers looked like shriveled grapes and my back was certainly the color of a red delicious apple that I exited the lake. Standing back on the dock and looking into the water was bittersweet. During my time in Palau my face had been covered in gray-colored clay, I ogled brilliant red coral on a cliff inside the sea, swam above a slew of sharks, and kayaked into the depths of caves. But nothing quite compared to being given the opportunity to share the water with these spellbinding creatures. I slowly began walking back up the hill, double-checking my body. Nope, not even one tiny little sting.

# CHECK IT OFF YOUR LIST

**Location/Facts:** Palau is an extraordinary archipelago in Micronesia with more than two hundred magical limestone and volcanic islands, lying eight hundred miles southwest of Guam. It is well known for its world-class scuba diving and snorkeling sites, plus fairy-tale scenery that ranges from dense jungles to glorious blue waters to pristine sandy beaches. Jellyfish Lake is located on Eil Malk, an uninhabited island off the coast of the main town of Koror. It is home to millions of stingless golden *Mastigias* and translucent moon jellyfish that migrate from one side of the lake to the other to follow the path of the sun.

**Getting There:** Most excursions to Jellyfish Lake begin from the state of Koror that is serviced by Palau International Airport (ROR). The main gateways to Palau are Guam, Manila (Philippines), Seoul (South Korea), Taipei (Taiwan), and Tokyo (Japan). Common flights are on United Airlines (www.united.com) from Honolulu to Guam to Koror or direct from Manila. From the airport, the city center can be reached by car or taxi in about twenty minutes, plus many hotels will offer shuttle service for about $20 USD each way. You should make arrangements with your chosen hotel prior to your arrival. A one-way fair for a taxi to Koror is approximately $25. Keep in mind that taxis are not metered, so confirm the cost beforehand.

**Language(s):** Palau has two official languages, Palauan and English. English is widely spoken.

The fruit bat is actually a delicacy in Palau, and fruit bat soup can be found on the menus of select restaurants

**Currency:** US dollar. You will find plenty of ATMs in Koror and major credit cards are accepted at most restaurants, stores, and hotels.

**Electricity:** Plug type A/B, 110 V. The outlets are the same as North America, so no adaptor is needed if traveling from the United States.

**When to Go:** Palau has a yearly average temperature in the mid 80s with high humidity, which makes it pleasant to visit any time of the year. But, considering that Palau is in the tropics, rainfall can occur at any time of the year. The best time to go is during the dryer months (November to April or February and March) when there's a decreased chance of rain. In September, we experienced sporadic rain throughout the day that did not affect any activities, and one storm on a snorkeling excursion that created choppy waters that prevented me from jumping in, but not the scuba divers I was with. The water temperature throughout the rock islands is generally between 81 and 84 degrees, perfect bath water.

**How to Visit/Planning:** Most water-based activities and exploration tours, including Jellyfish Lake, leave from the main city of Koror. For the most part, trips to Jellyfish Lake are not individual excursions; instead they are included in either group dive trips or snorkeling tours of the Rock Islands. With *Neco Marine* (www.necomarine.com) Jellyfish Lake is included in their all-day Rock Island snorkeling tour for $150, which can include such spots as Clam City or Cemetery Reef. *Sam's Tours* (www.samstours.com) offers a similar tour with additional snorkeling stops at places like Big Drop Off and Milky Way for $125. *Fish n' Fins* (www.fishnfins.com) has two tank dives with a stop at the lake for $210, or if you'd prefer snorkeling the cost is $175. There is also an option to charter your own boat starting at $1500 for a full day. Keep in mind that the $100 Koror State Jellyfish Lake permit is typically not included in the quoted price, but should be expected.

**Getting Around:** Getting around Koror can be done by rental car, taxi, or the evening BBI shuttle. Renting a car can be done at the airport terminal, as well as at some of the resorts. However, navigating your way by car may be tricky, as Koror does not have street signs or traffic signals, plus it's not really necessary to have a car. Taxis can easily be used when having one arranged beforehand by the concierge or restaurant host. Don't expect to be able to hail one while just walking along the street. The taxis are not metered; fares are based on your destination. Taxi fares within Koror roughly range from $6 to $8. In the evenings, you can also take the BBI shuttle that completes a round-trip service in an hour and stops at many of the main locations on the main street of Koror ($7 for a one-week pass). Ask your hotel where to get tickets. Most dive centers and hotels offer shuttle service to and from their locations during dive/tour days.

**Where to Stay:** Most tours begin in the main city of Koror, which makes it the best option choice for your lodging while you are visiting Palau. For the ultimate luxury experience after being in the water all day stay in an oceanfront room or overwater bungalow at the ***Palau Pacific Resort*** (www.palauppr.com; from $425), known as Micronesia's most luxurious resort. Sleep in a villa surrounded by the natural beauty of a tropical paradise at ***Palau Plantation Resort*** (www.palauplantationresort.com; from $180). For a more economical, no frills option book a room at ***The Penthouse*** (www.penthousepalau.com; from $76) or ***DW Motel*** (www.dwmotel-palau.com; from $82).

**Where to Eat:** For such an unknown place, the country has an eclectic mix of delicious restaurants with heavy Japanese, Korean, Filipino, and American influences. Indulge in fresh fish tacos at a favorite in Palau, ***Kramers Café*** (1 Pirates Cove, Koror City). Eat with the locals at ***Emaimelei Restaurant*** (Lebuu St, Koror) where the kitchen churns out a blend of Filipino, American, and local cuisine at a reasonable price. If you want your Japanese fix, head over to ***Tori Tori*** (Derbei, Ikelau Hamlet, Koror) for delicious sushi and sashimi. ***Elilai*** (www.elilaipalau.com/e/elilai) is a special treat, situated atop a hillside with lagoon views. Their fresh local ingredients are used to make Pacific Rim cuisine with Japanese, Thai, and Italian influences. At ***Taj*** (www.

tajpalau.com) you will tempt your senses with the smells and tastes of the spices of India. For the adventurous bucket list eater visit **Mog Mog** (www.mogmogpalau.com) to dine on a bowl of the local delicacy, fruit bat soup, where the whole bat (wings, fur, and head included) are cooked in a coconut broth. Not for folks who don't want their food staring them in the face!

## NEARBY MUST-DOS:

- Cover your body in the limestone clay at the bottom of the **Milky Way.** The creamy mud found on the floor of the inlet is known for its therapeutic properties. Most half- and full-day tours of the Rock Islands will make a stop here.
- Head forty minutes outside of the Koror city center to stand under the hundred-foot **Ngardmau Falls**. If you have a rental car you can navigate your way on your own, otherwise Palau Impac (www.palau-impac.com) offers a seven-hour tour for $95.
- Explore the thick jungles of Palau on an exciting four-wheel drive adventure. With **Palau Off-Road Jungle Tours** (www.offroadjungletours.com/index.html; from $160) you will be exploring otherwise inaccessible landscape; waterfalls, WWII relics, abandoned villages, and the lush rainforest.
- After you have explored the Rock Islands by day, take a night kayak excursion with **Rock Island Tours** (www.palauritc.com/english; $55). In the dark you will be able to see the bioluminescent organisms come alive. Their fluorescent glow along with the moon and twinkling stars will light up the calm waters.

## ESSENTIAL INFORMATION:

- You will need a Koror State Rock Island permit to scuba dive, kayak, snorkel, and swim in Jellyfish Lake. The cost is $100 and is valid for ten days. Your guide will typically take care of purchasing these permits, but it is not included in the cost of the tour.

- There is a per person fifty-dollar departure tax and green fee per person that can be paid in cash directly at the airport upon departure. A visa is not required for United States visitors staying for less than 365 days, though you must have a valid passport with at least one blank page.
- Protecting Jellyfish Lake is incredibly important, so be respectful while you are there; do not lift the jellyfish out of the water, enter the lake clean and free of sunscreen, do not use the lake as a restroom, and wear fins to slow your movements. Follow the rules of the lake in order to ensure that the jellyfish will be there for a long time to come.
- Scuba diving is not allowed in the lake because the bubbles can be trapped in the jellyfish's bell.

## PACKING TIPS:

- Palau is very casual, with a *relaxed island style*; shorts, tanks, and tees prevail. Leave your stilettos and sparkly dresses at home.
- Don't come to Jellyfish Lake (or Palau for that matter) without an *underwater camera*, you'll be disappointed at not being able to capture the underwater treasures. If your camera has video capabilities, that's even better as the mesmerizing pulsating moves of the jellyfish are fascinating.
- Pack a *rash guard* as an extra protection from the hot sun.
- A small *dry daypack* is helpful not only for the hike to Jellyfish Lake, but also the boat rides through the Rock Islands.
- Bring along comfortable *walking/water* shoes that have some traction. It can get slippery on the trail.
- Pack *light snacks* for the tours. Even though lunch is typically included, a granola bar or trail mix can ease some hunger.

**Helpful Websites:** Pristine Paradise Palau (www.pristineparadisepalau.com).

# 13. EAT YOUR WAY THROUGH BARCELONA

Leaning back into my aisle seat on the plane, I discreetly unfastened the button on my jeans and let out a long, loud sigh. My stomach happily rolled over the waistband, grateful for a release. Dreams of *crema catalana* and *pan con tomate* had been swirling in my head for weeks before we arrived in Barcelona, the capital of Spain's Catalonia region, but it didn't even compare to the reality of the food fest we had experienced. My protruding belly was proof, and so were the *carquinyolis* cookie crumbs scattered inside my carry-on.

We had embarked on a gluttonous tour of Barcelona—equipped with an itinerary that had us eating fresh Mediterranean seafood in the Barceloneta, traveling farther north through L'Eixample for trendy dining at award-winning restaurants, and on to the heart of the Barri Gòtic quarter to indulge in traditional Catalan tapas. We

A nice selection of housemade charcuterie for breakfast

Learning to cook paella at Cook & Taste in the Barri Gòtic

would break bread with the locals, sip sangría with new friends, and learn the art of creating paella, always planning our dinner while still eating our lunch. I've got news Italy: Spain may know a thing or two about food as well.

Eating remains one of Spain's favorite pastimes, an important social activity whether it's a quick stop for *raciones* (plates of cheese, pâtés, and cured meats), an afternoon three-course *menú del día* or a later dinner at one of the innovative Michelin-starred restaurants. This is especially true in Catalonia whose location on the Mediterranean coast results in impressive fish dishes, while the hills and fields nourish the livestock and garner fresh produce.

Off the plane we had headed straight to Barri Gòtic, the old Gothic Quarter packed with historical treasures and hidden culinary gems. Our main purpose there was to learn how to make what is quite possi-

Freshly cooked *langoustines* ready to be added to a dish of paella

bly the most well-known dish of Spain, paella. Being an Italian chef, I could easily whip up a creamy butternut squash risotto with Gorgonzola or prosciutto-stuffed ravioli topped with slices of black truffles. Change countries and that can pose a bit of a challenge. But, paella was similar to its Italian sister or rather distant cousin, risotto, so there was a shot I could find success.

Paella is a Valencia rice dish that has traveled the world. Most Spanish restaurants and beyond will carry a version on their menus. It starts with a *sofrito* of vegetables, usually tomatoes and garlic. Add the stock and *bomba* rice to this and leave it alone, letting the magic happen. Whereas in risotto you'd be continuously stirring the rice, in paella you simply let the boiling do the work. Less work is something I can easily get used to. What paella lacks is the Parmesan and heavy cream, plus the chicken broth is substituted for fish stock making it a healthier option. Traditionally, the expensive saffron spice is added to this to turn it that beautiful golden color, though due to the high cost some chefs are finding alternatives like turmeric, but it's just not the same and there was no imitation added to ours. Shellfish can be tossed in at the end, like the *langoustines* that we had added to ours in

Hanging jamón ibérico at the Boqueria Market

Sipping a fresh strawberry-mango fruit juice at Boqueria Market

class. Of course in the classroom we sampled our creation and the five other dishes that we constructed. This was the beginning of our food overdose.

From the lesson, we walked along the bustling La Rambla to the famed Mercat de la Boqueria, a cornucopia of fruit and vegetable stalls, plus limitless artisan cheeses, hanging meats, and fresh fish. It was a mixture of delicious colors, smells, and sensations—a great place to get a sampling of Catalonia's gastronomical specialties. We braved the throngs of tourists and locals alike to snack on freshly sliced *jamón ibérico* and *bacallà salat* (dried salted cod), as we sipped on freshly made mango-pineapple fruit juices costing only a couple dollars each. Hours were easily wasted admiring the carefully arranged stacks of eggs and orderly piquillo peppers. Not only can you buy perfectly organized groceries there, but there were also a few small tapas places to grab a quick meal. We stopped by Bar Pinotxo to order a dish they are known for, *xuxo*, a sugar-crusted, custard filled pastry that is deep-fried to perfection. We ate the delectable sweet while chatting with the mini celebrity in back of the bar, Juanito Bayen. He is the dapper man behind the fourteen-stool

Tapas of sauteed spinach with Iberian pancetta and chickpeas

bar that whips up such delicious Catalan classics that it has landed him in magazines and on television shows all over the world. He and his shop are a staple at the market.

Leaving Mercat de la Boqueria we headed north to L'Eixample to dine on what Spain is most known for, tapas. These small dishes are not a particular type of Spanish food, rather can be anything from a mini plate of tuna *conserva* to *jamon croquettes* to *patatas bravas*, the popularly served potatoes in a spicy tomato sauce. Going for tapas has long been a tradition in the Spanish culture, and a way of life. It is rumored that the concept began when bars would put a slice of ham or piece

The Bikini Comerc at Tapas 24 filled with buffalo mozzarella, jamón ibérico, and specks of black truffle

of bread on top of the patron's drink to keep the fruit flies out (tapa translates to lid or top). Now midday to early evening you will find packed bars, filled with sprightly customers noshing on green olives or roasted pardons. Tapas were meant to be a snack in between meals, but nowadays it's not uncommon for people to make a meal out of these bites.

Our tapas joint of choice that evening was the no-fuss basement restaurant of Tapas, 24, a place that typically has a lengthy queue in front of its doors during peak hours. The restaurant is owned by an alum of Ferran Adria's renowned El Bulli restaurant and creates unique, designer tapas. We sat at a tall table and ordered from the Catalan menu, printed on an off-white paper bag. Just like our itinerary told us where to eat, it also told us what to eat. There were signature dishes that this place was well known for. It started with the

Bikini Comerc 24, a crustless sandwich filled with jamón ibérico, buffala mozzarella, and delectable specks of black truffle. Next came the McFoie Burger, a tapa that played homage to the fastfood chain. A medium-rare beef patty served on an unexpectedly thin, crunchy bun with a side of creamy foie ready to be sparingly spread. Then the Bombes de la Barceloneta arrived, potato dumplings that were crispy on the outside with a smooth mashed potato center. Can you really go wrong with deep-fried potatoes?

This wasn't the only tapas stop on the trip, there were more than a dozen others in restaurants from every district in Barcelona. We ate everything from chargrilled *calçots* (a cross between a leek and an onion) to *ensaladilla rusa*, the Russian potato salad made with canned tuna, boiled eggs, and peas. It was always a feast for the senses; the tempting sound of crackling pork belly straight from the oven, the smell of freshly baked *empanadas*, and the sight of the crispy caramel-colored top of crema catalana. Plus, there was the taste of the one thing that every tapas restaurant had in common, *jamón ibérico*, a world-renowned dry-cured ham made from black Iberian pigs. This meat is almost the trademark of Spain; a leg held in a *jamonero* (ham-hock holder) on the counter of many bars waiting to be freshly sliced and washed down with a glass of sangría.

Beverages in Spain are almost as much a part of the culture as the food. Each morsel was always paired with a glass of sangría, cava, *orxata* or Spanish wine. Sangría is without a doubt one of the most popular beverages in the country. I rarely stray from drinking my beloved red wine, but on numerous occasions, I've freely abandoned it for sangría. Probably because it is a red wine-based punch, with the addition of select citrus fruits and lemon-lime soda or seltzer. Cava was also drunk on the regular, especially when venturing to the out-skirts of the city to Sant Sadurní d'Anoia in the Penedès wine region where you could find an eerie cava cave to drink it in. On the hotter days, there was always a refreshing *orxata* nearby, a beverage that originated in the Catalonia region and made with yellow nutsedge (tigernuts), sugar, and water. Last but not least, there was wine. Tiny wine shops and lounges line the streets, making it easy to pop in for a quick glass (or two).

We rolled into bed that night with a bottle of Tums, acutely aware that the next day the overindulgence would begin all over again. This time we'd be on a mission to find the best of a quintessential Catalan snack, *pa amb tomàquet* or *pan con tomate*. This toasted rustic bread is rubbed with tomato pulp and olive oil then sprinkled with a touch of salt. It is a classic side dish similar to the toast that is served with an American breakfast or table bread at an Italian restaurant. Truth be told, I don't like raw tomatoes. What a disgrace to my Italian heritage! I may be the only Italian restaurateur who will actually discard every slice of raw tomato in my caprese salad. But, there is an exception to every rule, and Spanish pan con tomate was it. My love of this dish and the tomatoes on it was like the perfect romance story.

My introduction to pan con tomate was at the paella cooking class where we learned how to make the dish from scratch. At that time it could have been considered just a blind date. The teacher assigned me the task of creating the toast, before I even knew it would be on the menu. He showed up to the class unannounced. He looked good. And he tasted good. Yet, I didn't know if I'd ever see him again; no second date was planned. But then he unexpectedly appeared at a Barcelona hot spot, Taller de Tapas. The restaurant set me up with complimentary pan con tomate and that's when I began to develop a little bit of a crush. Though at the time I couldn't give him the proper attention because sampling tapas was more important than exploring my chemistry with toasted bread.

It wasn't until this day, that I actually fell in love with pan con tomate. I had stalked him at every restaurant we visited; El Xampa-nyet, La Pepita, and Elsa y Fred. And my crush turned into something deeper. I could pinpoint the exact moment that I fell head over heels;

Disected pan con tomate ready to be turned into a popular Spanish tapa

it was while sipping a glass of the Brut Nature cava at the vineyard of Finca Valldosera. The table was perfectly set and there was a large loaf of crunchy bread on a pedestal. *Come to mama.* A plate of small vine-ripe tomatoes, a decanter of olive oil, and a small ramekin of salt were waiting in the wings. It was a deconstructed pan con tomate. You mean my new boyfriend can be created to have the exact characteristics I desire? I am officially in love. This relationship was simple. There was no drama, no heartbreak, and no socks left on the bathroom floor. It was just pure passion. That evening I laid in bed fantasizing about my next romantic date with pan con tomate.

My husband and I woke up deciding that we needed to survive on more than bread alone—enter *pintxos*. A traveler friend had told me about these bruschetta-style tapas with toothpicks stuck in them that I just had to try. She said, "I think they are called peen-chows or pint-oxe or pin-tox, something like that." Huh? Luckily, a Google search for Spanish "pin-tox" was enough of a clue to find the information I needed for pintxos. Pintxos (or pinchos) are small snacks typically served buffet-style in Spanish bars. They are particularly popular in Basque country, yet pervasive in Catalonia too. These finger foods have an array of toppings placed on a piece of crunchy bread, spiked with a toothpick and displayed on the bar tops of restaurants for easy grabbing. So, technically we would still be

*Anchoas y guindillas pintxos* - anchovy with pickled green peppers staked with a toothpick

eating an excessive amount of carbs, just covered with other goodies. That works. The system was easy enough: grab a plate, pick the snacks you would like to indulge in, and then return your barren toothpicks to the register to be counted. The number of empty skewers you turn in determines how much you will be charged. We started with four, the *Morcilla Cocida Pinchos*, *Piquillo* Pepper Jam, *Croquetas de Papas*, and a *Pulpo Pinchos*. I could have stopped right then with a mere four toothpicks, but with dozens of other flavors to choose from there was no hope for restraint. That's when the decision was made to turn this Spanish happy hour into dinner, simply a justification for eating more. I sensibly grabbed course two of my pintxos dinner, a cheese-stuffed pimento pepper, as if adding just one more would complete my full supper quest. There was a third course after that, two *chorizos* and one *angulas* (baby eel), which would lead to my eighth empty toothpick. Even though eight pintxos would have indicated the finish line for most skilled eaters, I went back to pick out one more, a slightly spicy chistorra sausage with a charred padron pepper. Definitely worthy of being toothpick number nine.

Sweet and spicy piquillo pepper jam pintxos

Sitting on the plane with my foil-wrapped rubbery chicken, hard bread roll, and plastic cup full of cheap French wine in front of me, I noticed how easy it was to forgo this meal—whereas, all the days in Barcelona were the same tug of war: our taste buds versus our belt buckles. When jamon, pintxos, and tapas were readily available, the waistband lost every time.

# CHECK IT OFF YOUR LIST

**Location/Facts:** Barcelona is the energetic capital of Spain's Catalonia region, known for its mix of modernist architecture, vibrant streets, sun-drenched beaches, and medieval roots. Catalonia is a region in the northeastern corner of Spain that borders France to the north, the Mediterranean Sea to the east, Valencia to the south, and Aragon to the west. This area is unique in its language, culture, and traditions. Barcelona is the capital of Catalonia and is known for its world-class food scene that ranges from buzzing tapas bars to gastronomically genius Michelin-starred chefs and colorful markets.

**Getting There:** The international Barcelona-El Prat Airport accepts numerous flights daily from all over the world. Though in some cases it may be cheaper to fly into Madrid and then take a cheap domestic flight to the Barcelona Airport on Veuling (www.vueling.com), Air Europa (www.aireuropa.com), or Iberia (www.iberia.com). The easiest way to get to the city center is by taxi, which will run you about $34 USD and take roughly twenty-five minutes. Taxis can be caught right outside any of the main terminal exits. A cheaper alternative is the Aerobus (www.aerobusbcn.com; $7 USD each way), which is a good option when you are traveling with less than three people (a taxi makes more sense if you have four or more). The buses are light blue with Aerobus written on the side and can be found outside the terminal 1 and 2 exit. There is almost always a bus waiting outside the terminals, but if not it is typically a less-than-ten-minute wait for one. The bus has four main stops in the city center: Plaça Espanya, Gran Vía, Plaça Universitat, and Plaça Catalunya. Keep in mind that from these stops you may still have to catch a taxi or the metro to your final destination, so calculate if the taxi may end up being cheaper in the long run. The RENFE train (www.renfe.com) also runs from the airport to the city center, making stops at Estacio Sants, Passeig de Gràcia, and El Clot where you can easily jump onto the metro from these stations.

**Language(s):** The region of Catalonia has two official languages, Spanish and Catalan. Many restaurants and hotels in the touristy areas will have a staff member who will speak English.

**Currency:** The currency in Spain is the euro. There are ATMs at the airport if you'd like to withdraw cash upon arrival or visit one of the many banks in the city to exchange your money.

**Electric:** Plug C/F, 220 to 240 V. Most outlets will be the same as the European with two round prongs. You will need an adapter and a converter if your devices are not dual voltage.

**How to Visit/Planning:** It is best to create your gastronomic itinerary well before you arrive in Barcelona, especially because many of the restaurant hotspots will require reservations in advance. Incredible food experiences are located throughout the city, which may require traveling a few miles from your hotel; so make sure to master the metro or selected mode of transport right away. Local food tours are a good option, especially in your first few days in town in order to get yourself acquainted with the area and the cuisine. *Taste Barcelona* (www.taste-barcelona.com; $118 USD) has a five-hour tour that is more than just food. You will cross through four neighborhoods learning about the local culture while sampling tapas and local gastronomic products, washing it down with a crisp rose or glass of cava. For a variety of tour options check *Devour Barcelona* (www.devourbarcelonafoodtours.com; from $84 USD) who gives you a few food tour options to choose from. The tapas and wine tour will have you learning about Spanish vinos from an expert while paring it with local cuisine. *Barcelona Slow Travel* (www.barcelonaslowtravel.com) will give you another perspective of Barcelona by taking you on a local market tour before learning to make paella at the chef's private home. They also offer a fun off-the-beaten-path gastronomic bike tour starting at $236 USD.

**Getting Around:** The individual districts of Barcelona are fairly walkable, but getting to each will require public transportation. The best way to get around the city is using the metro (www.tmb.cat). The underground system has eight color-coded lines, and the stations are easily recognizable by the big "M" at the entry, and the TMB symbol. You can choose to buy single tickets at any station's machine, but another option is the **Hola BCN!** card (www.tmb.cat/en/barcelona-travel-card). These are two- to five-day passes that give you unlimited journeys on Barcelona public transport starting at around $15 USD. Black & Yellow taxis can be found throughout the city, but will definitely be pricier than the metro. Prices start at around $8 USD just to get into the taxi and obviously go up from there.

**When to Go:** The best time to visit is May, June, and September when the temperatures are in the low- to mid-70s. The later summer months, July and August, will be humid with lots of tourists on the streets and the hotel rates at their peak. If you don't mind the cold weather (40s to 60s), you will escape the crowds and find a better deal by traveling in January through April.

**Where to Stay:** Barcelona has lodging for everyone's palate from trendy budget hostels to hoity-toity luxury. For budget travelers, check out **Hostal Barcelona Centro** (www.hostalbarcelonacentro.com; from $76 USD) in the center of Eixample district, a three-minute walk from Passeig de Gràcia metro station or the tranquil **U232** (http://www.u232hotel.com; from $110 USD) is just outside the city center, but just a few minutes' walk to the metro. Nearby the Ramblas is the modern **Hotel Jazz** (www.hoteljazz.com; from $140 USD) that boasts a rooftop terrace and bar. The kitschy **Chic & Basic Born** (www.chicandbasic.com; from $124 USD) is located in the trendy Born neighborhood, right next to the popular El Barri Gotic. The **Hotel Praktik Rambla** (www.hotelpraktikrambla.com; from $120 USD) is a fusion of Art Nouveau and tradition, or enjoy pure elegance at **The Serras** (http://hoteltheserrasbarcelona.com/; from $300) while overlooking the harbor on the rooftop terrace or swimming in the infinity pool.

**Where to Eat:** For tapas, indulge on *montaditos* (food on a slice of bread) at the typically standing-room-only **Quimet i Quimet** (Carrer del Poeta Cabanyes 25) or have the special bikini (toasted jamon and cheese sandwich) or the McFoie-Burger at **Tapas, 24** (www.tapas24.ca). Get your pintxos fix at *Maitea* (www.maitea.es) where they offer more than a hundred different varieties. Order *xuxo* (a sugar-crusted, custard filled pastry) and chat with local celebrities behind the bar of *Pinotxo* (www.pinotxobar.

A pan of Fideuà - a dish similar to paella except made with noodles instead of rice

com) at Boqueria Mercat. For a gastronomic experience head over to *Spoonik* (www.spoonik.com), *Informal* (www.hoteltheserrasbarcelona.com), or the Michelin two-starred *ABaC* (www.abacbarcelona.com), where the prix fixe sampler menu is the best way to experience things. Eating at *UMA* (www.espaciouma.com) is an adventure in dining. They serve a tasting menu in a charming environment that must be on every foodie's bucket list. Be prepared, it's cash only!

## FOODIE MUST-DOS:

- Learn to make Spanish and Catalan classics by taking a cooking class. Get your hands dirty at **Cook and Taste** (www.cookandtaste.net; $73 USD) where you'll spend a half day cooking traditional cuisine including paella (this is the place that taught me how to expertly make the dish). If you'd prefer some lighter cooking, try **Barcelona Cooking's** (www.barcelonacooking.net; $88 USD) Catalan Tapas & Wine Class that will have you assisting in the kitchen while learning about the local wines.

- Break away from an evening at the tapas bar to eat at a creative *molecular gastronomy restaurant*. This food-manipulation technique is where the science lab meets the culinary arts in the kitchen (think smoking liquid nitrogen cocktails, wasabi foam over seared tuna, or nutella powered with caramelized bananas). *Tickets* restaurant (www.ticketsbar.es) offers a cinema-themed entertaining way to eat and *Disfrutar* (www.en.disfrutarbarcelona.com) has a daring tasting menu that will surprise you with dishes like crispy egg yolk with mushroom gelatin and a deconstructed ceviche.

- Take a forty-minute train ride southwest and escape to the quaint seaside town of Sitges that is filled to the brim with incredible restaurants. Some of the favorites are *Nem* (www.nemsitges.com), *Komokieras* (www.komokieras.com) and *La Incidencia Del Factor Vi* (Bonaire, 25).

- *Visit the best food markets* in Barcelona. The popular La Boqueria Market (www.boqueria.info) is a well-known Catalan foodie haven; a mixture of delicious fruits, vegetables, meats, fish, and tapas stalls. Many of the cooking classes will include a tour here. The beautifully covered roof will catch your attention at Mercat de Santa Caterina (www.mercatsantacaterina.com), but the fresh foods and bars will keep you inside. There are several others that you can find at Visit Barcelona (www.barcelonaturisme.com).

- Take a short road trip to *Sant Sadurní d'Anoia* in the Penedès wine region to not only tour the depths of a cava cave, but to also sample the fruit of the vine while doing it. You can make reservations for a tour and tasting on your own at *Bodegas Freixenet* (www.freixenet.es), *Codorniu* (www.visitascodorniu.com) and *Gramona* (www.gramona.com/en). Or book a multi-visit tour with *Cava Emotions* (www.cavaemotions.com) who can take you to several different cava producers.

## ESSENTIAL INFORMATION:

- Many restaurants are closed on Sundays and Mondays, so check the hours of operation ahead of time before just popping in.

- Make reservations at reputable restaurants well in advance, especially if you want to go on the weekends.
- For a truly traditional taste of Catalan cuisine, stay away from dining in the touristy La Rambla. It will typically cost more and not be as authentic or enjoyable.
- Dining hours are much later in Spain than in the US. Lunch is the most important meal of the day and starts around two p.m. Dinner typically doesn't begin until after nine p.m., but many locals will have a tapas or pintxos snack at five or six.
- US citizens do not need a visa to enter Spain for stays under three months.

## PACKING TIPS:

- Bring comfortable **walking shoes**, especially if your main mode of transport will be the metro. Though there are several stations scattered throughout Barcelona they may be quite a few blocks from your final destination. Plus, the cobbled streets will require a sturdy shoe if you don't want to risk spraining an ankle!
- At most places in the city you can dress casually, but definitely pack a couple **dresses** or **button up shirts** for the fine-dining restaurants.
- Respect the Spanish churches by wearing clothing that will **cover your shoulders and knees** when entering.
- Though Barcelona has a beach, it is not a beach town, so before heading to a restaurant or on the metro, change out of your bathing suits and swim trunks.
- Wearing black is not quite as popular as it is in other European cities, so pack some **vibrant and muted clothing** in other colors too.

**Helpful Websites:** Tourist Guide Barcelona (www.barcelona-tourist-guide.com); Visit Barcelona (www.barcelonaturism.com).

# 14. TAKE AN OFF-ROAD TRIP THROUGH CENTRAL GREECE

When the country of Greece comes to mind many of us immediately think of the pure white buildings with brilliant blue rooftops of the islands, or the ancient citadel perched atop the Attica plateau in Athens. This is completely understandable if you have ever seen the enticing photos of the romantic sunsets that spread over the Santorini caldera, or how the Acropolis shimmers at night, providing the backdrop for the entire city down below. I am certainly guilty of sipping on a glass of dry Assyrtiko while intently watching both of these wonders as if they were the latest blockbuster movie release. But, there is another side to this intriguing country that is equally as picturesque with its crystal clear rivers that flow at the base of snow-capped

Quite possibly the best view in central Greece

mountains; equally as romantic with dazzling turquoise lakes that beg for a picnic filled with freshly made *dolmades*, crumbly feta, and plump black olives; equally as authentic with quaint villages where the mountain dwellers welcome you, bearing homemade Ouzo liquor and sweet baklava.

This was the unexpected part of the country that I explored on an adventurous jeep tour, a nine-day convoy from Athens through the Pindus mountain range in central Greece, about five hundred kilometers north of the capital city. The self-drive adventure was notorious for taking you on the roads tourists never know, exploring the nooks and crannies away from the typically well-traveled parts of the country. We drove on dirt paths with jaw-dropping cliffs and scenic switchbacks, we crossed rivers, stopping in villages to talk with the locals, visiting UNESCO world heritage sites, and marveling at the incredible vistas along the way.

◆ ◆ ◆

At a hotel in Athens, we were assigned our rugged ride for the week, an all-terrain vehicle equipped with a CB radio, so we were able to communicate with the rest of the convoy. There were four cars in this caravan, plus the lead where our trusty guide Yoav resided, a total of fourteen people. Each vehicle had a number, one through four, prominently displayed on the back window so we were easily identifiable and could stay in numerical order. This system wasn't always foolproof, serious situations arose throughout the journey that caused the sequence to be compromised.

"Car number two has stopped for a herd of goats, car number four is passing on the right."

"Car number three will be stopping to take photos of the goats as well."

"Car number one missed the goats and would now like to reverse."

Our off-road vehicle dubbed Aphrodite's Ass

"Car number four has now moved to the lead, we are not interested in goats."

"Copy that."

These mishaps didn't matter much high in the mountains of Greece, where the only other occupants of the gravel course were four-legged animals. Where it did matter was on the bustling streets of Athens, where cars would unexpectedly stop in front of one member of our procession in hopes that their ten-foot vehicle would fit into a six-foot parking spot, spending several minutes assessing the situation before realizing what we all knew behind them: It was not going to fit.

There were three of us in car number four, affectionately named Aphrodite's

One of the few living beings that you'll pass, high up in the mountains while on the dirt roads

Jawdropping cliffs to the right of the road, and sheer mountains to the left

Ass since we would be responsible for driving in the rear. Besides my husband and myself, there was Jessica, a freelance writer and the owner of an innovative cast tattoo art company in Oregon. Her witty (and sometimes vulgar) sense of humor had us often muting the radio to protect the innocent in the other automobiles. She became known for telling the kind of jokes that made you cringe, then quickly look around to see if it had offended anyone before uncontrollably snort-style laughing. We certainly were an adventurous trio, the first to scale the mountain tops in search of the best view, walk across tree branches that had fallen in the rivers, and speed through a twenty-four-kilometer portion of the Acropolis Rally Championship course, one of the toughest on the world rally circuits.

Most of the roads on the journey were not for the faint at heart. We encountered different terrains and levels of anxiety-producing elevations, reaching heights of 5,249 feet. At times, the driver had to hug the shoulder so tightly in order to not subject the passenger to the risk of getting vertigo from seeing the thousand-foot drop into the valley below. Other times the expert driving technique required maneuvering around obstacles blocking the path; rocks in the way of the road, collapsed tree stumps, and the occasional billygoat. The journey may have been heart pounding at times, but each frightening passage, steep incline, and strategic animal renavigation led to someplace truly incredible.

On one morning, the technical manipulation of steep dirt switchbacks led us down into the village of Delphi. Though there was a more direct route, it would not have produced nearly as breathtaking scenery, and be a waste of our all-terrain vehicles. The bumpy drive weaved back and forth a dozen times, only allowing the jeep to safely move at a turtle's pace. In the distance we could see the town, a blanket of olive trees along the mountainside stood between us. This

The Temple of Apollo at the Delphi archaeological site, where offerings to the gods were made

certainly is why Greek olive oil tastes so damn good; it is grown in a land of true beauty.

This modern town whose population is only fifteen hundred, made for the perfect base for exploring the ancient Delphi, a sacred UNESCO archaeological site. The archaic location is more than just another collection of ruins; it is the place in the mortal world where man is said to have been closest to God; a place where politicians, citizens, and kings came to consult the oracle. According to mythology, Zeus released two eagles from different ends of the cosmos and this is where they met, making it the center of the universe. It certainly was the center of my world at that moment.

At the site, we temporarily left our vehicles behind and took the upward path to the stadium—a route named the Sacred Way. This trail led to the highest point of the ancient ruins where the Pythian games were held quadrennially, every four years. The walk began by passing the Temple of Apollo, the grandest structure with six burly Doric

A monastery perched on the pinnacles of the Thessaly region

The meteora monasteries atop natural sandstone pillars

columns made of porous stone and limestone. Further up the hill from this temple, overlooking the valley below was the theater built in 4 BC. Its thirty-five rows had seated thousands of spectators who came to watch plays, festivals, and musical events. At the top of the mountain, the stadium's peak, we were rewarded with views of the breathtaking sanctuary beneath us.

The next afternoon, an uphill vehicle climb took us to Meteora. It was hard to compete with the sacred treasuries of Delphi, but this site did just fine. Meteora, meaning "suspended in the air" in Greek, is a magical complex of six active monasteries that are strategically built on natural sandstone pillars, some that rise up to thirteen hundred feet in the air. Perched on the pinnacles of the Thessaly region, worshippers came here to discover peace and absolute isolation. Many years ago, access to these monasteries was strenuous, using handmade ladders and baskets with a pulley system to hoist the monks and their

Niala Summit is the perfect place to contemplate life

goods up. This was a system that had long been abandoned by the time we had arrived.

The most challenging and frightening drive of the week required top-notch skill. It was a rocky climb with sheer cliff drops to one side, plus several sections of road that were beginning to crumble away. We cautiously ascended the road that led to what I have since called my favorite place on Earth, Niala Summit. It is a location that many have never heard of and fewer have ever seen.

After parking the Jeep on the side of the road, I continued to climb to the peak on foot, away from the group. From the tippy-top it was a complete 360-degree view of natural, peaceful beauty with greenery and scattered spots of leftover snow. There was not a tourist in sight. Many times while traveling there is one point during a trip where a sense of gratitude overwhelms me, literally bringing tears to my eyes (and I swear that I am not a drop-of-the-hat crier, my tears are almost always reserved for sappy Kleenex commercials and weddings). I sat

Dubbed as one of my favorite places on earth: the top of Niala Summit

at the highest point with a feeling of being completely blessed to be at that exact spot at that exact moment as a tear rolled down my face.

The roads weren't always treacherous, nor did they always lead to incredible heritage sites and peak views. On most days, sometimes two to three times a day, the route brought us to some of the most charming villages in Greece. Many of them were so small that they did not even register on the map and their names were more of a suggestion than an indication of a municipality. These pit stops were not only a chance to sip on a Greek coffee or patronize the shops for trinkets, but also a time to immerse with the locals. We drank frothy frappés with the residents in a petite café in Lidoriki, a town built at the foot of Mount Giona. Here we also bought a bag of pastries for less than a euro and listened to the native patrons share stories of the love for their village in their broken English. In Mega Holio we walked through the cobbled streets shopping for homemade liquors and dried flower wreaths. When our feet tired, we popped into a local bar

My husband walking through one of the small villages along the route

for a bottle of cold Mythos beer. Hiladonia was a peaceful place whose vacant town center was reached by walking down a narrow, overgrown path. There was not a resident in sight as we walked through the brush passing impressive stone homes along the way. There were several other adorable village stops, too many to mention, and each with its own character and charm.

The town visits were also where we typically indulged in a meal, and no two eating-places were alike. Each experience was as unique as the destination and the road that got us there. We ate at traditional tavernas where only family members made up the modest staff. At some of these small restaurants, the matriarchs invited us into their delicious-smelling kitchens to be engulfed in the tempting aromas and get a glimpse at their cooking secrets. Dozens of handwritten family recipes were taped to the walls and big bubbling pots were filled with the day's menu items. If no one were watching, I would have dunked my head into every one of those pans to get a closer sniff.

Drinking a frappé with the locals in the village of Lidoriki

After a picnic lunch, my husband and I took in a very romantic view

When we weren't dining at a local taverna we were picnicking in nature: on the top of a mountain, alongside a stream, or under a tree. A portable table was pulled out of the vehicles and a delicious spread was laid on top of it. Even at these informal settings, all the Greek culprits were present; tzatziki, hummus, kalamata olives, and so on. On one day the afternoon lunch setting was on a bluff where only a tiny stone church was perched. We dined on a rickety bench in front of it, overlooking the rolling hills of the green valley below while taking turns ringing the old chapel bell. Another memorable outdoor meal was on the sandy shore of a crystal-blue flowing stream. We ate while either sitting on large rocks that poked out of the ground or over the water on a thick tree branch that had fallen.

After over a thousand kilometers on the road, we ended up back where we started, in Athens where we all shared one last dinner table. Just one week before, the people who surrounded us were total strangers and now they were friends. We were bonded by food, experience, and adventure. We held hands as we all took to the dance floor in the center of the restaurant, laughing and whirling around in a circle to the Greek music that played. It was a journey that proved without a doubt that Greece's beauty went beyond pure white buildings with brilliant blue roofs. It was also an expedition that built lasting relationships.

# CHECK IT OFF YOUR LIST

**Location/Facts:** Greece is a southeastern European country sharing borders with Albania, Macedonia, Bulgaria, and Turkey. It is also bordered by one of the longest coastlines in the world. Bustling Athens is the largest city and capital of Greece, located in the southeastern corner. The Pindus mountain range is known as the spine of Greece, because it runs from northern Peloponnese all the way up to the Greek-Albanian border. The terrain is varied with deep canyons, dense forests, and steep peaks, the highest being Smolikas at 2,637 meters (8,651 feet).

**Getting There:** Most off-road tours begin in Athens, which can be reached by air, train, car, or ferry depending on where you are coming from. The best way to arrive from oversees is by air, flying into the Athens Eleftherios Venizelos International airport located in Spata. Several international airlines fly into this airport daily. Getting into Athens' city center (or the meeting location of your tour) can be done via metro, bus, or taxi. A taxi queue can be found outside the terminal and costs about $35 from early morning to evening and $50 after midnight. The metro is easy and economical; it is connected to the airport. A one-way trip costs under $10 and takes roughly forty minutes to the city center. The bus can be caught opposite the main exit on the arrival level of the airport. Tickets can be purchases at the ticket-kiosks outside the arrivals and costs about $4. Depending on where your meeting location is, you may need to catch a taxi from the metro or bus station.

**Language(s):** Greek is the official language. English is widely spoken in the larger cities and touristy towns, but not in many of the smaller villages.

**Currency:** The euro is the national currency.

**Electricity:** Plug Type C/D/E/F, 220 V. In Greece you will need an adapter and a voltage converter for electronics that are not dual voltage. Note that many outlets in Greece are recessed so some larger universal adapters may not fit.

**When to Go:** The best time for an off-road tour of central Greece is spring to early summer (April to mid-June) or autumn (September or October). The temperature can range from mid-50s to low 70s, which is comfortable for driving and exploring. My trip was in mid-May when the wildflowers were in full bloom and temperatures were mild. A light jacket was only needed in the mornings and at the tippy tops of mountains. Avoid the scorching summers, where temperatures in Athens can exceed 100 degrees, unless you don't plan on spending any time at all exploring the city. Plus, even though you will find milder temps in the mountains, July and August are peak months, which cause inflated prices and hordes of tourists. Winter is not recommended and many tours won't be available since there may be heavy snow in the mountains, making it dangerous to pass some parts.

**How to Visit/Planning:** Though you are able to rent an off-road vehicle and take a trip through central Greece on your own, it is not recommended unless you want a serious adventure. There are limited road signs, and not many passing cars to help if there is an emergency. Also, a large part of the exploration is about the history, nature, and food—having an expert to explain all of it enhances the experience. It is important to book with a reputable company who is concerned for your safety, plus are educated on the area. My excursion was the "Athens to the Pindus" self-drive tour with *Tripology* (www.tripologyadventures.com), who offers four-wheel drive tours around the world, including throughout Greece. Not only did they make me feel secure, but they were also informative and accommodating.

**Getting Around:** No need to worry about getting around throughout the trip as you will have a vehicle and a guide leading the way. While in Athens, the Metro (www.amel.gr) is easily accessible and can get you almost everywhere you need to go, especially the main attractions. If your plan is to visit the Acropolis and Plaka area the metro has stops close by each, Akropoli and Monastiraki accordingly. Once in central Athens, it is very walkable from Plaka to the Acropolis, taking roughly twenty to thirty minutes. It is an uphill walk, but not very steep. Taking a taxi is possible, but it's best to make arrangements ahead of time, as they can be difficult to hail on the streets. You can use the bus system (www.athenstransport.com) for cheap transport, but beware that it may be confusing unless you have studied, and understand, the bus schedule.

**Where to Stay:** Most off-road tours will include lodging, but if you're spending a couple extra days in Athens (and you should) opt for a hotel in the Acropolis and Plaka area. This will put you in the center of all the action. Have a good night's sleep and evening cocktails at the rooftop bar of the *Plaka Hotel* (www.plakahotel.gr; from $75) where you'll get a panoramic view of the Acropolis. Choose to stay in the Mighty Aphrodite or The Betty Boop Suite at *Alice Inn Athens* (http://www.aliceinnathens.com/; $102), the cute names are fitting for this charming inn at the foot of the ancient citadel. For a funky five-star experience, try the *New Hotel* (www.yeshotels.gr; $171) where the curious artwork and unusual custom-made furniture will have you in awe.

**Where to Eat:** Along with hotels, most tours will also include meals. Plus, they will have plenty of snacks in the vehicles just in case you get hungry along the way. But, don't miss the opportunity to dine at some of the delicious and unique restaurants in Athens. *Dinner in the Sky* (www.dinnerinthesky.gr) is a once-in-a-lifetime dining experience, where you'll be suspended in the air while eating a gourmet meal. If you are a wine lover like me, *Scala Vinoteca* (www.scalavinoteca.com) serves a creative Mediterranean menu and more than a hundred wines to choose from. You will be dining on traditional Cappadocian and Byzantine dishes amongst a plethora of hanging meats and cheeses at **Karamanlidika** (www.karamanlidika.gr). For a

Feeling on top of the world in Meteora

Michelin experience, **Funky Gourmet** (www.funkygourmet.com) serves up playful, funky food that is a treat for the senses. **O Kostas** (5 Pentelis, Syntagma) is an unpretentious hole-in-the-wall known for the best *souvlaki* in Athens.

## MUST-DOS:

- You can admire the ***Meteora Monasteries*** (www.visitmeteora. travel) from afar, but also take the opportunity to tour the interiors and get a glimpse into a monk's lifestyle one thousand years ago. Entrance fee for the monasteries are three euros.
- Take the ***Sacred Way*** walk at Delphi archaeological site (www. ancient-greece.org). It will take you from the temple of Apollo all the way up to the ancient theater to the stadium.
- Schedule an extra day or two in Athens to visit the ***Acropolis*** (www.acropolisofathens.gr; 12 euros), the ancient citadel sits high up on a rock overlooking the city.

- It's easy to sit in the passenger seat of your four-wheel drive, but don't be afraid to take the wheel and **do the driving**.
- There are many opportunities in the quaint villages to **connect with the locals.** Take advantage of these precious moments; listen to their stories and share your own.

## ESSENTIAL INFORMATION:

- Most self-drive four-wheel drive tour companies will require **travel insurance** that allows for you to drive a vehicle off-road. My policy was purchased from World Nomads (www.worldnomads.com) for about $100.
- You will need an **International Driver's License**, which is very easy to get. You can apply for your international driving permit through the American Automobile Association (AAA; www.aaa.com) or the National Automobile Club (NAC; www.thenac.com). In most cases this can be done through the mail, but contact your local office to double-check.
- Though your guide will be navigating you through the mountains, and will usually pull out a map to show you the route each day, I would recommend getting a good **map of central Greece** and a highlighter. It's fun to mark off where you are going and where you have been to get a sense of the area that has been covered.
- Plan on having **no Wi-Fi or cell phone** service during much of your time on the road. Some hotels will have spotty Internet, but don't count on being connected with super speed.
- For United States residents, a **visa** is only required for stays over ninety days or if you are traveling on an official or diplomatic passport.

## PACKING TIPS:

- Bring *motion sickness medication*; there are times you may not be the driver or be able to sit shotgun and will have to ride in the back seat.
- *Dress in layers*, the bottom of the mountain can be much warmer than the top.
- Bring a pair of light *hiking boots* or *tennis shoes*, some stops will allow for short hikes.
- Off-roading lends itself to very *casual attire*; jeans, shorts, and T-shirts are fitting for most of the trip. The only exception may be for dinners at the starting and ending point in Athens.
- You'll be on the road for long periods of time without electrical outlets. Invest in an *external charger* that can load up any electronics you need while on the road.
- Though not essential, using a *duffle bag* as luggage will help to save storage in the vehicle's trunk.
- Don't forget the *sunglasses*, you will need a pair almost every month of the year.
- Bring a *conservative outfit* for touring the monasteries (shorts are not allowed). If you forget, most will lend men oversized pants and ladies a wrap skirt.

**Helpful Websites:** Ministry of Culture and Sports (www.culture.gr); Visit Greece (www.visitgreece.gr); Greek Embassy (www.mfa.gr).

# 15. VOLUNTEER AT AN ELEPHANT RESCUE IN THAILAND

Ladies stood outside of the parlor doors along the crowded streets waving their magic hands, beckoning me inside. My fatigued feet instinctively ached, like the response of one of Pavlov's dogs. Attempts to pass the shops without entering were almost always futile. I had picked up an addiction since arriving in Thailand, and the city of Chiang Mai easily fed that addiction once a day, sometimes twice. The five-dollar foot massage was my vice and getting a fix was easy, it could be done on just about every street corner. I would question how anyone couldn't be hooked on their feet being delightfully soaked, rubbed, and scrubbed, taking the stresses of life away. But on this day instead of entering the threshold for relief, my

Wat Chedi Luang in the Chiang Mai city center

tootsies would be subjected to the pains of withdrawals. Rather than being pampered myself, I would be the one doling out the rubs and scrubs. It would just not be done to the typical two legged clients, instead to a ten-thousand-pound Asian elephant.

The city had been filled with local treasures, plus it was the gateway to explore northern Thailand and the starting point for many tours. Since I had arrived, beyond the orgasmic foot massages, my time had been filled will unexpected adventures. An evening at the notorious Sunday Night Market in the old city center led to semi-reluctantly munching on a variety of fried insects, and then chugging a glass of grass jelly milo, a malt powder beverage that perfectly washed down a pair of bug's legs. An afternoon Segway tour took me through the ornate Wat Chedi Luang temple where you could participate in a Monk Chat, a time where the worshipping Buddhists would have enlightening conversations with willing visitors. There were wild *tuk tuk* rides, cooking classes to perfect the art of Panang curry, afternoons noshing on algae-green thousand-year-old eggs, and a transgender ladyboy show that left me yearning for their beauty secrets. Venturing outside of the city led to an excursion to the Long Neck Karen hilltop tribe, where women of all ages are known for their elongated necks surrounded by numerous spiral brass coils, plus a stop at the White Temple of Chiang Rai, which was a vision of purity.

It was practically adventure overload, even for me whose passion is trying something for the first time. But, today there would be something truly memorable added to my new

Taking a tiny nibble of a traditional Asian century-old egg

A herd of ellies roaming free on the Elephant Nature Park grounds

experience repertoire, something so special that it would cause me to willingly forgo a foot massage. Today I would be getting up close and personal with some of the many resident elephants known to be in the country. Munching on toasted crickets couldn't quite compare.

Thailand, as well as other Asian countries, has capitalized on the elephant industry, offering an array of interaction opportunities for visitors. You can ride on the back of a giant one while trekking through the rivers or have an ellie paint you an artistic picture using just its trunk. There are even circus-themed shows where a display of tricks will be performed to entertain you. But, after much research, the decision was made against any of the aforementioned presentations. There were one too many stories about the horrific training techniques of these precious animals in order for them to perform at these sorts of tourist attractions. Many are torn from their mothers as babies and then put through an ancient six-day *Phajaan*, a ritual also known as the crush. This training technique confines the animal to a cage where he is restrained by ropes, not able to move his legs or head. It has also been reported that during a Phajaan abuse with bullhorns, nails, sticks, chains, and sleep-deprivation has been used in order the crush the elephant's spirit so they become submissive to their owner. This is not to say that there are not ethical companies using humane training techniques, but I wanted to go to a place where it was well known that the elephants were celebrated, loved, and treated with the respect that they deserve. So instead of watching an elephant show or another type of display, the easy choice was made to volunteer at a highly recognized elephant sanctuary, The Elephant Nature Park. It is an elephant rescue and rehabilitation camp located in Northern Thailand, a place where volunteers not only get an ellie education, but also are able to interact with them through feeding, bathing, and simply appreciating.

The park was started in 1996 by Lek, a beyond-impressive woman whose life mission is to create a natural environment for these

The vast landscape allows plenty of space for the elephants to roam

rescued animals to live. Her bond is deep; over the years she has been their midwife, mother, savior, friend, protector, and provider. She has also travelled great distances to negotiate fees with loggers and trekking companies in order to have their injured elephants join the safety of her herd. Her love and respect is evident. *And* it is inspiring. One of the most impressive things is that unlike the harsh techniques used to break an elephant's spirit, the training style here is to reward them for good behavior, not punish them for bad. This is the reason the *mahouts* (elephant caretakers) will always have a bushel of bananas with them. Elephants will do almost anything for a banana, similar to me and what I'd do for chocolate.

The rescue is located about an hour north of the Chiang Mai city center, and the park provided free transportation with the entrance fee. I was punctually picked up at my hotel in a comfortable air-conditioned van filled with about a dozen other volunteers that day. On the short ride over we passed several companies that were offering one of

Two of my new friends at the Elephant Nature Park

the most common Thailand attractions, elephant trekking rides. Some of the animals on these premises were tied up outdoors, with a short chain around their leg that prevented them from straying within a couple of feet from where they stood. They were occupying their time with a small pile of hay that lay in front of them. It was difficult not to wonder how many hours a day that they had spent tethered there. The thought passed as we hit the end of the long dirt road where the fields opened up to endless stretches of lush, green rolling hills. We drove just a few minutes on this path before seeing the gorgeous sight of elephants roaming free. We had arrived and I immediately knew that this wasn't going to be any ordinary experience.

When we entered the headquarters on this expansive piece of land we were assigned one of the passionate guides who started the morning at the park with an informative tour of the grounds and an introduction to its four-legged residents. The inhabitant ellies were an eclectic bunch; some old, some young, some blind, some injured from working in the illegal logging industry, some abused, and some rescued from the circus—all incredibly beautiful.

One of my favorites of the herd was Lucky, a big girl who was blind in both eyes and had been rescued from a circus show. This was not an uncommon fate for such animals. She had been the star in the Lucky Circus for three decades; many years after, the effects of performing under the harsh spotlight had taken away her sight. There were no more show-stopping tricks for her to perform here. Her days were filled with love, compassion, and a couple hundred pounds of pineapples. It was also hard not to get emotional as Malai Tong limped by, a medium sized elephant that was victim to a landmine that left one leg shorter and disfigured. Unfortunately, this outcome was quite familiar in the illegal logging industry and Malai was one of the luckier ones who survived the explosion. Though she was not productive in the logging industry after the injury, her mahout found her disfigurement to be valuable at street begging, which is now criminal in Thailand. Not long after, Lek rescued her, bringing her to the safety of the park. Even though she was in a better place, every step she took looked like an extreme effort filled with pain.

There were so many other heartbreaking stories of animal cruelty that these elephants could probably tell, ones that would have undoubtedly had them begging for death instead of carrying on. But, now they have found that silver lining they didn't know existed, a heartwarming place with people who cared about their comfort and well-being.

Despite the name, the Elephant Nature Park does not limit its residents just to these massive, endearing creatures. It is also home to over two hundred dogs that were either rescued from catastrophic flooding in Bangkok, local surrounding villages, or the dog meat trade. This was evidence that Lek's compassion has no boundaries. You will see the pups all over the property, lounging on wooden chairs in the sun, barking at strangers, and roaming in the fields. Many just want a little love and a belly scratch, which most of the visitors were happy to give. I even tried rubbing their tiny paws to see if they enjoyed foot massages as much as I do. Apparently they did, because there was always a furry four-legged companion by my side.

After the initial forty-five minute get-acquainted tour, it was feeding time and everyone in the herd was hungry. Bulging buckets of fresh watermelon, bananas, and pineapples were ready to be devoured, and the ten of us in our group were in charge of the feeding. Doling out one piece of fruit at a time, we fed the elephants, putting their nourishment at the end of their trunks as they grabbed it and skillfully maneuvered the food into their mouths. The precise capability of their trunks was impressive, sometimes even more so than myself with the use of a fork. Though their appetites seemed endless, the barrel of fruit was not and when the bucket was empty, they retreated back into the fields for some more relaxation.

The animals were not the only ones who needed to eat lunch, so did we. The rescue center had provided all the volunteers a seemingly endless buffet with a line of chafing dishes that were filled with both Asian and American vegetarian cuisine. It was quite a selection, everything from a traditional Thai papaya salad to American-style French fries. Being a fan of variety, I put a little of everything on my dish. After overloading our plates, the group sat at one of the several picnic tables, joined by dozens of other volunteers. Some of them were here just for the one-day educational experience and others for a weeklong volunteer program that required spending the night in cabins on the premises. The lengthier experiences definitely required more intensive work like preparing the fruit for feeding, cleaning the poop in the pens, and cutting down corn stalks. We all chatted randomly, sharing our own origins and favorite Thailand experiences so far, agreeing that this one would be among our most memorable even though we were only halfway through day one.

Dirty elephants heading to the shallow river for their bath

As we were finishing the last of the aluminum container of French fries, there was an indication that the bathing of the elephants was about to commence: a herd of dirty ones passed by, heading toward the river. Their backs and heads were covered with a thin layer of self-applied mud, a sun block and insect control technique. This slight hint was more than enough for me; I quickly brought my unfinished plate to the dishwashing stand, not wanting to miss any part of the cleansing event. I happily saw my lunch leftovers being put into a bin and then being fed to the random nearby dogs. Nothing goes to waste here.

Our assigned group walked alongside our new four-legged friends, down to the shallow murky water where the elephants knew to stand in the middle of the narrow stream. Empty plastic pails were distributed, as well as a piece of bark that was used to exfoliate their rough skin. We all, including the elephants, stood in the knee deep river as one person scrubbed the massive surface of the elephant and the other rinsed by throwing buckets of water. All the while, the ellies

Trying my hand at bathing one of the residents with a piece of bark

An elephant washes himself as he gets splashed by a mahout

were being entertained by a basketful of bananas. Some diverted their attention from the food to participate in the cleansing process by submerging their trunks in the river, sucking in water and then spraying themselves. The waving trunks and flying sprinkles was an entertaining spectacle that had to be better than any circus show.

As we bathed several of the larger elephants, the mahouts escorted some of the smaller juveniles to a clear space in the river and supervised as they completely submerged themselves underwater. With this bathing technique they rolled their bodies from one chubby side to the other, which seemed to be as much fun as practical.

After about an hour, everyone was squeaky clean, and it was time for one more feeding. Apparently, these gentle giants never get full. We went back to the feeding station, took fruit from the full baskets and fed them until there was nothing left. At that point, the elephants turned from the platform and peacefully strolled back into the fields, undoubtedly knowing that the process would start all over again tomorrow, just like my foot massages back in the Chiang Mai.

# CHECK IT OFF YOUR LIST

**Location/Facts:** Chiang Mai is the second largest city in Thailand, located roughly 700 km north of Bangkok in Thailand. It is an escape from the bustle of its larger counterpart, plus a little bit cheaper. It is a popular place amongst expats who can live there for a fraction of the cost of living in the US. The Old City center and the surrounding area is home to hundreds of ornate temples, fabulous food, and a laid-back vibe. The Elephant Nature Park is in the Mae Taeng District, about sixty km north of Chiang Mai city.

**Getting There:** In most cases, volunteer trips to Elephant Nature Park begin from Chiang Mai. Many flights into the city arrive via Bangkok to the Chiang Mai International Airport, which is roughly a ninety-minute flight. The airport is located less than fifteen minutes from the city center. Some hotels will offer free shuttles, but the city is also easily reached by taxi. Once in the arrival hall, you will need to go to the coupon booth (or speak to someone carrying a coupon book). It's very simple, just tell them where you are going and they will give you a slip to give to the driver. For locations within the city center, it is a flat fee of 150 baht (a little over $4) and takes about fifteen minutes. The Elephant Nature Park offers pickup/drop-off from your hotel in Chiang Mai's city center. Their comfortable shuttles take approximately ninety minutes.

**Language(s):** The official language of Thailand is Thai. English is widely spoken in the large cities, including Chiang Mai. Most elephant volunteer programs are led in English.

**Currency:** Thai baht.

**Electricity:** Plug Type A/C, voltage 220. You will find either outlets that are the same as the United States or a two round prong outlet; usually the design is made to fit both. It is recommended to bring an adapter just in case and a converter is necessary for devices that are not dual voltage.

**When to Go:** March through June are the hottest month in Thailand with temperatures near the hundreds and high humidity, so it will be pretty miserable to be outdoors with elephants during this time. The *rainy season* (May through October) will bring a little bit cooler temperatures than the hot season, but you may experience sudden torrential downpours. Overall the *cool season* (November through February) is the best time to visit when the temperatures will be pleasantly chilly in the evenings and warmer during the day.

**How to Visit/Planning:** The Elephant Nature Park offers volunteer programs from one day in length to one week. In addition to feeding and bathing, the longer visits may include cleaning shelters, harvesting crops, and building fences. Trips to the park typically begin and end in Chiang Mai where you will need to spend at least one evening since the included hotel pickups are early in the morning. The actual length of time you spend in the larger city depends on how much time you have and how long you plan on spending with the elephants. For those who have more free days, four days in Bangkok and a couple in Chiang Mai should be good enough to explore. It is recommended to book your experience in advance which you can easily do online (www.elephantnaturepark.org). Another option would be to book at your chosen hotel upon arrival, but know that the park restricts the visitor count and its popularity (people love ellies!) can cause sell-outs on certain days.

**Getting Around:** While in Chiang Mai it is very easy to get around; within the city center walls it is very walkable. But, when your feet get tired or you need to venture a little further there are a few options. Tuk tuks are typically the quickest and easiest way to get around. The three-wheeled carts can be found lingering around almost everywhere and are relatively cheap, rarely costing over 150 baht ($4.25 USD). But, be sure to negotiate the fee before hopping in. Be warned that if they know you're a tourist they may hike up the price a bit, but you can negotiate. *Songthaews* are red passenger trucks fitted with bench seats. They are similar to buses, except have no specific route. When you see one, flag it down and tell them where you are going and they will tell you whether they are headed in that direction. If they are, you hop aboard and pay a flat rate of 20 baht ($0.57 USD). *Warning*: If you ask the songthaew driver how much it costs, they will typically charge you more. Also, when you are giving them your destination, if it's not a main attraction, it's easier to give them the name of the closest temple. You can also get a taxi at your hotel, just negotiate the price before jumping in.

**Where to Stay:** If you are doing an extended program at the Elephant Nature Park you will be housed in their onsite cabins. Otherwise, most tours start in Chiang Mai where there are plenty of lodging options. Inside the city walls is a desired place to be as you will be able to easily access most of the hot spots on foot. I stayed in the historic city center at *3 Sis* (www.the3sis.com; from $43 USD), which is right across the street from Wat Chedi Luang. The ***Ketawa Stylish Hotel*** (www.ketawahotel.com; from $54 USD) is a fun and funky hotel along the Ping River where each room has a color theme. If you want to be in the heart of the city's bustling night bazaar choose *dusitD2* (www.dusit.com/dusitd2; from $97 USD). Built to mimic a Mandalay palace, you will believe you are living in a fairytale on the sixty acres of **Dhara Dhevi** (www.dharadhevi.com; from $425). Though palace living comes at a hefty price, living like a king or queen for the night won't disappoint you.

**Where to Eat:** ***The Ginger & Kafe*** (www.thehousethailand.com) is an eclectic and quirky restaurant where you can relax on colorful couches while indulging in creative Asian fusion dishes. I spent many evenings here eating bowls of *khao soi* and using their free Wi-Fi. Support local organic farmers by having a meal at **Pun Pun** (www.punpunthailand.org) which is located on the grounds of the Wat Suan Dok temple. For super-cheap eats and a unique experience dine at the popular lunchtime canteen ***The Vegetarian Society*** (42 Mahidol

The ornate White Temple in Chiang Rai

Road, tel: 053 271 262). For an elegant treat spend the evening at **David's Kitchen** (www.davidskitchenat909.com) where the sophisticated menu highlights French, Italian, and Thai food. After several days or weeks in Thailand, you just may want a pizza and the **Secret Learning Restaurant** (www.secretlearningchiangmai.wordpress.com) is the place to get a tasty one.

## NEARBY MUST-DOS:

- Take a tour about two and a half hours from Chiang Mai to see the peculiar **White Temple of Chiang Rai**. Wat Rong Khun is an unconventional Buddhist Temple that is a vision of pure white meant to symbolize purity. A full-day tour will typically include other stops such as the Long Necked Karen Hilltop village, Monkey Temple, and Golden Triangle. Tours start at roughly $30 USD and can be booked through All Chiang Mai

Tours (www.allchiangmaitours.com) or Authentic Thai Tours (www.authenticthaitours.com).

- Take a taste of Thailand back home with you by taking a cooking class where you'll learn how to make traditional dishes like Pad Thai and Panang Curry. ***Thai Orchard Cookery*** (www. thaiorchidcooking.com) is the place that helped me to perfect my skills, plus it included a trip to the market where we were dared to eat a thousand-year-old egg. Challenge accepted.

- Plan your trip so you will be in the city of Chiang Mai over the weekend so you can visit the notorious ***Sunday Night Market*** (Rachadamnoen Rd, Mueang Chiang Mai District). This eclectic and crowded evening bazaar is a place where you can eat tasty street food, buy artisan crafts, shoot BB guns, and get an airbrushed tattoo.

- ***Wat Chedi Luang*** (103 Phra Pok Klao Road) is an eye-catching Buddhist temple that is centrally located inside the Chiang Mai city walls. It is worthy of your bucket list to explore its large *viharn* (sermon hall), naga dragons at its doorstep, and the ruined brick *chedi* that sits behind the grand assembly hall. At this temple you can also participate in the "Monk Chat" program where curious visitors are able to speak to the monks about almost any aspect of life. This is the perfect opportunity to get insight into their lifestyle and beliefs.

## ESSENTIAL INFORMATION:

- The Elephant Nature Park is in a remote location, so you must bring everything that you need with you.
- You can book online with a deposit, but the balance must be paid in cash (either Thai baht or USD) when you arrive.
- A vegetarian lunch is included in the one-day project cost and all meals are served buffet style. There are a variety of Thai and

American dishes that will accommodate most dietary restrictions.
- US citizens are not required to get a visa for stays less than thirty days.
- Chiang Mai is blessed with free and moderately fast Internet access almost everywhere.

## PACKING TIPS:

- For the one-day project, you are allowed **one small daypack** per person.
- Pack versatile **water shoes**, because you will be standing in the riverbed as well as hiking through the fields.
- The day can get muddy, so bring an extra **change of clothing** just in case.
- You will be in direct sunlight much of the day. Make sure to **bring a wide brimmed hat** and a **high SPF sunscreen**.
- Bring **discreet clothing** for touring the temples while in Chiang Mai, ones that will cover your elbows and knees.
- Carry a **pack of tissues** with you unless you want to drip dry; some toilets in the area will be squat style.

**Helpful Websites:** One Stop Chiang Mai (www.1stopchiangmai. com); Amazing Thailand (www.tourismthailand.org).

# 16. FEED THE SWIMMING PIGS IN THE BAHAMAS

Our speedboat glided through the translucent aquamarine waters of the Exuma Islands. Bordering the endless shades of blue were the powder-white sand beaches of crescent-shaped shallow islands. There are 365 of these cays along this section of the Bahamas, covering 130 brilliantly turquoise miles. Some are privately owned by famous stars like Johnny Depp who fell in love with the area while filming *Pirates of the Caribbean*, and David Copperfield who was so enamored he purchased Musha Cay, a 150-acre piece of paradise that has been transformed into a luxury resort costing just under $40,000 per night. For that price, you'd expect that he'd be on site performing a few magic tricks, but that is not the case.

Conch shells hanging from driftwood along the turquoise beach

Drinking a Bahama Mama and taking in the best view in Exuma, on the deck of
Haulover Bay Bar & Grill

It wasn't hard to see the attraction of the Exuma Isles. It is a laid-
back archipelago where the time seemed to move slower, a place
where unwinding came naturally. Much different than our starting
island of Nassau, where the cruise ships dock and Senor Frogs was
packed to the rim with tipsy twenty-somethings toting around two-
foot-tall cocktails. A quick half-hour flight from the busy duty-free
shops, tour buses dropping off hordes of people in front of the Atlan-
tis casino, and blaring music from the second floor of the downtown
bars, was this pint-sized version of its capital counterpart.

On the main isle of Great Exuma, name-brand bars are traded in
for the clear turquoise waters that surround outstretched sand bars
and beachfront grills, where visitors sip on a chilled bottle of Kalik,
the official beer of the Bahamas. If you drive far to the south into Little
Exuma you may find yourself at Santana's, where tourists and locals
alike fill the handful of seats at the counter for a plate of their

specialty, the cracked spiny lobster. Right next door in a teeny build-ing, you can get dessert at Mom's Bakery, where Mama herself might sell you a loaf of her to-die-for rum cake that crumbles to the touch and melts in your mouth. It is so delicious and she is so charming, that you will want to make that half-hour trip from the main city of George Town again and again. Far to the north, a stop at Big D's Conch Spot will get you a bowl of conch salad, a Bahamian tradition that you can't possibly leave the islands without trying. In Rolle Town, a stop at the Haulover Bay Bar & Grill for a leisurely Bahama Mama cocktail will reward you with one of the best views in the world. We sat on their peaceful deck for hours watching the kite surfer's drift over the flat waters. This spot may very well be the best-kept secret in Exuma. If you do end up missing the party atmosphere of Nassau, you could take a five-minute ferry ride from the big island to the nearby Stocking Island for the Sunday afternoon pig roast at Chat 'N' Chill. Here boats line the waterfront, and there's always a large group of people indulg-ing in Goombay Smash cocktails, playing sand volleyball, or sunbathing on the beach. If all that weren't enough, the islands are also home to a quirky anomaly—swimming pigs.

It hasn't been until recently that instead of travelers talking about the translucent blue waters and picturesque cays of Exuma, they're talking about the aquatic four-legged porkers. People flock to this part of the Bahamas for a chance at feeding the newest famous resi-dents, the skinny-dipping pigs. I was absolutely no different.

There are two uninhabited island locations to accomplish this goal; one is Big Major Cay and the other White Bay. The former of the two is also known as Pig Beach and is roughly sixty-five miles from the north end of Great Exuma, about a two-hour boat ride. This was the original location for the swimming pigs, and there are a couple beliefs as to how they actually got there. One thought is that they were left by sail-ors who wanted to return to eat them, but never did. The other legend is that their owner put them on this vacant cay years ago because his neighbors were complaining that they were stinking the area up near his home. He would come every day to feed them and eventually they would greet his boat in the water in order to be fed first. The competing porkers on White Bay Cay are located just a ten-minute boat ride from the mainland. It's a knockoff of the first location, but that doesn't mean it is inferior.

The difference between the two depends on whom you talk to. The Major Cay supporters say that it is the original and you shouldn't accept imitation pork, where as The White Bay Cay supporters claim that the piggy pioneers have gotten lazy due to an influx of tourists and now many will wait on the shore for tourists to come to them. No matter which one you should choose one thing is for certain: you will see swimming pigs.

Our boat was on a half-day tour that included a swine stop at White Bay, a choice made due to the choppy waters that day and my husband's affliction of seasickness. It was his birthday and a dose of

Getting stuck near a blow hole on the Blow Hole Cay

seasickness would be a terrible gift. This was guaranteed to be a smoother ride where the rocking of a parked boat would be limited.

We started our powerboat tour by flying through the cays, exploring the nooks and crannies before the main attraction. There was a quick stop right where the Caribbean Sea meets the Atlantic Ocean, the water between the two violently swooshing around in a battle of where it wanted to reside. At this stop the visibility was so lucid, the sea of the floor fifty feet below could clearly be seen. The range made it easy to watch three dolphins as they played around the boat, jumping in the air and giving a spectacular show. Next there was a short uphill hike on one of the cays that resulted in a breathtaking 360-degree view, where standing at the cliff's edge gave the opportunity for a photo worthy of *National Geographic*. Another isle boasted a blow hole where the water forcefully blasted up in the air through the rocks. After stepping too close to get an Instagram selfie, I was caught in its spray, ending up

One lonely reptile on Iguana Island in Exuma

Making friends with a reptile on Iguana Island

drenched from head to toe. It had been an entertaining excursion thus far and we hadn't even seen one curly tail.

Just prior to the stop at White Bay Cay, there was another oddity that rivaled the pigs—Iguana Island. This islet was home to roughly a hundred of these gentle reptiles. When our boat approached the beachfront, one lone lizard stood on the sand. But, as the sound of the boat's engine got closer to the shore, the cay came alive. Iguanas of all sizes started to fill the shoreline waiting for the boat to dock. Unlike the pigs, they will not swim out to accost you (although they can swim). It was still a greeting quite like no other.

Armed with a handful of purple grapes, I dropped one onto the ground at my feet and a small group of reptiles immediately swarmed me. I then made a short grape trail, leading the critters away from the crowd of tourists and behind a rock. Sitting on this stone, I had a dozen mesmerized iguanas all to myself. But, when my grapes were done they started to scatter. It was a no food, no love policy just like the felines at the cat cafés in Tokyo. One last little straggler came toward me in hopes that there was one leftover morsel for him. He looked up at me, and then walked over to my pink-painted toenails mistaking them for grapes. He gave them one little lick before realizing that they didn't taste quite as good. He lazily turned around, headed back toward the crowd who still had food left to dole out.

One little swimming pig tried to climb onto the boat

It was finally time for the grand finale and as we pulled up to the piggy paradise of White Bay Cay, it looked more desolate than our arrival to Iguana Island. Not a swine in sight. The boat stopped a few meters away from shore and we quietly waited, barely breathing in anticipation. Nothing. Then the captain gave a little jingle of the bell and the bushes started to move. Everything on Exuma up until that point had been relaxed; people and things moved at a snail's pace. No one was in a hurry, until the ring of that bell. A dozen pigs and piglets came running out of the low shrubs, some stopping at the shoreline and others making their way into the water knowing that they would be fed first.

The captain said, "If you want to feed the pigs go ahead and jump in." I hesitated for a moment taking in the oddity that lay before me—pigs were swimming. I squealed like one of them that this was actually

A swimming pig heading straight for me, looking for a hot dog

Feeding hot dogs to the adult pigs on White Bay Cay

happening. I jumped off the side of the boat into three feet of water and two nostrils came straight for me; a round nose perched slightly above the translucent blue water level. Backing up trying to avoid a collision was futile, his trotters were moving underwater way faster than my feet. We were nose to nose playing a weird game of chicken, which I regretfully lost. He barreled into me and after realizing I had no food, turned the other direction and moved on.

For the next swimmer I was better prepared, holding a few chicken hot dogs (because of course it'd be wrong to feed pigs pork) in one hand and my GoPro in the other. The next porker came at me with the same amount of tenacity and went straight for the camera which was yanked away just in time. Finally seeing the hot dogs in my hand, three pigs doggy paddled around me taking turns snatching them from my fingers. It was then a bit of a frenzy, the captain throwing us hot dogs from the boat and us trying to grab them before the pigs stra-tegically swiped them, losing the battle half of the time. Some brilliant

Cuddling my favorite piglet on White Bay Cay

ones even tried to hop aboard the boat after spotting the keeper of the food.

When the dogs were done, the small group of us moved to the shore where our guide was filling large troughs. He loaded them with cabbage, rice, and fruits, plus fresh water. This sight and their hefty size was evidence that these pigs ate well . . . very well. They flocked around these food-filled containers, gulping up the slop as if they hadn't just eaten a slew of hotdogs minutes earlier. They were bottomless pits.

As we explored the small island we saw that the little piglets had retreated back into the bushes seeking shade. One or two would sporadically make their way out into the open to get a little attention. I picked up a teeny black and white girl who gave out a little squeal. Holding her close to my chest and petting her course head soothed this little one until it was asleep in my arms. If it were possible, she would have been my only Exuma souvenir—the best one ever.

Reluctantly leaving my piglet behind, we got back into the boat and waved goodbye to our new porky friends who could really care less since their snouts were still deep in food. Gliding away it made me wonder if pigs can now swim, should we rethink ever using the term "when pigs fly"? I suppose you just never really know.

# CHECK IT OFF YOUR LIST

**Location/Facts:** The Bahamian Islands of Exuma lie thirty-five miles southeast of Nassau and are divided into three major sections; Great Exuma, Little Exuma, and the Exuma Cays. The largest is Great Exuma, running thirty-seven miles in length, plus Little Exuma is attached to the south end by a small bridge. The Exumas consist of over 350 small, low islands called cays. The swimming pigs can be found on two of these cays, the original being the Big Major Cay and the other at White Bay.

**Getting There:** The most popular way to reach Exuma is via a non-stop flight from Nassau, Miami, or Fort Lauderdale. There are daily direct flights to Exuma International Airport (GGT) on Bahamasair (www.bahamasair.com) and Sky Bahamas (www.skybahamas.net) from Nassau, which is a quick half-hour flight. American Eagle (www.aa.com) offers direct flights from Miami, and Silver Airways (www.

The Exuma waters are a hundred beautiful shades of blue

silverairways.com) has nonstops from Fort Lauderdale. You can save a little money by taking the night ferry through Bahama Ferries (www.bahamasferries.com), which will take over twelve hours. The cost of a round-trip fare is $130. These boats are technically for transporting freight, and there are no sleeping compartments. Most riders will bring a blanket or sleeping bag and stretch out on the deck or in a chair.

Once you get to GGT airport you will find car rental shops right across the street or there are plenty of taxis that will take you to the main city of Georgetown for roughly $30 USD.

**Language(s):** English is the official language, though you will also hear Bahamian English, a dialect influenced by various African languages and Haitian Creole. The "h" is often dropped so "thing" would be pronounce "ting."

**Currency:** The currency is the Bahamian dollar, though US dollars are used just as frequently and the exchange rate is of equal value. There's no need to change any money, though you may sometimes get your change in Bahamian coins. Many restaurants and gas stations are cash only, so make sure you bring enough or there are also ATMs available.

**Electricity:** Plug Type A/B, 120 V. The voltage and socket are compatible with the US, so there is no need for an adapter or converter.

**How to Visit/Planning:** Unless you book a private charter, which runs just under $1000 for four hours, in order to go feed the swimming pigs, you will need to book a half-day or full-day tour that includes other stops as well. Most people will stay on the mainland of Great Exuma and then hop on an organized tour from there. There are quite a few companies to choose from with the itineraries slightly varying with each. I did the half-day Ocean Safari tour with Exuma Water Sports (www.exumawatersports.com; $150); it leaves from the settlement of Barratarre, but also does a shuttle pickup at the Grand Isle Resort. The trip included the pigs at White Bay Cay, a stop at iguana island, a cliff hike, the blow hole and a few other incredible cays. Four C's Adventures (www.exumawatertours.com; $172 USD) and Coastline Adventures (www.coastlineadventuresexuma.com; $200 USD) also offer full-day tours that will take you to the pigs at Big Major Cay, Thunderball Grotto (where the James Bond movie *Thunderball* was filmed) and to swim with docile nurse sharks.

**Getting Around:** If you plan on exploring the Great Exuma Island it is smart to rent a car, because the cost of taxis will add up quickly and they are not plentiful (though hotels can call you one if you need to go somewhere). You won't find any of the popular American name-brand car rental companies; we rented ours online with no issues through Exuma Car Rental (www.exumacarrental.com) for roughly $75 per day and picked it up right across the street from the airport. You can also try Don's Rent A Car (242-345-0112) which is right next door, but it doesn't have a website. Be warned that they drive on the other side of the road than the United States!

If you decide not to rent a car, the main city of George Town is very walkable and some of the hotels will provide a shuttle service to get there. But, don't expect lots of entertainment in this town, it's a quiet waterfront village with only a few restaurants, minimal shopping, and a grocery store.

## WHERE TO STAY:

For a luxury experience, book a room at the AAA four-diamond **Grand Isle Resort** (www.grandisleresort.com; from $369) where you can walk the mile-long private white sand beach and dine at their romantic Palapa Grill overlooking the pool. **Peace & Plenty** (www.peaceandplenty.com; from $155) is a charming hotel centrally located in the middle of the "big city" of Georgetown. **Coral Gardens** (www.coralgardensbahamas.com; from $99) is a simple B&B near Hooper's Bay with charming innkeepers. **Regatta Point** (www.regattapointbahamas.com; from $176) is an all-suites hotel where sitting on your porch gives you exquisite views of Elizabeth Harbor, the marina, or Crab Cay.

**Where to Eat:** It's tough to find anything other than fish fries, conch, and grills, so you may as well succumb. Head south to **Santana's** (William's Town, Great Exuma; tel. +1 242-345-4102) for the cracked lobster or eat like the locals at **Shirley's at the Fish Fry** (Queen's Highway, Great Exuma) in George Town. If you want to try a traditional conch salad stop at **Big D's Conch Spot** (Steventon, Great Exuma; 242/358-0059). For fancier fare that pushes the limits of modern Bahamian, snag an outdoor table at the **Palapa Grill** (www.grandisleresort.com) at the Grand Isle Resort. If you spend any time in Nassau before heading to Exuma, indulge in the local flavors of **Lukka Kairi** (www.lukkakairi.com) where fresh lobster tanks line the entrance.

## OTHER MUST-DOS:

- Take the five-minute water taxi ride over to Stocking Island to enjoy the weekly **Sunday Pig Roast** at Chat 'N' Chill (www.chatnchill.com). You can catch the boat at the Government Dock in Georgetown for $12 round-trip (www.elviswatertaxi.com). Make sure to head over early; they've been known to run out of pork by the early afternoon.

- Swim through a hidden underwater opening to enter the famed *Thunderball Grotto*, an intricate cave system that was the site of the 1965 James Bond movie of the same first name. Once inside, snorkel through schools of fish and the brilliant coral reefs that create a breathtaking aquarium. It will be easy to see why Hollywood is attracted to this site! It's best for snorkelers to plan their outing at low tide when it's easier and safer to enter. Some of the full-day tours that go to Big Major Cay will offer a stop here, like Coastline Adventures (www.coastlineadventuresexuma.com).

- See what is known as the best sunset in Exuma at ***Catch a Fire Restaurant*** (www.catchafireexuma.com) that sits just south of Georgetown on the mainland. Get there early, order some of the best conch fritters and grab a cocktail just before the sun goes down.
- Take in the five-star view from the outdoor patio at ***Haulover Bay Bar & Grill*** (tel. 12425242108) that is hidden away in the settlement of Rolle Town. It is a place that you will enter as a patron and leave as lifelong friends of the sweet family who freely doles out hugs to visitors. Plus, every Wednesday you could drink cocktails and belt out a karaoke tune from eight p.m. until late.
- Face your fears and ***swim with the nurse sharks*** at Compass Cay Marina. Don't worry, these shark-infested waters are filled with ones that are friendly and docile. If that still scares you, then just give them a quick pet when they swim up on the dock. Coastline Adventures' (www.coastlineadventuresexuma.com) full-day tour makes a stop here.

## ESSENTIAL INFORMATION:

- If you have a preference, confirm with your chosen tour company about which swimming pigs cay you will be taken too. It's typically not advertised which one you will be going to, especially if it's not the original Big Major Cay.
- Taking photos of the pigs without other tourists in them will be tricky. But, don't be afraid to break away from the crowd to follow a lone pig in the distance instead of sticking near the cluster of them right at the boat.
- Be careful of your fingers and camera equipment, pigs bite and can mistake those for their next meal.
- Pigs poop, and swimming pigs poop in the water—watch for floaters and keep your mouth closed!

- The pigs love fresh water almost as much as hotdogs. Bring a water bottle with a bowl and they will be in piggy heaven.
- Bahamians drive on the left side of the road, which can take some getting used to especially if you are renting a car.
- US citizens will need a valid passport to enter the Bahamas, but a visa is not required for short trips.

## PACKING TIPS:

- It can get windy and chilly when you are zipping through the cays on a boat, so pack a ***light jacket.***
- The sun can be deceiving in the Bahamas, bring a ***higher SPF sunscreen*** than you normally would.
- The Exumas are very laid back; ***T-shirts, shorts, sandals, and sundresses*** are fine 99 percent of the time.
- Though you will be able to get some decent photos from the boat, a ***waterproof camera*** will allow you to take shots at the swimming pigs' level and of their cute little feet underwater.
- Many tours involve the boat parking itself on the water during snorkeling excursions (not the Ocean Safari with Exuma Water Sports that we took), which can cause seasickness for some so be sure to pack your ***motion sickness medication.***
- A good pair of ***water shoes*** is helpful because sometimes the little piglets like to hide in the bushes of the cay.
- A ***waterproof daypack*** or a ***tote bag*** is not only helpful at the beaches, but also on the boat.

**Helpful Websites:** The Islands of the Bahamas (www.bahamas.com); The Out Islands of the Bahamas (www.myoutislands.com).

# EPILOGUE: WHAT WILL YOU ACCOMPLISH NEXT?

The other evening a group of friends were having an enlightening discussion, answering the million-dollar question, "If you won the lottery, what would you do differently?" Everyone went around the circle sharing his or her wishes and dreams. Some would go see the Northern Lights in Alaska, while others would quit their job to pursue their passion or buy a fancy new bright red Ferrari, and so on. When it came to my turn, the others looked at me in anticipation expecting my aspiration to be something beyond extraordinary, considering my current lifestyle of exploring the world as a travel writer. They were all surprised when I replied, "Not much would change for me, because I am living my dream."

I may not be rich, I don't wear designer clothing or drive a luxury sports car, but bathing elephants in Thailand doesn't require Louis Vuitton, just a passport and a desire. My ultimate goal was to design a life that I love to live, one filled with new experiences, travel, and adventure. I have accomplished that and it didn't require a million dollar lottery—it simply required the belief that I could.

When I think back at how this lifestyle came to be, one thing is incredibly clear: I believed it was possible. There may have been fear, intimidation, and self-doubt on the surface, but underlying it all was a quiet confidence that made me think, "If there is someone else in the world doing it, then it is possible for me too." From the very first post that was ever written for my blog (which was absolutely terrible by the way) to climbing an active volcano in Guatemala, to writing this book, the deepest question was never if I would succeed, but rather *how* I would. This is not to say that there weren't momentary (and sometimes drawn-out) uncertainties. You can ask my husband how many times he has heard me say that I wanted to give up blogging because my numbers were never going to be good enough, or that this book would never be finished on time because the words didn't flow easily. The point is that I didn't quit. I kept plugging away, one tiny step at a time, even when my belief was shoved way deep underneath the doubt. The outcome of simply putting one foot in front of the other, even on days when it was a tip-toe instead of a leap, resulted in a career surrounded by everything that I adore: world travel, delectable food, photography and, of course, bucket lists.

I am not telling you all of this to toot my own horn (though I feel an extreme sense of pride for everything I have accomplished), it is simply to let you know that I am not the exception to the rule—you too can live a life like this. Just like many of you, I was dealt some pretty crappy cards in life. There was definitely no Mercedes in the driveway on my sixteenth birthday, my parents divorced in my youth, there was addiction and dysfunction surrounding me, I suffered anxiety for more years than not, had to put myself through college and almost lost everything in the last market crash. There have been deaths and disappointments and failed businesses, some of which I had to literally pick myself up off the ground from. My life is simply the example of what can happen when you have a dream, work hard to accomplish it and believe in yourself. Then what is the difference between you and me? Instead of listing the thousands of reasons that I can't do something, I find the half dozen reasons to believe why I can. I find solutions instead of making excuses.

Too many people drift through their life aimlessly, without a plan or even a loose sense of direction. They mindlessly accept what comes next without making any effort to change the path. These people are sitting in the back seat, instead of taking control as the driver of their own lives. This may be because they don't believe in themselves, or are just too lazy to put in the hard work. In many cases they will end up regretful and bitter for not having achieved the incredible things that others have. Don't be that person.

Spending the afternoon with the African children at Esa school in Tanzania

Many of you will put goals on our bucket list without ever really believing that they will be ticked off. A bucket list isn't much of an inspiration unless you start putting check marks next to the things on it. But, if you don't trust in yourself, chances are that that will never happen. You can do what you believe you can, but also you become what you do. You will not be able to dive the Great Barrier Reef without putting in the effort to learn to scuba dive, or hike the four-day Inca trail without training beforehand. You may be given the best opportunity to achieve a goal, but a lack of belief will limit your success. Sometimes your lack of confidence is the result of listening to what others say. There will always be people who crush your spirit, telling you that you can't be an artist because it is not a viable way to make a living, or laughing at your idea of selling all your belongings to travel the world as an English teacher. Why are you listening? One of the most valuable lessons I have learned in life is to only take advice from someone who has achieved what you desire. I would never take marriage guidance from someone in a continuously rocky relationship, or ask career advice from someone who hates his or her job. So why take coaching on how to live your life from someone who is not leading *their* ideal one?

I challenge you to play the million-dollar game, asking yourself how your life would be different if money wasn't a factor. When you know your answer, ask yourself why you aren't on the path to live that dream. Then make a plan, go out there and be an explorer of life, see the world—turn your wanderlust into a reality. It is all at your feet if you will just take the first step. What will you accomplish next?

Relaxing on stone steps in Lake Atitlan, Guatemala

# APPENDICES

# APPENDIX A:
# 50 MORE IDEAS FOR YOUR BUCKET LIST

The world is filled with an endless amount of incredible experiences that go way beyond the featured ten. With this list of fifty more ideas, and the ones you'll come up with for yourself, your bucket list will never be empty.

1. **Dogsled Through the Alaskan Forest** — Alaska is home to the strenuous Iditarod Sled Dog Race, a journey that spans 1,150 miles across the rugged wilderness from Anchorage to Nome. You'll be able to experience the thrill of this sport first hand by meeting Iditarod racers and their powerful pooches, plus

Cruising through the 1,600 islets of Vietnam's Halong Bay

sledding along some of the mountainous terrain that their dogs train on. (visit www.alaska.org/things-to-do/dog-sledding)

2. **Go Gorilla Trekking in Uganda** — Trek through the dense rain forest of Uganda to get a close encounter with the mountain gorillas of the jungle. The fact that these species are on the brink of extinction and you need to travel to far-away lands to see them adds to the experience. (www.bwindiforestnationalpark.com)

3. **Cruise on a Junk Boat through Halong Bay** — A three-and-a-half-hour drive from the bustle of the city of Hanoi lays a peaceful set of 1,600 islands and islets, Halong Bay. This UNESCO World Heritage site has been the backdrop to many movies, including the Oscar-winning *Indochine*. Spend a day or a week cruising through the green-topped limestone islands and emerald waters on an ancient-style junk boat. (www.indochina-junk.com)

4. **Sleep in an Ice Hotel in Sweden** — Each year in the village of Jukkasjärvi, in northern Sweden, the IceHotel is built from natural ice and snow. It is an art exhibition as much as a hotel, where the canvases span from floor to ceiling. Spend the night in one of their negative-five-degree rooms, where you will be surrounded by artistically chiseled ice. It's a bonus that there is also a chance of seeing the Northern Lights from their location on the bank of the Torne River. (www.icehotel.com)

5. **Hike the Inca Trail to Machu Picchu** — Machu Picchu is an Incan citadel that stands 2,430 meters above sea level in the mountain forest of Peru. Getting to this ancient city can be done by train, bus, or a four-day trek along the same paths that the Incans did years ago. People choose the challenging hike not only to see other ruins along the way, but for the sense of pride when reaching this UNESCO World Heritage Site by foot. (www.incatrailperu.com)

6.   **Hot Air Balloon over Cappadocia, Turkey** — See the surreal landscape of Cappadocia from high above in a sky dotted with colorful balloons. Cappadocia is the land in central Turkey known for its fairy chimneys (rock formations), rolling vineyards, and troglodyte dwellings that are best seen from three thousand feet in the air. (www.butterflyballoons.com)

7.   **Walk the Great Wall of China** — The Great Wall of China winds up and down a series of fortifications, stretching from Shanhaiguan to Lop Lake in the Gobi Desert. The wall is one of the most recognizable and extensive construction projects built to prevent attacks of the Chinese Empire. Take a walk along a portion of the 13,170-mile-long wall, stopping at scenic spots that overlook flowing rivers and to view precious historical relics. (www.travelchinaguide.com)

8.   **Drive Route 66 in the United States** — Get your kicks on Route 66, the iconic 2,400-mile route from Chicago to Santa Monica. Also, known as the Main Street of America, it was one of the original US highways, a means for the nation to move about for work or pleasure. Today it keeps old traditions alive with neon-signed motels, mom-and-pop diners, and kitschy roadside attractions. (www.theroute-66.com)

9.   **Dive the Great Barrier Reef** — Australia's iconic Great Barrier Reef stretches for more than 1,200 miles, running parallel to the Queensland coastline. It is the world's largest coral reef system with over 2,900 reefs, 1,500 fish species, 400 types of coral, and 900 remote islands. Scuba divers flock here to glide with hundreds of manta rays, marvel at the colorful sea fans, and swim with schools of blackfin barracudas. (www.oceanfree.com.au)

10.  **Go Truffle Hunting in Tuscany** — Traveling to Italy is absolutely about the pasta and the wine, but it's also about the truffles. Walk through the Tuscan forests with a Lagotto

Exploring the depths of a cave in the Penedès region of Spain

Romagnalo breed of dog sniffing out a culinary treasure—the white truffle. Though there are over sixty varieties of truffles worldwide, this is the most coveted, at times bringing in over $800 per 100 grams. (www.giuliothetrufflehunter.com)

11. **Explore the Depths of a Cava Cave in Spain** — The cava caves of Spain feature dark narrow tunnels, steep spiral staircases, a labyrinth that would challenge anyone's sense of direction, and are filled to the stone ceiling with a winemaker's dream. Some cava caves would make the perfect location to film a horror flick, while others could be used as a skilled mathematicians puzzle. Exploring the seemingly endless channels can only be topped by tasting the bubbly at the end. (www.spanishwinecountry.com/spanish-wine-regions/cava-wine-region)

12. **Climb Africa's Mount Kilimanjaro** — Standing at over 19,000 feet, Mount Kilimanjaro is Africa's highest peak. The

once-in-a-lifetime trek to the summit will have you hiking through lush rainforests, over glaciers, and across the Tanzanian landscape, plus traveling through four different climatic zones. It takes roughly six days to reach what has been called "the roof of Africa," where the stunning view will be worth the challenge. (www.basecamptanzania.com)

13. **Eat at the French Laundry in Napa** — The French Laundry is arguably the most well-known French restaurant in the world. A meal for two at this Michelin three-starred eatery will set you back close to a thousand bucks, but your taste buds will be dazzled. In order to indulge in the nine-course dining experiences the chefs create, you'll need to get a reservation—and that's the tricky part. (www.thomaskeller.com)

14. **Travel the Trans-Siberian Railway** — For those that believe getting there is half the fun, travel the legendary Trans-Siberian railway, an epic train journey that spans from Moscow to Vladivostok. Traverse one third of the globe, enjoying the scenery from the window of your train car, plus make stops to different cities along the way. (www.transsiberianexpress.net)

15. **Drink Steins of Beer at Ocktoberfest in Germany** — Put on your traditional Bavarian outfit and drink a stein (or two) at the world's largest beer festival, Ocktoberfest held in Munich. Each year this sixteen-day festival draws over six million people from around the world. (www.oktoberfest.de)

16. **See an Opera at the Sydney Opera House in Australia** — There is nothing quite like the Sydney Opera House overlooking the harbor, its exterior an iconic vision from all angles. Don't just admire one of Australia's most recognized buildings from afar, step inside to spend a magical evening at one of their acclaimed operas. (www.sydneyoperahouse.com)

17. **Helicopter over a Volcano in Hawaii** — Feel the heat radiate when you fly over an active Hawaiian volcano in an open-door

helicopter ride. Your ride will cross the Kilauea Volcano that has been continuously erupting for the last thirty years. With the doors off, there's nothing but five hundred feet between you and this hot natural wonder of the world. (www. paradisecopters.com)

18. **Sleep in an Overwater Bungalow in Bora Bora** — You've seen the photos of a string of bungalows perched atop the azure waters below. A memorable trip to Tahiti's Bora Bora must include a night in one of these overwater hideaways where you can wake by diving into the warm water and go to sleep to the sound of the swish of the water beneath you. One of the most luxurious ones you will find is at the Four Seasons. (www. fourseasons.com/borabora)

19. **Take the Walk of Faith at Tianmen Mountain in China** — In the Zhangjiajie National Forest Park you will find a 196-foot-long see-through glass path that stands over 4,000 feet above sea level. This adrenaline-producing walkway clings to the side of the Tianmen Mountain. A stroll along this path is only for the most adventurous, who will marvel at the crystal-clear view below their trembling feet. (www.zhangjiajietourism.us)

20. **Throw Tomatoes at La Tomatina in Spain** — La Tomatina is a weeklong festival in the town of *Buñol* thats highlight is on the last Wednesday in August, when thousands of people fight in an innocent battle using tons of over-ripe tomatoes. Trucks come to the city hauling more than one hundred metric tons of ammunition and the world's biggest food fight begins with the throw of a single squished tomato. (www.latomatina.info)

21. **Walk the Spanish El Camino de Santiago de Compostela** — El Camino de Santiago was originally a pilgrimage leading to Santiago de Compostela, to the tomb of the apostle St. James. Now, scores of people on a personal journey walk this five-hundred-mile network of routes across Spain and Europe. Whether the

motivation is spiritual or adventurous, many choose to take this monthlong challenge. (www.caminoadventures.com)

22. **Attend the Kentucky Derby** — It isn't just the world-class horses that set the Kentucky Derby apart from other horse races, it's the spectacular hats. Let your inner Southern Belle emerge, and don your most dramatic bonnet while watching what has been called the "greatest two minutes in sports." (www.kentuckyderby.com)

23. **White Water Raft Through the Grand Canyon** — Get a thrilling perspective of the Grand Canyon by touring it from the Colorado River. In your raft, you will navigate the greatest whitewater in North America while marveling at the multicolored layers of the eroded rocks. (www.oars.com/grandcanyon)

24. **Attend a Tea Ceremony in Japan** — The refined Japanese Tea Ceremony is the ritual of preparing and serving the powdered

The marching of the uniformed men at the changing of the guard at Buckingham Palace

green tea, matcha. This warm, thick beverage is served with sweets to balance the bitter taste of the tea. The host may spend years mastering this art, learning every detail from utensil placement to the perfect angle for the tea bowl. (www. japanese-tea-ceremony.net)

25. **Get Scrubbed at a Hamam in Turkey** — The hamam has been popular in Turkey for thousands of years, not only as a relaxing bathing ritual but also as a social center. Today the healthy hot steam bath, followed by a body scrub and massage, is still a major part of the Turkish culture. (www.ayasofyahamami. com)

26. **See the Changing of the Guard in London** — The Changing of the Guard at Buckingham Palace is a mesmerizing spectacle where the Old Guard hands over the security responsibility to the New Guard. This is combined with synchronized marching, precision drills, and the band playing. It's a show like no other, but get there early! (www.changing-guard.com)

27. **Relax in the Blue Lagoon Hot Springs in Iceland** — The warm geothermal, milky-blue waters of the Blue Lagoon draws visitors worldwide. Many float in the mineral-rich waters for the reputed skin benefits, while others go there for the relaxation, ducking into a grotto with a beverage in hand from the float-up bar. (www.bluelagoon.com)

28. **Experience Istanbul's Call to Prayer at the Blue Mosque** — Five times a day throughout the streets of Istanbul you can hear the trilling call to prayer, also known as ***ezan***. During this time the voice of the bellowing ***muezzin***, the man who calls the Muslims to prayer from a minaret, can be heard over the loudspeakers at different mosques in the city. One of the best locations to witness this is while sitting on the benches between the Blue Mosque and Hagia Sophia as a quavering musical battle begins. (www.bluemosque.co)

Atop Sigiriya Rock in Sri Lanka

29. **Climb Sigiriya Rock in Sri Lanka** — Sigiriya is an ancient palace built in 480 AD, located in the central Matale District of Sri Lanka. This UNESCO World Heritage site is known for its beautifully landscaped gardens, well-preserved frescos, and twelve hundred different anxiety-producing levels of stairs to reach the summit. These steps will bring you to the sky palace that sits atop the rock, a royal residence built sixteen hundred years ago. (www.seelanka.net/sigiriya)

30. **Go Volcano Boarding in Nicaragua** — The adventure starts with a rocky forty-five-minute hike up the 2,388-foot Cerro Negro (Black Hill), an active volcano just outside of León, Nicaragua. Once at the top you will sit on plywood boards, and go racing down at speeds up to 30 mph. (www.leon.quetzaltrekkers.org)

31. **Cross the Salar de Uyuni in Bolivia** — Blanketing more than forty-five hundred square miles, the Salar de Uyuni is a flat salt dessert that seems to go on infinitely. It is the remains of a

lake that once covered the southwestern corner of Bolivia, but is now a vastness of white that plays an optical illusion on you. During the wet season, the shallow water that collects acts as a mirror of the sky, showing reflections of the sky and clouds, making the world seem endless. In the dry season, you can walk or drive across it, taking goofy photos that play with the lack of perspective created by the continuous sheets of hexagonal tiles. (www.latorretours-tupiza.com)

32. **Kayak Through Icebergs in Greenland** — Lose contact with civilization while paddling your kayak through a labyrinth of icebergs along the pristine Greenland waters. You may encounter a curious seal or giant whale, but the real treat is the peacefulness of listening to the crumbling of the icebergs in the distance. (www.greenland.com)

33. **Hike Between the Towns of Cinque Terre in Italy** — Cinque Terre is a collection of five charming villages that are linked by a network of picturesque hiking trails. The trails go through each town, giving you a chance to peruse through the quaint shops, drink a glass of Chianti at a café, or both. (www.cinqueterreonline.com)

34. **Attend Mass at Notre Dame Cathedral in Paris** — You don't have to speak French or be religious to be blown away by a powerful mass at the Notre Dame Cathedral in Paris. The sound of the preacher's voice will billow through the cavernous cathedral and into your body. It may not be the largest Catholic cathedral in the world, but it is one of the most beautiful and famous with an estimated 14 million visitors a year. (www.notredamedeparis.fr)

35. **Tour the Hanging Temple of Mount Hengshan in China** — The Hanging Temple is an architectural wonder, built into a cliff of Hengshan Mountain. It is said to have been built by a monk during the Northern Wei Dynasty (386–534 AD). Inside

Getting some puppy love after dogsledding in Norway

is a labyrinth of passageways connecting forty pavilions and halls, plus more than eighty bronze, iron, and clay statues. (www.travelchinaguide.com)

36. **Let Go of a Floating Lantern in Taiwan** — Watch the sky ablaze as over a hundred thousand luminous lanterns are simultaneously released at the Pingxi Lantern Festival. The launching began as a means to signal refugees of the town's safety; today participants decorate them with their wishes and release them into the moonlit sky. (www.fest300.com/festivals/pingxi-sky-lantern-festival)

37. **See the Northern Lights** — The Northern Lights (Aurora Borealis) are mysterious twists of multicolored lights that can only be seen in a handful of locations in the world, mostly in the Arctic Circle. To witness them is a once-in-a-lifetime experience whether you do it while relaxing in a thermal spa in

Taking a float in the salty Dead Sea in the Middle East

Iceland, cruising on a yacht through Alaska, or night dogsledding in Norway. (www.theaurorazone.com)

38. **Swim with Whale Sharks in Mexico** — Don't let the name "whale shark" scare you, these enormous fish are gentle giants. During the warm season, hundreds migrate to the waters of the Caribbean Sea. A boat ride from Cancun will take you to a place where you can swim with several of the largest fish in the world that grow up to sixty feet long and can weigh over forty thousand pounds. It is a thrill to be face to face with their gigantic mouths that can extend five feet when open. (www. cancunwhalesharktours.com)

39. **Watch the Grand Prix in Monaco** — Each year the ritzy streets of Monaco are turned into a challenging Formula 1 circuit for one of the most prestigious races in the world, the Monaco Grand Prix. It's one of the slowest tracks, but probably the most glamorous, bordering the yacht-filled harbor and studded with movie stars. (www.monaco-grand-prix.com)

Spending a snowy day at Romania's Dracula Castle

40. **Float in the Dead Sea in Israel** — The Dead Sea is a salt lake over thirteen hundred feet below sea level, making it the lowest elevation on Earth. Nestled in the Judean Desert; the unusually high salt concentration (8.6 times saltier than the ocean) causes a natural buoyancy that makes people float. Many people use this oasis as a chance to aimlessly drift while reading a newspaper. (www.deadseaguide.com)

41. **Visit Dracula's Castle in Transylvania, Romania** — High above the valley of Romania, in the principality of Transylvania, there lies an unusual castle that is said to have once been occupied by Count Dracula himself. You will find the gothic Bran Castle near the town of Brasov, which has long been linked to this ancient vampire, though Dracula *probably* won't be there when you arrive. There is a mystical atmosphere surrounding Bran Castle; it looks like the perfect setting for a vampire novel, perched on top of a hill and filled with dozens

of tunneled stairs, dark wood paneling, and stark white walls. (www.bran-castle.com)

42. **See a Broadway Musical in New York City**—Along and nearby Broadway, in the heart of New York City, between Forty-second and Fifty-third, people have been dazzled by gleaming lights, powerful voices, and some of the world's best theatrics. There's nothing quite like a Broadway show. The theater district has also been called "The Great White Way," because of its flashy marquees that light up the sky. Many Tony awards have been earned on these streets. (www.broadway.com)

43. **Interact with the Penguins of Antarctica** — A highlight to any trip to the chilly continent of Antarctica is interacting with the many penguin colonies; Adélies, emperors, chinstraps, and gentoos. Watch as they clumsily waddle to the sea, slide on their bellies and curiously approach you, sometimes coming so close they shuffle right over your feet. (www.coolantarctica.com)

The Catacombs Underground Ossuaries in Paris

44. **Get Spooked at the Catacombs in Paris** – The Catacombs is a labyrinth of caves underneath the heart of the city and the resting place for the bones of six million Parisians. Starting in the late eighteenth century, remains were transferred to the ossuary as overcrowded graveyards were closing due to the risk to the public. Though the underground maze is extensive, the portion that is open to the public is an eerie two-kilometer-long walk filled with skulls, bones, and stones (www.catacombes. paris.fr)

45. **Attend Burning Man in Nevada** — For one week each year over sixty thousand dreamers, artists, and partygoers converge at Black Rock City in Nevada for the ultimate desert art festival. This bash is not for idle spectators, it is expected that you participate by creating art, performing, volunteering, and dressing up. The hedonistic homemade community centers around "The Man," the sixty-foot-tall mascot who is burned to the ground on the final days. (www.burningman.org)

46. **Zip Line through the Rain Forest of Costa Rica** — Imagine the thrill of gliding along the treetops in the Costa Rican rain forest attached to cables. The zip lines bring you to different height platforms, crossing an extraordinary landscape on the way. You will find adrenaline-pumping zip lines all across the country that will fly you next to a waterfall and through the forest with the monkeys, giving you a different perspective from the air. (www.visitcostarica.com)

47. **Trek to Mount Everest Base Camp in Nepal** — At over twenty-nine thousand feet, Mount Everest soars above Khumbu in northeastern Nepal. Though a rare few attempt to reach the summit, the trek to Everest Base Camp at 17,590 feet is still a challenging adventure and an achievable goal for the rest of us. Along the way the stunning Himalaya views, hospitability of the village people, and spectacular glimpse of its peak will take you aback. (www.nepalecoadventure.com)

48. **Attend the Palio Horse race in Siena** — Twice a year, the central piazza (Il Campo) of Siena is turned into a track for the most important event in the city—Palio. The Italian town is stuffed to the brim as ten of the neighborhoods (*contrades*) each compete in a bareback battle of the best racehorse. The event is just as much about the thrill of the seventy-five-second race as it is about the pageantry and pride. (www.ilpalio.org)

Walking on the Waianapanapa Black Sand Beach on the Road to Hana in Maui

49. **Drive Maui's Road to Hana** — With flowing waterfalls, picturesque hiking, and a black sand beach, the fifty-three-mile Road to Hana drive is one of the most popular in the world. Most travelers will take the road to the town Hana, then turn around and head back the same route they came. For the more adventurous traveler, do the continuous loop, which takes you over the unpaved, bumpy part of the road with the zigzagging turns that tour books warn you about. (www.roadtohana.com)

50. **Wear a Mask at Carnival in Venice** — Each year the Venice canals come alive as roughly three million visitors flock to this colossal masquerade party. It is one of the biggest celebrations in Italy that starts two weeks before Ash Wednesday and ends on Shrove Tuesday. Partygoers parade through the city donning elaborate bejeweled masks and costumes while enjoying an array of festival events. (www.venice-carnival-italy.com)

# APPENDIX B: RESOURCES

I have spent several years living the bucket list life and traveling the world, testing hundreds of websites, companies, and gear along the way. This is a collection of the best resources, ones that I personally use and recommend.

## BUCKET LIST RESOURCES

**Bucket List Journey** (www.bucketlistjourney.net)
This is my personal bucket list and travel blog documenting my once-in-a-lifetime experiences around the world. In my most humble opinion, it is a great source for inspiration to living the bucket list lifestyle.

**Bucketlist** (www.bucketlist.org)
The most popular bucket list community, a place where you can record your life's ambitions, chronicle your accomplishments, get inspired by other member's goals, and encourage people to accomplish theirs.

**Bucket List** (www.bucketlist.net)
Another community where the ideas seem endless. What I like about this one is the "swap" tab where you can ask others for help in achieving a goal.

***The Bucket List* Movie**
Though this movie isn't the best, nor is it how the term bucket list originated, it is what put the term bucket list on the tips of more people's tongues.

**BuckitDream App** (www.buckitdream.com)
This downloadable app helps you build your own bucket list, plus share your dreams to inspire others.

**iWish App**
The iWish app helps you discover your dreams with over twelve hundred bucket list ideas, then assists you in achieving them. You can create reminders, prioritize goals, and even make your own vision board.

## AIRFARE

**ITA Matrix** (www.matrix.itasoftware.com)
Though you cannot book directly through this site, it is one of the most efficient flight search tools. Search by specific dates or peek at the calendar to see the best pricing of several airlines based on an entire month.

**Tripadvisor** (www.tripadvisor.com)
The largest online travel community that compares pricing from big sites like Expedia, Orbitz, and Priceline. Also check their Bargain Travel Forum (www.tripadvisor.com/ForumHome) where the public shares tips on travel discounts, flight glitches, and last minute deals.

**Kayak** (www.kayak.com)
Kayak searches hundreds of travel sites to find you the best bargain, a one-stop shop for airline deals. Also, go to Kayak Explore (www.kayak.com/explore), where you can enter departure city and month, and it will return flight deals from around the world.

**Skyscanner** (www.skyscanner.net)
This website searches several travel agents and different airlines, including many of the budget airlines that the other booking sites don't include.

**Momondo** (www.momondo.com)
Momondo seems to be the perfect blend of all the rest, pulling from over seven hundred travel sites to give you the best deal.

## ACCOMMODATIONS

**Airbnb** (www.airbnb.com)
Airbnb connects homeowners with travelers, offering unique accommodations in every price range and style. You can rent an entire apartment or, for the budget-minded, a shared room in someone's home. Plus, they have a good review section that will tell you about renters' past experiences.

**Booking.com** (www.booking.com)
This is the accommodation site that I visit first and typically last since their hotel pricing is usually the lowest. Their extensive review section is helpful in making your decision.

**Expedia** (www.expedia.com)
After hitting up Booking.com, I go to Expedia to compare pricing and read their reviews. All things the same, I book through Expedia because I earn points that accumulate to discounts on future bookings.

**Couchsurfing** (www.couchsurfing.com)
You can save hundreds of dollars on accommodations with this site that connects you with locals, offering a couch to sleep on or spare room for free. Not only are the hosts reviewed, but the surfer gets reviewed too. Besides the cost, the benefit to this is meeting locals who can share the off-the-beaten path tips to their city.

**HostelWorld** (www.hostelworld.com)
The world's leading place to book a hostel, with the largest selection. They have also expanded to include campsites, B&Bs, and budget hotels.

**Home Exchange** (www.homeexchange.com)
Simply take a few minutes to list your home or apartment, then find another property in a location you'd like to stay in and contact the owner to make the exchange.

## TRAVEL APPS

**Evernote** (www.evernote.com)
Evernote makes it easy to collect travel information when planning a trip. It can store maps, photos, and links that can be accessed on any of my devices. It is what I use for creating all my itineraries.

**Google Translate** (www.translate.google.com)
Google Translate is really versatile when it comes to interpreting; it can translate paragraphs of text, images with words, and speech. It has been my savior when trying to order from a foreign menu or attempting to get directions from a local.

**PackPoint** (www.packpnt.com)
If you're the person that forgets to pack sunscreen on a beach vacation or gloves on a ski holiday, PackPoint is the perfect app for you. By inputting your destination, trip length, and the basic nature of your visit, the app will customize a packing list.

**Snapseed**
Snapseed is an easy photo-editing app with a powerful collection of tools for touching up your pictures. Its Healing tool can fix blemishes and the Brush tool brightens people or props in a photo. There are only a handful of filters, but I use the Drama one often.

**Skype** (www.skype.com)
Skype is a cheap, and often free, way of staying connected on the road. Through Wi-Fi it is free to message, video chat, and call as long

as the person on the other end also has an account. If you need to make a phone call to someone who is not on Skype, you can load money onto your account and make the call for a fraction of the cost.

**VSCO** (www.vsco.co)
This is a powerful photo-editing app that offers a multitude of downloadable filters. Plus, the strength of each filter can be adjusted to your liking. I use VSCO for every photo uploaded to Instagram in order to keep the tone consistent.

**WhatsApp** (www.whatsapp.com)
WhatsApp is another way to keep in contact with friends and family while on the road. Using Wi-Fi, it offers individual or group messaging with other WhatsApp users. It is free for the first year, than costs $0.99 per year subscription after that.

**XE Currency Converter** (www.xe.com)
The XE Currency Convertor app makes it easy to find out how much my dollar is worth wherever I am traveling to. It easily calculates the foreign currency exchange rates in countries all over the world. You can also use it on the fly to find out how much something costs while shopping at an open-air market. There are times that I am in three different countries in a week and it can be difficult to keep track of how many rupees or dongs equal a dollar. There is no need for me to worry about that with this app.

## TRAVEL DOCUMENTS

**The US Department of State** (www.travel.state.gov)
For US residents, this website has a plethora of valuable travel information. It informs you about visas, passports, vaccination requirements, travel security alerts, and so much more.

**American Automobile Association - AAA** (www.aaa.com)
If you are in need of an International Driving Permit, visit this website or National Automobile Club (NAC; www.thenac.com). In most cases, one can be gotten through the mail.

## TRAVEL INSURANCE

**Allianz** (www.allianztravelinsurance.com)
Allianz is a leader in travel insurance when it comes to providing financial safeguards for things like trip cancellation and emergency medical coverage.

**Clements Worldwide** (www.clements.com)
Many travel insurance policies don't cover damage to your expensive travel gear, which can be heartbreaking when your DSLR falls off the side of a boat or laptop gets dropped in front of a chicken bus. Clements is a property insurance that can cover pricey mishaps like these.

**World Nomads** (www.worldnomads.com)
World Nomads is the perfect travel insurance for the adventurer, covering everything from hot air ballooning to scuba diving. They have extensive coverage with competitive pricing.

## TRAVEL REWARD CARDS

**Chase Sapphire Preferred Card** (www.creditcards.chase.com)
The Chase Sapphire Preferred card isn't airline specific, but offers some great benefits. It features a frequent flier point transfer with a wide selection of its partners. So instead of being able to use your points for only one specific airline, you can choose where they go. Of course, just like most others, it offers no foreign transactions fees and a good-sized sign-up bonus.

**Hilton HHonors** (www.hhonors3.hilton.com)
There are many hotel rewards credit cards, but the one of my choice is the Hilton HHonors. I don't stay at the Hilton hotels every time I travel, but rather for one-night stays close to the airport or special deals that they may have. I once stayed in the five-star Conrad in Istanbul for twelve bucks a night combined with points. What I like about Hilton is that they have hotels in the centers of most major cities.

**MileagePlus Expolorer** (www.theexplorercard.com)
With the United MileagePlus Explorer (www.theexplorercard.com) card, there are no foreign transactions fees, which are usually between 2 to 3 percent. Plus, I receive one free checked bag, priority boarding, two lounge passes per year, and luggage protection. When my luggage recently got lost for twenty-four hours in Switzerland, they immediately reimbursed me $200 to purchase clothing and other essentials.

## VOLUNTEERISM

**Kiva** (www.kiva.org)
With as little as twenty-five dollars, you can lend money to an entrepreneur across the world to help achieve their dream. This is especially rewarding if you have plans of traveling to the specific country, as it helps to build a stronger connection.

**Pack for a Purpose** (www.packforapurpose.org)
Pack for a Purpose is a non-profit organization dedicated to helping travelers make a difference around the world by using empty space in their luggage for supplies. Simply check the communities you will be visiting and the projects will list what items they need.

**GVI** (www.gviusa.com); **Projects Abroad** (www.projects-abroad. org); **Global Volunteers** (www.globalvolunteers.org)
If you would like to spend an extended period of time giving back, these three organizations offer volunteer projects around the world. The programs range from teaching English in Bangladesh to participating in marine conservation projects in the islands of the Seychelles.

## OTHER RESOURCES

**Ask the Pilot** (www.askthepilot.com)
This website has just about everything you need to know about air travel, from the latest media news to how to handle an emergency.

**Fear of Flying School** (www.fearofflyingschool.com)
Don't let the fear of flying stop you from traveling to your dream destination, head over to this website instead. It contains dozens of articles that cover things like relaxation techniques, air turbulence, and why the wings on your plane won't snap off.

**FlyerTalk** (www.flyertalk.com)
FlyerTalk is an incredibly popular online community dedicated to flying travelers. Their news category reports the most up-to-date articles from passenger complaints to airline strikes, while the chat boards cover tips and tricks from the once-a-year traveler to the elite frequent flyer member.

**SeatGuru** (www.seatguru.com)
SeatGuru is a database of seating diagrams searched by airline flight number. Simply key in your flight and it will return the best (and worst) seat choices.

**T-Mobile** (www.T-Mobile.com)
If you are an avid traveler who lives in the US, T-Mobile offers plans that include free international data and texting to over 140 countries.

**The Man in Seat 61** (www.seat61.com)
Before traveling by train anywhere in the world, pay a visit to The Man in Seat 61 who provides a comprehensive guide on routes, fares, and times.

**The Points Guy** (www.thepointsguy.com)
This site is a useful guide to navigating the world and earning points along the way. You will learn the best rewards programs and credit cards, plus how to rack up the most points possible.

**Travelzoo** (www.travelzoo.com)
Each week, Travelzoo publishes their Top 20 list of the week's very best travel deals. Sometimes it's just a flight and other times it's a full-on ten-day luxury vacation. By signing up for their newsletter you will get the latest and greatest bargains sent to your inbox.

**Weather** (www.weatherchannel.com)
A weather website seems too simple, but often people forget to check the temperatures before leaving for their destination. I always check this site before leaving to know what to pack, but it's great for other reasons too. It can tell you what time to catch the sunset, what months see the most rainfall, and up-to-date weather news.

**Zozi** (www.zozi.com)
Think Groupon for adventurers—Signing up for their email list will get you daily discounts centered around adventurous activities, outdoorsy experiences, and travel getaways.

# ABOUT THE AUTHOR

**Annette White** is an author, photographer, serial adventurer, and creator of the award-winning travel blog, *Bucket List Journey*. Her popular site has over a hundred thousand monthly readers, and Frommer's named her Instagram @bucketlistjrny one of the best travel accounts to follow. She has been recognized by and worked with a multitude of top companies, such as Tripadvisor, Sandals Resorts, and LAN Airlines—while exploring more than forty countries on five continents. When she's not on the road, you can find Annette whipping up delicious dishes at her Michelin-recommended restaurant, Sugo Trattoria in Northern California, that she co-owns with her husband, Peter. Learn more at www.BucketListJourney.net.

For more inspiration, visit Annette's Blog:

BUCKET LIST **JOURNEY.**

dream it. do it.

www.BucketListJourney.net

Instagram: @BucketListJrny
🅵 BucketListJourney
🐦 BucketListJrny

# INDEX